A HISTORY OF PHYSICAL EDUCATION
AND ATHLETICS AT OBERLIN COLLEGE

A HISTORY OF PHYSICAL EDUCATION AND ATHLETICS AT OBERLIN COLLEGE

LEE C. DRICKAMER
WITH FREDRICK D. SHULTS

TRILLIUM, AN IMPRINT OF
THE OHIO STATE UNIVERSITY PRESS
COLUMBUS

Copyright © 2022 by The Ohio State University.
All rights reserved.
Trillium, an imprint of The Ohio State University Press.

Library of Congress Cataloging-in-Publication Data
Names: Drickamer, Lee C., author. | Shults, Fredrick Davis, 1932–2020, author.
Title: A history of physical education and athletics at Oberlin College / Lee C. Drickamer with Fredrick D. Shults.
Description: Columbus : Trillium, an imprint of The Ohio State University Press, 2022. | Includes bibliographical references and index. | Summary: "Examines the development and history of the first program for physical educators and athletics at Oberlin College, from the mid-nineteenth century to the present"—Provided by publisher.
Identifiers: LCCN 2022017119 | ISBN 9780814215234 (cloth) | ISBN 9780814282311 (ebook)
Subjects: LCSH: Oberlin College. Physical Education Department—History. | Oberlin College—Sports—History. | Physical education and training—Study and teaching (Higher)—Ohio—Oberlin—History.
Classification: LCC LD4168 .D75 2022 | DDC 378.771/23—dc23/eng/20220616
LC record available at https://lccn.loc.gov/2022017119
Other identifiers: ISBN 9780814258439 (paper)

Cover design by Angela Moody
Text design by Juliet Williams
Type set in Adobe Garamond Pro

For all of the students at Oberlin College, many of whom took part in Physical Education classes, some as majors and others for enjoyment.

For the students who participated in intercollegiate athletics.

For the students who engaged in intramural and club sports.

For the students who enjoyed and benefitted from the many recreational activities of the college.

For the faculty who engaged in the Physical Education Major.

For the faculty, coaches, and administrators who have made physical activities an important part of an Oberlin College education.

For the late Fredrick D. Shults.

CONTENTS

List of Illustrations ix

Preface and Acknowledgments xiii

INTRODUCTION 1

CHAPTER 1 Learning and Labor: 1830s–1870 16

CHAPTER 2 Gymnastics: 1871–1895 30

CHAPTER 3 New Physical Education: 1896–1925 64

CHAPTER 4 Sports as a Cultural Phenomenon: 1926–1950 104

CHAPTER 5 Athletics as Competition: 1951–1974 129

CHAPTER 6 Title IX, Inclusion of Women, and Sports as Entertainment: 1972–1990 153

CHAPTER 7 Worldwide Sports and Winning Dominates: 1991–2010 178

CHAPTER 8 The Present and Future Directions: 2011–2021 and Beyond 202

Appendices

    Appendix A.1: Timeline for Pertinent National and International Events 223

    Appendix A.2: Timeline for Physical Education and Athletics at Oberlin College 229

    Appendix B: Administrators for Physical Education and Athletics 235

References and Sources 239

Index 247

ILLUSTRATIONS

FIGURE 0.1	Oberlin Hall	2
FIGURE 0.2	Arthur Tappan	3
FIGURE 0.3	Physical education and athletics pyramid	10
FIGURE 0.4	Map of the south campus	14
FIGURE 0.5	Map of the north campus	15
FIGURE 1.1	Asa Mahan	21
FIGURE 1.2	Lucien C. Warner	22
FIGURE 1.3	James H. Fairchild	23
FIGURE 1.4	Gymnasium certificate	25
FIGURE 1.5	Resolutes baseball team	27
FIGURE 1.6	Tappan Square and baseball diamond	27
FIGURE 2.1	Interpretive dance at Memorial Arch	34
FIGURE 2.2	Delphine Hanna	36
FIGURE 2.3	Frederick E. Leonard	39
FIGURE 2.4	Second Ladies Gymnasium—exterior	45
FIGURE 2.5	Second Ladies Gymnasium—interior	46
FIGURE 2.6	Aerial view of the women's sports facilities	47
FIGURE 2.7	Second Men's Gymnasium—exterior	48
FIGURE 2.8	Second Men's Gymnasium—interior	48

x • Illustrations

FIGURE 2.9	Athletic Park	50
FIGURE 2.10	Luther Halsey Gulick	51
FIGURE 2.11	Thomas Denison Wood	53
FIGURE 2.12	High wheel bicycle club	55
FIGURE 2.13	Baseball team—1890	56
FIGURE 2.14	Football team—1892	57
FIGURE 2.15	Women's field hockey	59
FIGURE 2.16	Baseball team—Moses Fleetwood Walker	60
FIGURE 2.17	John Heisman	61
FIGURE 3.1	Seniors from Women's PE—1910	73
FIGURE 3.2	Start of sprint race and pole vault	75
FIGURE 3.3	Basketball team—1921	78
FIGURE 3.4	Woman golfer	80
FIGURE 3.5	Women fencing	80
FIGURE 3.6	First Yale–Princeton basketball game	82
FIGURE 3.7	Rockefeller Gymnasium—games in progress	82
FIGURE 3.8	Aerial view of campus	84
FIGURE 3.9	Warner Gymnasium and Warner Center	85
FIGURE 3.10	Warner Gymnasium—hanging track	86
FIGURE 3.11	Savage Stadium	88
FIGURE 3.12	Jesse Feiring Williams	95
FIGURE 3.13	Charles W. Savage	96
FIGURE 3.14	Four Horseman of Oberlin football	96
FIGURE 3.15	John Herbert Nichols	98
FIGURE 3.16	Whitelaw Reid Morrison	99
FIGURE 3.17	Gertrude E. Moulton	100
FIGURE 4.1	Navy V-12 unit	108
FIGURE 4.2	Lera B. Curtis	110
FIGURE 4.3	Guy C. Throner	110

FIGURE 4.4	Helen Edwards Domonkos	111
FIGURE 4.5	Katherine S. von Wenck	111
FIGURE 4.6	Crane Pool	118
FIGURE 4.7	Hales Memorial Gymnasium	119
FIGURE 4.8	Physical Education Library—Hales Gymnasium	120
FIGURE 4.9	Jones Field House	121
FIGURE 4.10	George M. Jones	121
FIGURE 4.11	Aerial view of athletic complex—north campus	122
FIGURE 4.12	Tennis courts and baseball diamond	123
FIGURE 4.13	Students collecting wood at Camp Hanna	123
FIGURE 5.1	Betty F. McCue	132
FIGURE 5.2	Lysle Butler	135
FIGURE 5.3	Bill Tidwell	137
FIGURE 5.4	Julian Smith	137
FIGURE 5.5	J. William Grice	137
FIGURE 5.6	Robert W. Fuller	140
FIGURE 5.7	Jack Scott	140
FIGURE 5.8	Cass Jackson	142
FIGURE 5.9	Patrick Penn	142
FIGURE 5.10	Tommie Smith	143
FIGURE 5.11	Joe Horn	143
FIGURE 5.12	Sara Houston	143
FIGURE 5.13	Aerial view of campus and Galpin Field	148
FIGURE 5.14	Hales Gymnasium Annex	149
FIGURE 5.15	Williams Ice Rink	150
FIGURE 6.1	Mary J. Culhane	160
FIGURE 6.2	Ruth Brunner	161
FIGURE 6.3	Barbara Calmer	161
FIGURE 6.4	Janet Wignall	162

FIGURE 6.5	Claudia Coville	162
FIGURE 6.6	Philips Physical Education Center	176
FIGURE 7.1	Donald Hunsinger	187
FIGURE 7.2	Michael Muska	187
FIGURE 7.3	James (J. D.) Donovan	188
FIGURE 7.4	Heisman Club Field House	195
FIGURE 7.5	Field House track and Field House tennis courts	196
FIGURE 7.6	Williams Field House	197
FIGURE 7.7	Kahn Track and Shults Field	198
FIGURE 7.8	Fredrick D. Shults	199
FIGURE 7.9	North Fields	199
FIGURE 7.10	Hunsinger Tennis Courts	200
FIGURE 8.1	Joel Karlgaard	205
FIGURE 8.2	Natalie Winkelfoos	205
FIGURE 8.3	Carr Pool—renovated	208
FIGURE 8.4	Dill Field	209
FIGURE 8.5	Dolcemaschio Stadium with Culhane Field	209
FIGURE 8.6	Knowlton Athletics Complex	210
FIGURE 8.7	Shanks Center—exterior	211
FIGURE 8.8	Shanks Center—interior	212

PREFACE AND ACKNOWLEDGMENTS

Lee C. Drickamer graduated from Oberlin College in 1967 with a degree in biology, obtained a doctorate in zoology from Michigan State University in 1970, and pursued a career teaching and doing research at three institutions of higher education. He has, with co-authors, published thirteen monographs and textbooks pertaining to areas of zoology. Some of his interests and writings shifted to history more than thirty years ago and include several titles pertaining to academic history, among them *A History of the Department of Biology at Oberlin College* and *Northern Arizona University: Buildings as History*. In the course of this work, and after retiring to a house in Oberlin, he became interested in the story of physical education and athletics at the college.

Fredrick D. Shults graduated from Oberlin College in 1954 and returned to the college in 1957, where he taught the History of Physical Education, Sport Sociology, the Competitive Ethic, and Methods and Techniques as part of the Physical Education Major. He spent his entire career as a member of the Physical Education faculty and coached soccer, lacrosse, and several other sports. He earned a master's degree from Ohio State University in 1959, writing a thesis on "The Life of Fred Eugene Leonard, M.D., His Contributions and Influence on the Profession of Physical Education." During his early years at Oberlin, he completed a doctoral degree in physical education at Indiana University in 1967, with a dissertation entitled, "The History and Philosophy of Athletics for Men at Oberlin College." That work serves as the basis for portions of chapters 2 through 6 and inspired Drickamer to pick up the threads of the story. Sadly, Fred Shults died in June 2020 as revisions of this book were underway.

Together, we sought to provide a comprehensive narrative of the history of physical education at Oberlin. The faculty, students, and proteges of these individuals frequently were pioneers in the development of physical education, from the 1880s until the 1950s; some of the graduates continue to be influential into the twenty-first century. Carefully placing their accomplishments into the historical context of the timely and often overlapping philosophies of both physical education and education in general, became a primary focus for us. Comparing these benchmarks against the backdrop of changes in American higher education and current events, and attempting to elaborate upon them using newly acquired information, we provide answers to questions such as: How did these changes occur? What prompted these transitions? We furnish the reader with a unique and close examination of conditions that facilitated and promoted the long-standing traditions of physical education at the college.

The narrative traces significant developmental and philosophical shifts in American higher education from the 1830s to the present. These provide the backdrop and context for changes witnessed at Oberlin and other similar institutions. While Oberlin physical education faculty and graduates played critical roles during the past 130 years, they frequently incorporated innovative ideas and concepts drawn from the leaders prominent in northeastern US schools. Changes in society often proceed, hand-in-hand, with physical education and athletics.

It is noteworthy that the "mind–body" duality was prevalent from the college's establishment in the 1830s. We can follow this thread continuously to today's emphasis on health and wellness. Current developments are manifested on campus in the facilities and in the curriculum. We touch on this same mind–body tenet in several chapters and explore it more fully as a major part of the final chapter.

To facilitate the flow of the narrative, no footnotes or endnotes are used. Our primary goal was to produce a useful book for scholars, while at the same time to attract a wider audience of faculty, graduates, and others concerned with the development of physical education and athletics. There is also an audience among those who follow the myriad aspects of the history of higher education. We listed pertinent sources at the end of each chapter, with a comprehensive bibliography at the end of the book. While writing we discovered gaps, both in knowledge and written records. These gaps are not catastrophic in nature, and we will acknowledge them as they occur.

Many people contributed to making this effort a success. Four of these deserve special recognition: (1) Nancy Hawley Morrison (OC 1967) was a classmate of LCD and a cheerleader for two years. When we contacted her about her cheers, she not only provided useful information and photos, but took on the job of editing the entire manuscript multiple times. She did a superb job. (2) At the Oberlin College Archives, Anne Salsich provided the best service imaginable, in terms of searching for and scanning photographs. As you will rapidly detect, the book is filled with excellent visual material. (3) James D. (J. D.) Donovan lived up to his reputation as the historian of all things athletic at the college. His enormous efforts to mine materials, organize them, and explain so many aspects of the programs at Oberlin, were a major feature of compiling parts of the book. (4) Mike Mancini, Assistant Athletics Director for Communications, gave me valuable time, in terms of knowledge about the facilities and teams. Further, he delivered a pair of volumes, compiled with the assistance of J. D. Donovan, that contained all of the records for the men's intercollegiate sports teams, beginning in the 1890s. Nancy and Anne were Yeowomen, and J.D. and Mike were Yeomen. Thank you!

Ken Grossi, Director of the Oberlin College Archives, was partly responsible for getting LCD involved in this effort, and his valued inspiration throughout the several years of work involved is gratefully acknowledged. Louisa Hoffman, also with the College Archives, readily provided materials and assistance. Clara Margaret Flood drew the two excellent maps of the Oberlin College campus for chapter 1. Roland Baumann kindly read some of the revised chapters. He also led efforts to write the biographical and informational guides that introduce the individual sections of materials in the college archives.

Three people who wrote about physical education and athletics at Oberlin were of great importance to understanding both the earlier and more recent history: Molly Murphy and Lisa Pruitt wrote the introductory essay for the Physical Education Records in the college archives. Leland Brandt wrote a senior honors thesis on "The Evolution of Women's Intercollegiate Athletics at Oberlin College" under the guidance of Carol Lasser. A list of names of the many wonderful people who assisted by sharing knowledge in both written and oral forms with this project includes the following: Natalie Winkelfoos, George Andrews, Roland Baumann, J. D. Donaldson, Don Hunsinger, Norman Craig, Norman Henderson, Michael Mancini, Ann Stevens, Dick Michaels, Margaret and John Erickson, Deborah Horn Roosevelt, Alexia Hudson-Ward, Anne Salsich, Betsy Bruce, Yago Colás, Kevin Willbond, Carolyn Briggs, Megan Mitchell, Judith Sellers, Haley Antelle, Rebecca Sparagowski, Anne Elder, Prudy Hall, Tim Cross, Eileen Dettman, Ann Butler, Maureen Donnelly, Carl Brown, and David Eisner. My sincere apologies to anyone who was inadvertently left off this list—we thank you as well.

All of the figures and photographs in this book are the property of the Oberlin College Archives or the Department of Athletics and Physical Education at Oberlin College; this includes photographs taken by Lee Drickamer which are the property of Oberlin College, and Figures 1.3, 1.4, and 1.5, which were drawn for this book and are the property of Oberlin College.

We thank Director Anthony Sanfilippo at the Ohio State University Press, Tara Cyphers, Robert Ramaswamy, and Juliet Williams for their assistance throughout the publication process. John Jacobs did an excellent job copyediting the entire manuscript. Elizabeth Zaleski was superb with editing the proofs and making corrections. Eileen Allen provided a comprehensive index. We also thank Angela Moody, who designed the cover. The Press's careful attention to detail most certainly made the book better. Two excellent reviews inspired the revision of the original manuscript. As a journal editor and author, I give a superb thanks to the reviewers, R. Scott Kretchmar and Jason R. Edwards, for their excellent and most helpful comments.

INTRODUCTION

The first forty years of the nineteenth century were characterized by several significant changes as the US continued to expand into the Western Frontier. These events included the Industrial Revolution and the Second Great Awakening. The latter, which began in the 1790s, was characterized by a Protestant religious revival in New England; it continued into the first thirty years of the nineteenth century, spreading westward through the 1820s. This movement had a significant influence on the founding of several small liberal arts colleges. In Ohio, for example, Kenyon College (1824, Episcopalian), Denison College (1831, Baptist), Oberlin College (1833, Congregationalist), and Ohio Wesleyan College (1842, Methodist) were each dedicated, in part, to educating pastors and training missionaries.

The Oberlin Collegiate Institute was chartered in 1833 and opened its doors in the fall of 1834. It was a unique experiment, the establishment of a small college in the swampy wilderness of north central Ohio (fig. 0.1, fig. 0.4). Through the vision of John J. Shipherd (1802–1844), and with assistance from Philo P. Stewart (1798–1868), the institution began a journey committed to admitting and training people of both genders. From its early years, Oberlin included men and women with African origins. Around the same time Oberlin opened, the Lane Seminary in Cincinnati was struggling with a lack of funding. The student body banded together under the aegis of "Lane Rebels" and staged a protest. This unrest was recognized by the Oberlin founders, and in 1834, the

FIGURE 0.1. Oberlin Hall, the first building on campus, was completed for classes in 1834. It housed all aspects of the school, including classrooms, lodging for students and faculty, and a chapel. By the end of the decade, several more buildings appeared on the fledgling campus. The structure stood on the southwest corner of the present intersection of Main and College Streets. (Oberlin College Archives)

Lane school merged with and relocated to Oberlin. The college's student numbers were bolstered, and the fundraising benefitted from efforts by Arthur Tappan (fig. 0.2). Tappan (1786–1865) was a New York businessman and abolitionist, and his support was welcomed. With new-found dedication and assistance from like-minded individuals, the Institute survived some difficult early years. By the 1850s, when the name was changed to Oberlin College, the school was literally "out of the woods" and graduating students for the ministry, medicine, teaching, and other career pathways.

As societies developed in both Europe and Asia, various activities provided training for individuals and for groups destined to engage in military endeavors. The Greeks were likely the first westerners to provide a form of physical education involving running, jumping, swimming, and wrestling. Writers as early as Plato recorded that for the mind and body you could not fashion one without the other. Juvenal, in Roman times, listed his qualifications for a "good man"—first of which was "Mens sana in corpore sano," or "A sound mind in a sound body." This duality was relegated to the backdrop, when, during the millennium cov-

FIGURE 0.2. Arthur Tappan, from Northampton, MA, lived his adult life primarily in New York City, where he and his brother Lewis engaged in a number of commercial ventures. Arthur, an ardent abolitionist, aided the organization of several antislavery societies. He was associated with the Lane Seminary in Cincinnati and then became a benefactor of Oberlin College when the Lane Rebels moved north in 1834. He provided funds for a campus building bearing his name. The campus green was named Tappan Square in his honor.

ering the fifth through the early fifteenth centuries, people focused on the afterlife. All humans were presumed to be sinners. Thus, matters of the mind prevailed over physical development, and bodily aspects of the duality were generally ignored. The Renaissance, emerging early in the fourteenth century, restored the mind–body tenet and brought with it new forms of exercise and games.

The first Olympics were held in the eighth century BCE and were staged every four years annually until the fourth century CE. While some forms of physical education occurred during the next 1,500 years, it was only in the eighteenth century that any real organized physical training was developed in various European countries. Depending on their geographical locations, the different countries' schools could be identified by their training regimes. As society progressed, there was now adequate time each day to devote to physical development, which included, along with manual labor, gymnastics and athletic games. Once again, the prevailing philosophy of education included the age-old principle of combining "a sound mind in a healthy body." This philosophy was in vogue during the 1830s when Oberlin College was founded.

This narrative presents Oberlin College as an excellent example of an institution founded in the nineteenth century that survived through decades of change into the twenty-first century. This is accomplished in the context of historical shifts in philosophy, differential growth and expansion for some larger schools relative to smaller colleges, and transformations in American higher education. The book is the story of a small college with a mission to integrate physical activity as a vital element of the overall educational experience. The college logo, impressed on its seal—"Learning and Labor"—signifies a firm belief in mind–body harmony. The founders fully appreciated the need for development of both mind and body if both were to function effectively within each student. The "Labor" portion of the motto was part of the daily routine of students, who devoted a half day to studies in the academic classroom, and a half day to constructing buildings, general maintenance of the campus, and tilling the farmland surrounding the campus to provide food for both humans and livestock. Other chores included a variety of domestic activities. Together, these daily routines provided a living pattern that embodied the mind–body connection. The resulting exchange benefitted the college through the student labor, while students earned money or credit toward tuition, room, and board.

As occurred at other institutions of higher education, there was a sequence of changes in terms of the predominant nature of physical activities at the college. The chronology that began with manual labor progressed in stages, through intensive programs of gymnastics, to games and sports, and eventually to modern physical education and intercollegiate athletics. As with similar schools, Oberlin College recognized that a liberal arts education is foremost an individual effort, while physical education, when applied in games and sports, is more often a team experience. Today, students at Oberlin, upon completing an academic exercise, sign the Honor Pledge: "I have neither given nor received aid in this examination." Though there is no extant pledge for a member of an athletic team, orchestra, theater troupe, or dance group, the pledge might read: "I have both given and received aid in this performance."

A key emphasis in this story is the many ways in which Oberlin was a leader in the development of physical education. To form a more complete picture, events and innovations in physical education and athletics from other institutions are integrated into the narrative. Accomplishments at Oberlin help set the stage for some chapters and give insight into the prominent role played by a liberal arts college in Ohio regarding a major feature of American culture: the pursuit of exercise and physical activity. (1) Delphine Hanna, M.D., was the first female professor of physical education with tenure at any American institution of higher education. At Oberlin, she set the stage for many of the developments in physical education that would follow, well into the twentieth century. (2) Warner Gymnasium (1901) was an early structure designed specifically for physical education and with an indoor running track. (3) Fred E. Leonard wrote the first book on the history of physical education, published in 1923 (and reprinted in 1947). Others from Oberlin wrote textbooks and monographs on aspects of physical education and sport; this continues up to today. (4) Oberlin was the first institution to award a four-year physical education degree as part of a liberal arts degree. (5) The college was the first school to have a director of athletics with faculty status, and Oberlin was one of the first institutions where coaches were given faculty status. (6) Oberlin served as a key location for the introduction of the New Physical Education, involving organized sports and games. (7) Several Oberlin-related individuals played important roles in the formation of organizations like the National Collegiate Athletic Association (NCAA) and the founding of groups such as the Playground Association of America. (8) Moses Fleetwood Walker, who attended Oberlin, was the first individual of African American heritage to play professional baseball. (9) John Heisman began his football coaching career at Oberlin.

Taken together, these accomplishments attest to the importance of the college in the history of physical education. While Oberlin men's athletic teams were early participants in some sports, the college had a lesser role in the emergence of American collegiate athletics than it did with developments in physical education, organizations of schools involved in athletics, and the expansion of recreation as a lifelong experience.

Themes and Rationale

Oberlin serves as a case study to examine changes in physical education and athletics across almost two centuries in the context of developments in higher education, society, and underlying philosophies. The approach involves several interwoven themes, which provide the rationale for the current need for such a book. All of these themes could be used to explore histories like Oberlin's for other institutions of higher learning. That research would eventually allow for useful comparisons and lead to a more comprehensive perspective on how physical education developed, matured, and evolved to what exists today.

(1) Examining the philosophies that served as foundations for physical culture leads to two fundamental questions noted earlier and which are addressed in each chapter. What changes occurred in the types of physical activities characterizing a step along the path to where things stand today? Why did the particular philosophy and activity routines change? Placing the transitions in broader perspective, including national and international events, trends in higher education, and shifts at other schools broadens the context. In an evolutionary scheme, new philosophies arise, or old ones are modified by trial-and-error steps, and one or several new approaches emerge. Oberlin and similar schools are good examples of how philosophies shift and, in turn, their application to physical activities produces changes.

(2) Chronological divisions followed periods when different forms of physical activity predominated. In this way, the interconnected nature of transitions in physical education can be interpreted in the context of societal events. History does not occur in discrete time periods; rather, there are overlaps in terms of philosophies and practices in physical education. Thus, in reading the narrative it is important to integrate across chapter boundaries on numerous topics, such as philosophy or physical education at Oberlin. In this way the flow connects similar subjects through time.

(3) Philosophy forms an integral part of this story, providing a sense of underlying thought processes. One focus examines the duality of mind and body, something that is addressed by physical activity combined with academic study and scholarly pursuits. From this perspective the body (physical) is controlled by the mental (nervous system) and, consequently, being fit physically influences and enhances the capabilities of the brain. In the last portion of the twentieth century a "new" philosophy often called "win at all costs" emerged. The basic tenet is that programs of athletics and individual athletes must strive to win sparing no effort, which can include, for example, putting aside safety issues, verbal abuse from coaches, and cheating. This approach soon migrated downward to affect youth sports as well as college and professional games. This last topic is covered in more detail in chapters 7 and 8.

(4) There are numerous books detailing the philosophy of physical activity and sport incorporating national and international trends, including some by alumni of the physical education program at Oberlin College. However, there do not appear to be any full histories of

the changes in physical education and athletics at a single institution which address the progression in the philosophy of physical education and sports. Oberlin can thus serve as an example of schools during the lengthy period covered by the book. A history like this is unique in terms of a scholarly approach to the growth and diversification of a program of physical education and athletics, including attendant discussions and controversies. This theme is enhanced by the important roles played by individuals with relationships to the college. People with Oberlin connections were leaders in terms of training physical educators, helping initiate organizations that grew up around physical activity and recreation in the late nineteenth and early twentieth centuries, and providing textbooks and manuals used in physical education classes. They were not, however, generally, the innovators in terms of introducing new sports or activities or with putting forth sets of rules for new sports as they emerged. Other schools, largely those in the eastern states and some elsewhere in the country, provided the locus for "inventing" new sports or modifying those adopted from Europe. For example, basketball originated in Springfield, MA; volleyball at the YMCA in Holyoke, MA; baseball likely originated with cricket or rounders adapted from England; and football has a long history extending to ancient times and was modernized first as soccer and rugby.

(5) On a more provincial level, the histories of people, places, and events that together comprise the Oberlin experience are brought together as a story. By incorporating the people and their varied roles, time periods come to life, and relationships are examined involving individuals at the college and at other institutions. The evolution of the physical facilities at the college follows a path that is typical for the schools of the period, eventually leading to modern athletics complexes with multiple, sometimes specialized, buildings and outdoor venues. Particular events are more time- and place-based and serve as foundations for or are manifestations of key happenings over the 188-year history of the college up to 2021.

(6) Recent decades involve reevaluations of the roles of college sports in education and the relationships involving the dominance of intercollegiate athletics at many schools. How did this progression lead to the present, varying priorities at different institutions? Health and wellness studies are becoming more important, and quite popular in college curriculums. What is the future of these nascent programs, and how will they be integrated with the existing physical education and athlet-

ics programs? There is a need to reassess the role of athletics at undergraduate liberal arts colleges: a common thread in the answers to these questions is a return to the duality of mind and body as necessary for a complete individual. This may take different forms for each individual, but at its core the renewed emphasis will provide a basis for better health and increased productivity.

(7) Finally, sharing the rich history of an aspect of the Oberlin College experience which integrates with all other facets of the institution is a real pleasure. Individuals who examine aspects of American higher education and those studying physical education and athletics will benefit from the approach and materials used. By offering the broader context of a more complete history of physical education, athletics, and recreation at Oberlin, this book can serve as a stimulus for similar efforts at other institutions. The course of events and underlying rationales for changes will vary at each school.

Terms and Definitions

Different terms are employed at various, overlapping time periods to describe the topics covered. These include physical training, physical culture, and physical education, listed in the chronological order of their common usage. For example, gymnastics led into physical training when anthropometric measurements were introduced to assess students' bodily health and fitness. Physical fitness was the goal while gymnastic exercise remained the primary means to accomplish that end. After gymnastics was replaced by games and sports, physical education was the primary term. It included the goal of fitness, but added social values, competition, and winning. Today, physical education is the primary term used.

Physical education has been defined in several ways. Two men with Oberlin connections, Jesse Feiring Williams and Whitelaw Reid Morrison, defined the term as follows: "Any motor activity that trains the individual to control and direct his body is a form of physical education. . . . Physical education is a very old method of education" (Williams and Morrison, 1939, 19. Williams also defined the term as follows: "Physical education should aim to provide an opportunity for the individual to act in situations that are physically wholesome, mentally stimulating and satisfying, and socially sound" (Williams 1922, 16). In an encyclopedia on the subject we find another definition: "Physical education is the art and science of human movement as expressed through participation in exercise, games, sports, and dance" (Bosco and Turner 1981, 420). Lastly, in a more recent book by C. A. Bucherm physical education is defined as "the process of education that concerns activities that develop and maintain the human body" (Bucher 1972, 6). Physical education is a vital part of the overall educational experience.

Modern definitions for the expanded fields of physical education, exercise science, and sport are provided in a recent textbook by D. A. Wuest and J. L. Fisette, who suggest that "today, physical education is defined as an educational process that uses physical activity as a means to help individuals acquire skills, fitness, knowledge and attitudes that contribute to their optimal development and well-being" (2012, 8–9) and that "exercise science is the scientific analysis of exercise or, more inclusively, physical activity. To study activity, exercise scientists draw upon scientific methods and theories from many disciplines, such as biology, biochemistry, physics and psychology. Sports are highly organized, competitive activities governed by rules. . . . Sports provide meaningful opportunities to demonstrate one's competence and to challenge one's limits. Competition can occur against an opponent or oneself" (2012, 9). In the present book, the focus is on physical education and sports.

Games, sports, and athletics have individual, often overlapping, definitions. "Games" is often used to denote a broad grouping of low-level, loosely organized activities including party games, children's games, and others. This could include, for instance, jacks, bridge, or hopscotch. Here, games are any recreational activity done alone or with others, usually with few rules, and involving self-enjoyment or competition. A game is also an event in which an activity is the central focus. "Sports," a more expansive term, are physical activities, carried out with prescribed rules and a more competitive spirit. Basketball, volleyball, and golf are examples. Last, "athletics" refers to any sort of games or sports that are highly organized and regulated, with an emphasis on human physical strength, endurance, and skill. Athletics may be performed either individually or as a team. Athletes at this level participate in a game as a competitive event. An examination of human history reveals that all three of these terms apply to physical activities common for thousands of years.

The pyramid (fig. 0.3) represents several aspects of the history of physical education and athletics during the progression from the nineteenth into and through the twentieth century, following the years when "Learning and Labor" was the normal student routine. Refer-

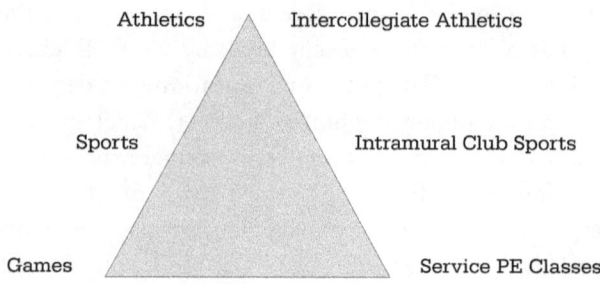

FIGURE 0.3. Pyramid of stages and activities in the history of physical education. (Lee C. Drickamer)

ence is made to this pyramid several times in later chapters. Games were introduced to the masses, the beginners who simply wanted to play. As players became more skilled, more refined rules and competition developed, and games turned into sports directed toward the more adept and dedicated players. The top of the pyramid was restricted to the most expert individuals. Anyone not proficient or sufficiently motivated to be included in games, sports, or athletics, was relegated to being a spectator. To prepare students to become active in games, sports, and athletics, physical education instructors developed their own pyramid with service classes as the base, intramural and club sports in the middle, and intercollegiate athletics at the top, as seen on the right side of the pyramid. Though there were fewer athletes at the top of the pyramid, the number of coaches and the financial resources needed increased. This often weakened the support for the service classes and the intramural and club sports programs. This also had the consequential effect of obscuring and deemphasizing the mind–body harmony that was the original foundation for physical activities among the entire college community.

Organization and Chapter Flow

The narrative follows a chronology from 1833 to the present. The organization within each chapter varies at times, but generally has similar subsections in a logical flow. Each begins with coverage of pertinent background events in the US and world that influenced higher education during that period. This sets the context for presenting the current philosophy of education for that period with an emphasis on how that influenced physical education and athletics.

People and programs form the bases for the next sections. Though coverage of some individuals is interspersed within other parts, key people are sometimes grouped in a separate heading. These individuals and their colleagues are the ones who carried on the activities just noted with the pyramid (fig. 0.3). The programs, which change over time, provide the structure for interactions between the faculty, students, and coaches in both physical education and athletics.

For many chapters, the last section deals with the facilities and other venues. It is these structures and playing fields where the activities are conducted. Shifting needs usually drive the construction of new buildings, but it is also the case that a new venue can provide an opportunity to bring in additional activities or sports. Some chapters conclude with coverage of the roles played by faculty at and graduates from the college in the history of physical education. In addition, some students who graduated from the college and later served as mentors of the next generation are introduced. Each chapter concludes with a brief summary.

Comparisons

To provide some sense of what was happening with physical education and athletics at small colleges, comparisons between Oberlin and peer institutions are made at several key junctures in the narrative. Principal among these are the other four schools in the Five College Consortium: Denison University, Kenyon College, Ohio Wesleyan University, and the College of Wooster. Several other small liberal arts colleges are used at particular places, most notably schools from the North Coast Athletic Conference (NCAC), of which Oberlin was a founding member in 1984. References to some larger schools provide bases for assessing similarities, differences, and changes over time. While Oberlin holds a prominent place in the history of physical education, other institutions made major contributions and played prominent roles in many of the developments of this discipline and particularly with regard to athletics.

Special Notes

The history of physical activities at colleges and universities generally encompasses four types of programs: (1) service classes, sometimes required, for most students; (2) courses toward a major in physical education; (3) extracurricular activities—intramurals, club sports, and recreation; and (4) intercollegiate athletics. To this may be added, for some time periods, a fifth category called "corrective physical education," or adapted physical education. This last was designed for students with disabilities or similar issues that precluded their participation in regular physical education classes. As appropriate, the four numbered categories are examined during the chronological journey through history.

Like many similar liberal arts colleges founded in the nineteenth century, Oberlin College opened a training academy soon after the institute began operations, comparable to a high school. It was called the Preparatory School from 1834 to 1892, at which time the name changed to Oberlin Academy. The academies served several purposes; a primary one was to prepare younger students for admission to the college. Another was to prepare teachers for primary and secondary school classrooms. The academy at Oberlin closed in 1916. For many years, academy students enjoyed limited participation in college athletics, including varsity teams. In addition, Oberlin undergraduates often served as coaches for sports teams at the academy.

Finally, as with any endeavor of this type, writers are limited by the nature and depth of the available information. The Oberlin College Archives have extraordinary collections of pertinent materials. The staff provided access to records of the physical education departments, athletic teams, personal papers of faculty and staff, and myriad other topics. The use of online materials from other repositories, which now exist in great abundance, and visits to several institutions aided the work. Discrepancies for findings on the same topic—for example, with dates for a building's construction—occur with some regularity. Where possible, information used came from primary sources.

Timelines and Maps

To assist the reader down multiple pathways, two timelines were created (see Appendix A). The first includes dates and events that are important to the overall history of physical education and athletics, primarily at the national level, but also with a few international hallmarks. The second timeline is specific to events pertaining to Oberlin College and its role in this experience. These provide a set of guideposts for our story.

In order to place the coverage into a physical framework, there are two maps. Using two maps, rather than a single one, avoids confusion with overlapping structures and field locations across the years and enhances the scale, aiding in readability. The best way to do this is to use one map for buildings and related structures on the south or main campus (fig. 0.4), and a second map covering the north campus with today's athletics facilities (fig. 0.5). References will be made to these maps in most chapters with regard to specific structures and playing fields. Aerial views of the campus at different times are found in figures 3.8, 4.11, and 5.13.

Sources Consulted for Introduction

Full citations are found at the end of the book.

Fairchild, J. H. *Oberlin: The Colony and the College, 1833–1883.*

Fletcher, R. S. *A History of Oberlin College from Its Foundation through the Civil War.*

Gerber, E. W. *Innovators and Institutions in Physical Education.*

Hackensmith, C. W. *History of Physical Education.*

Kretchmar, R. S., M. Dyerson, M. P. Llewellyn, and J. Gleaves. *History and Philosophy of Sport and Physical Activity.*

Shults, F. D. *The History and Philosophy of Athletics for Men at Oberlin College.*

Thelin, J. R. *A History of American Higher Education.*

Weston, A. *The Making of American Physical Education.*

Wuest, D. A., and J. L. Fisette. *Foundations of Physical Education, Exercise Science, and Sport.*

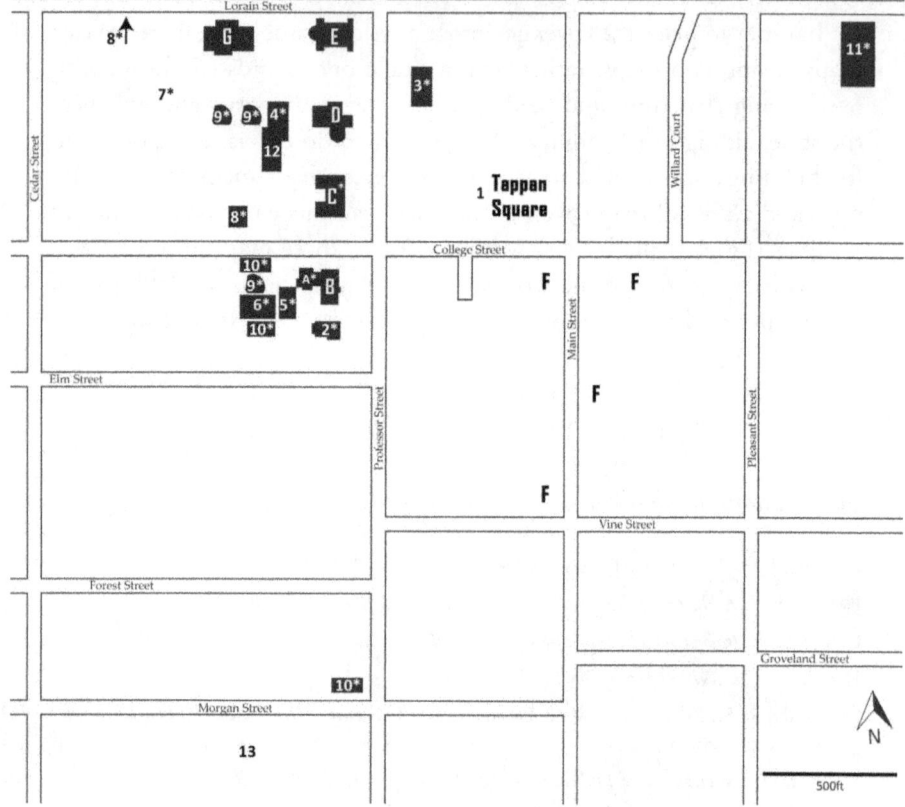

FIGURE 0.4. Map of the main (south) campus of Oberlin College showing the structures associated with physical education and athletics. The dividing line used for the two maps is Lorain Street; everything in this map is south of that road. Numbered structures encompass all buildings since 1833. Those no longer present are noted with an asterisk in the key below. Some current structures as indicated at the bottom of the map key are shown with letters to aid in orientation. Outlines of buildings are not drawn to scale. (Clara Margaret Flood)

1 Tappan Square–cricket, rugby, football, tennis, baseball, and other sports
2 Music Hall (First Ladies Gymnasium)*
3 First Men's Gymnasium* (No photo available)
4 Second Men's Gymnasium*
5 Rockefeller Skating Rink and Gymnasium*
6 South Campus outdoor playing areas for sports*
7 Outdoor Skating Rink–Dickinson Field*
8 First and Second Dickinson Houses*
9 Tennis Courts*
10 Tennis Courts*
11 Gayter's Ice Skating Area*
12 Warner Gymnasium (Warner Center)
13 Ladies Grove and Arboretum
A First Church
B Second Ladies Hall*
C Talcott Hall–built on site of the Second Ladies Hall after fire (1888) destroyed the earlier structure
D Warner Conservatory
E Finney Chapel
F Downtown Oberlin
G Wilder Hall (Men's Building)

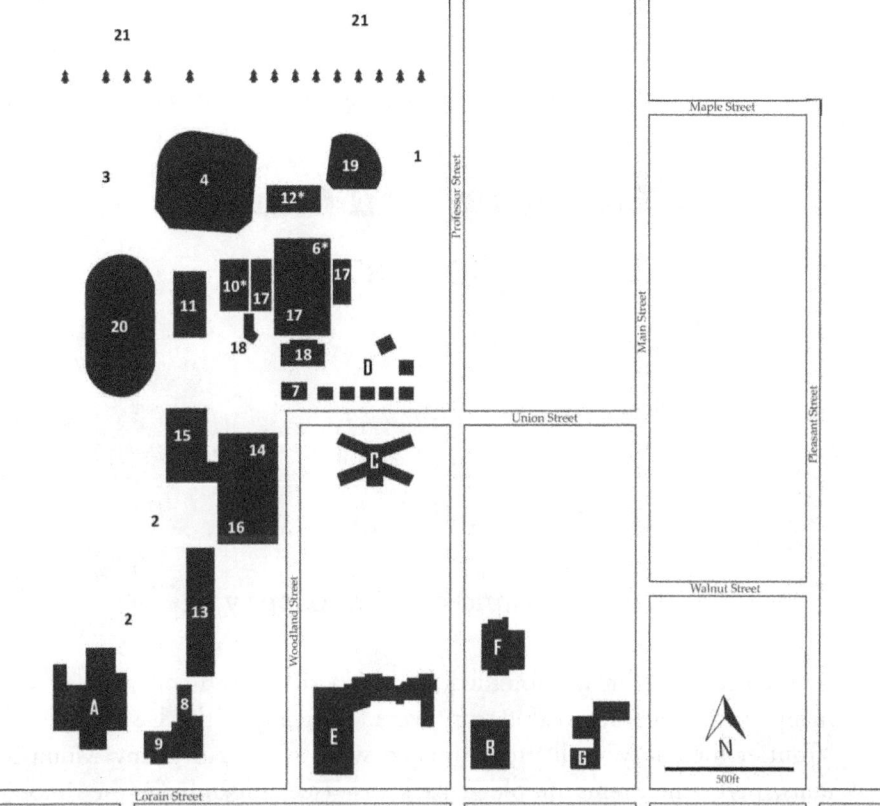

FIGURE 0.5. Map of the north campus of Oberlin College showing the structures associated with physical education and athletics. The dividing line used for the two maps is Lorain Street; everything in this map is north of that road. Buildings and playing fields no longer present are noted with an asterisk in the key below. Some current structures as indicated at the bottom of the map key are shown with letters to aid in orientation. (Clara Margaret Flood)

1   Athletic Park
2   Galpin Field–Women's Sports and Intramurals
3   Dill Fields & Old Dill Field Football Grounds
4   Dill Field Baseball Stadium
5   Track and Field–area for some field events
6   Savage Stadium*
7   Nichols Gateway
8   Crane Pool
9   Hales Gymnasium and Annex
10 Jones Field House*
11 Williams Ice Rink/Field House/Training Facility
12 Tennis Courts–clay*
13 Tennis Courts–hard surface (multiple locations)
14 Philips Physical Education Center
15 Heisman Club Field House
16 Shanks Health and Wellness Center
17 Knowlton Stadium and Dick Bailey Field
18 Knowlton Athletic Complex–Locker Rooms and Social Spaces
19 Dolcemaschio Stadium and Culhane Field
20 Robert Lewis Kahn Track and Fred Shults Field
21 North Fields for Soccer, Lacrosse, Intramurals, Club Sports, and Team Practices
A   Mercy Allen Hospital (Allen Memorial Hospital)
B   Carnegie Library
C   North Hall (now Langston Hall)
D   Union Street Apartments
E   Science Center

CHAPTER 1

Learning and Labor

1830s–1870

Background and Philosophy

By the time Oberlin was founded, both as a village and college in 1833, many events relevant to this story were occurring in the US. While a "frontier mentality" still predominated west of the Allegheny Mountains, pertinent events unfolded back east (see Appendix A for timelines). Some of those developments in New England were, in turn, based on changes transported from various locations in Europe, where several philosophical approaches predominated. Among these, some contained tenets involving the mind–body duality. The Enlightenment produced a variety of philosophies, among which the duality played a role. The most prominent of these was likely that postulated by René Descartes and often called reductionism. This promoted the viewpoint that the body could influence the mind, but the reverse was not true. It is noteworthy that some aspects of this dichotomy persist in today's stereotypes of athletes and intellectuals, referred to as "jocks" and "geeks."

The importance of the connection between mind and body, as envisaged by the ancient Greeks, again moved to the forefront by the start of and throughout much of the nineteenth century. Later, in the last third of the century, fostered by the Darwinian theory of evolution, pragmatists held that the human body was shaped as a response over time to its environment. Melded onto this was the notion that the mind was part of the body and was thus affected by environmental influences in concert with changes in the body. The roots of what became known as "muscular Christianity" are found in the middle of the nineteenth century in both Europe and America. It is against this background of shifting philosophies that modern physical education was born, slowly replacing manual labor as the locus for daily exercise. How did these various influences affect the development of physical activity in the US and particularly at smaller colleges like Oberlin?

Toward the end of the eighteenth century, elementary forms of calisthenics and gymnastics developed in Europe. During the first quarter of the nineteenth century, these movements spread to America. During the 1820s and 1830s, these began to take hold in New England. It was not until the 1860s, however, as manual labor declined in emphasis, that calisthenics and gymnastics appeared in places like Oberlin. The New England influence can be felt in the schools of thought and practice regarding the best methods for instruction. Soon, gymnasiums dedicated to this purpose were widespread across the Midwest. The two closely related forms of exercise dominated at Oberlin and elsewhere among small colleges in Ohio for the last three decades of the nineteenth century.

Calisthenics consists of various synchronized routines; these generally do not require apparatus or equipment, though weights and wands may be used. Much of calisthenics involves using the body's own mass for weight and resistance. Examples include jumping jacks, push-ups, sit-ups, and lunges. Some calisthenics consist of rhythmic movements, not unlike particular forms of dance, and as was the case at Oberlin and other schools, often accompanied by music. These exercises can be done individually or in groups. Many have participated in or observed large groups doing morning routines consisting of calisthenics; for example, these are observed in many Asian countries and among workers at industrial plants. Today, many athletes engage in forms of calisthenics as a warm-up prior to a full workout or participation in an event. Calisthenics can be viewed as complementary or preparatory to gymnastics.

In broad terms, gymnastics includes systematic exercise using various forms of apparatus, tumbling, and acrobatics. In the nineteenth and early twentieth centuries, this functioned as a way to build strength, agility, and fitness. Today, gymnastics is a competitive sport. As it developed in several schools in Europe, there were several forms, two of which influenced what occurred at Oberlin. German gymnastics was based on a nationalist and militaristic philosophy and involved different types of apparatus including parallel bars, horizontal bars, stationary rings, and vaulting horses. The exercises, prescribed and usually executed individually, were designed primarily for men. Swedish gymnastics, by contrast, involved groups performing movement exercises, including some with clubs and wands, and bore some similarities to calisthenics. When apparatus was incorporated into the routines, strength building was the goal, especially using weights and pulleys. This system was used by both women and men. More of these forms of exercise are covered in chapter 2, at the time when they became the foundation of physical culture. Most nineteenth-century photos of gymnasiums show pieces of apparatus or groups performing exercises or both and often include neatly stored clubs, wands, and mats.

Friedrich Jahn (1778–1852), a German schoolteacher, is credited with formulating the German tradition called the *Turnverein*, which consisted of a gathering of groups to perform their various exercises, most often in a location called a *Turnplatz*. Several of his followers, reacting to repression of the movement in Germany, emigrated to the US. Pehr Henrik Ling (1776–1839) was most responsible for developing the Swedish gymnastics tradition. Early in life, he was exposed to the nascent Danish gymnastics. This, coupled with other experiences, led him to create a system that used exercises as a means of attaining correct body development based on science and medicine.

A significant facet of the educational philosophy which developed in the northeastern US was that a general education should incorporate physical exercise. The dichotomy, established early by Plato, involved a distinction between "education of the physical" and "education through the physical." Both schemes end up with individuals who are physically fit, but they provide different patterns of integration of the mind and body. Most American colleges and universities had required forms of physical activity as an element of their curriculum, comprising part of the general education for each student. Today, as discussed in the final chapter of the book, there is a resurgence in the desire to have physical exercise form a part of the daily routine for all students.

American Schools and Colleges

German gymnastics was introduced by Charles Beck (1798–1866) at the Round Hill School in Massachusetts in 1823. Calisthenics was brought to the Hartford Female Seminary in 1832 by Catharine Beecher (1800–1878). The first YMCA in the US was opened in 1851 in Boston with both forms of gymnastics present. In 1866, a group of women created the first YWCA. When the Oberlin Collegiate Institute opened for classes (1834), the early beginnings of organized exercise were underway. However, the predominant physical activity at that time in more rural areas, away from the eastern states, remained manual labor.

In the northeastern US, several institutions established the foundations for the emergence of modern physical education and aspects of modern sports. New gymnasiums and outdoor areas for use as playing fields were established at a number of schools. These included an early gymnasium at Harvard University (1860) and Barrett Gymnasium at Amherst College (1860), where Edward Hitchcock (1828–1911) was a prominent figure in athletics for five decades. Others were to follow in the ensuing decades covered in the next chapter.

Oberlin College

Oberlin College serves as a useful example of how the various philosophies and patterns of organized physical activity emerged from the 1830s and were maintained, though in ever-reduced use, until the years after the Civil War. John Jay Shipherd (1802–1844) directed the work of the Oberlin Collegiate Institute for two years before its first president, Asa Mahan (1799–1889; fig. 1.1), was installed in 1835. Shipherd's ambitious aspirations set the standard and guided the development of the educational process even after the early presidents officially assumed executive control of the school. Shipherd sought to offer the most useful education at the least expense of health, time, and money to young people who hoped to be Christian ministers and schoolteachers. His means of accomplishing these objectives incorporated the manual labor system. In a circular sent to publicize the new institution, Shipherd wrote:

> In the Oberlin Institute prominence is given to the Manual Labor System. All of its Students, rich and poor, male and female, are required to labor four hours daily, little children, peculiar cases and providence excepted. The principle objects of this are health, bodily, mentally, and moral; the students support; and the formation of industrious and economical habits. (Fletcher 1943, 129)

The Oberlin Institute had its own farm to provide food for the campus and residents. For male students, there was much to be done in terms of the varied farming activities, cutting down trees for building materials and heating, constructing businesses and dwellings, and providing local infrastructure including roads and streets. Female students, following the customs of the time, were involved with cooking, cleaning and maintenance activities, and crafting clothing and household linens. Students committed half of each day to academics and the other half to their labors. This meant that they paid for much of their education through physical efforts that benefitted them and all others at the school as well as citizens of the new village of Oberlin. Generally, four hours of daily work (later changed to three hours per day) were expected from each student each day except for Sundays. Prescribed work often occurred in blocks, including those in the preparatory school and school of theology, in addition to those in the college curriculum. For example, in 1841, the hours from 2:00 to 5:00 p.m. were set aside for all to do manual labor.

A major concern driving the need for this manual labor system was the feeling among educators and theologians that many people were not getting enough exercise during their sedentary daily lives. This was not only detrimental to their physical well-being, but also affected their mental, moral, and spiritual health. Given our modern world and the emergence of "couch potatoes" and with many younger people devoting significant amounts of time to computers and social media, there is a movement today to introduce more activity through additional recreation as part of health and wellness programs. Achieving sufficient physical activity became a recurring problem for humans once people settled into an existence where food was plentiful, and our other needs were met with minimal physical exertion.

Manual labor remained an integral feature at Oberlin College (the name changed in 1850) through the Civil War period. Asa Mahan (fig. 1.1), Oberlin's first president, and the second president, Charles Grandison Finney (1792–1875), who served 1851–1866, both believed in the inherent value of manual labor. They strived to maintain the system even when it became a financial strain on the college after clearing lands and constructing buildings was no longer necessary. The manual labor–mental faculties philosophy remained a central focus from the opening of the college until the decade after the Civil War.

FIGURE 1.1. Asa Mahan, first president (1835–1850) of the Oberlin Collegiate Institute. Mahan graduated from Hamilton College (1824) and then from Andover Theological Seminary (1827). He was the pastor for the Lane Seminary in Cincinnati, OH, at the time the Oberlin Institute opened. After being forced out at Oberlin over differences with the faculty concerning his intense religious views in 1850, he spent time in Cleveland and later became president of Adrian College in Michigan. (Oberlin College Archives)

Oberlin College was not unique in having a program of manual labor, as Denison College also used this as one of its founding principles. Wabash College, in Indiana, founded a year before Oberlin, also began with manual labor as a principal component of the educational philosophy. However, other small schools (e.g., Ohio Wesleyan College and Kenyon College) and Ohio University, founded in the first half of the nineteenth century, did not rely on students for construction and operations, but used local farmers and laborers for these tasks. Many of the colleges and what later became larger institutions like Ohio State University were founded after other forms of physical exercise had replaced the manual labor system.

An excellent example of the benefits of the manual labor system at Oberlin during the period is Lucien C. Warner (fig. 1.2). Originally from the state of New York, Warner attended the Preparatory Academy and then Oberlin College, receiving a degree in 1865. Brief service in a Civil War regiment was followed by a medical degree from New York University. Warner had a distinguished career in business, with his brother Ira, involving a variety of industries ranging from clothing to chemicals. He became a long-serving member of the Oberlin College Board of Trustees and was a major benefactor along with his wife, Karen Osborne Warner. Their gifts included funds for the gymnasium and original conservatory of music buildings. His early years, including those at Oberlin, which

FIGURE 1.2. Lucien C. Warner (1841–1925), shown here as an older gentleman, was an Oberlin graduate who attended the college during the period of learning and labor. His business career enabled him to donate considerable sums to his alma mater, used for a variety of purposes including two major buildings, one of which remains as part of the campus today. The former Warner Gymnasium is now home to the Warner Center, which houses the Dance Program. (Oberlin College Archives)

involved manual labor, provided a foundation for a productive and philanthropic career.

The Civil War brought a temporary end to student enthusiasm over gymnastic exercises; the war also delayed the decline of the manual labor system. Presidents Mahan and Finney had upheld Shipherd's concept of physical labor. But, soon after the war, Oberlin's third president, James H. Fairchild (1817–1902), who served from 1866 to 1889, faced the reality that continuing the old system was no longer feasible. Other avenues for physical activity were needed to promote and foster the harmony of mind and body. Fairchild's belief in this philosophy is summed up by the following quote from a book he authored, *Oberlin: The Colony and the College, 1833–1883*:

> The body is the instrument and organ of the mind, and our intellectual and spiritual activities and movements are dependent upon the conditions of the body. A sound mind comes with a sound body. Every disturbance of the physical condition produces a reaction upon our highest and noblest powers. Duty to the soul involves duty to the body. (1883, 188–189)

Further in the same book Fairchild voiced his skepticism concerning the possible use of gymnastics as a form of exercise to replace manual labor:

FIGURE 1.3. James H. Fairchild, third president of Oberlin College. Fairchild was raised in Lorain County, graduated from Oberlin (1838) and served on the faculty, teaching several subjects. He returned to the faculty upon resigning as president in 1889, serving briefly as president again for 1896–1898. He hid an enslaved fugitive, John Price, in his home, which was one segment of the Oberlin-Wellington rescue in 1858. (Oberlin College Archives)

It is by no means clear that muscle is not sometimes cultivated at the expense of the brain, animal strength at the sacrifice of nervous energy and power. It is at least questionable whether he who makes a gymnast of himself is not sacrificing the higher to the lower nature, and whether, in the end, he is not the loser, even in the domain of power and achievement. (1883, 194)

Later Fairchild (fig. 1.3), as recorded in his annual report for 1879–1880, accepted exercise as a necessary replacement for manual labor:

The two gymnasiums, one for young men and the other for the young women, are still sustained, and attendance upon their exercise is required of the students, except as they make regular provision for it in manual labor. This attendance is by class, four days in the week. A more thorough organization, under the charge of an officer of the College, would doubtless secure better results.

Thus, the philosophy of this period remained centered on the need for mind and body as equal elements in the physical, mental, and spiritual health of the individual. At Oberlin, the 1860s was a period of transition from primarily manual labor to more recreational forms of physical exercise including calisthenics and gymnastics as well as some early athletic competitions. Similar shifts occurred at Denison and Wabash during the 1860s and as students returned from the Civil War. Schools that were not founded based on the manual labor system shifted to gymnastics a bit sooner than those that were. A foundational philosophy requiring a combination of academic rigor with regular and purposeful physical exercise was embodied in the physical training that gradually replaced manual labor.

Physical Infrastructure at Oberlin

Near the end of President Finney's administration (1851–1866) at Oberlin, manual jobs were difficult to find, so the male students formed a Student Gymnasium Association as a response to their need for physical activity. They collected funds to erect a crude gymnasium (1861) where they engaged in various exercises (no photo or drawings of this structure exist). Whereas manual labor was introduced and organized by the college founders, it was gradually replaced by calisthenics, gymnastic exercises, and later games and sports which were the product of student enthusiasm and organizing efforts. Their energy drove the expansion of outlets for physical activities. Once the college faculty and administration realized the goal of good health—bodily, mentally, and spiritually—could be maintained and advanced through these new activities, they eventually gave their full support.

This first gymnasium, with a footprint measuring about 90' by 120', was located on College Park (Tappan Square), and was built in 1861 by the Student Gymnasium Association through student subscription (fig. 1.4). The gym was positioned northwest of where Tappan Hall was and, on the site, where Society Hall was later constructed. This site was on the west side of Tappan Square opposite today's Finney Chapel (map, fig. 0.4). The gymnasium housed several types of apparatus common to that era, including ropes for climbing, ladders, weights, sets of parallel bars, and Indian clubs used for rhythmic exercises. The students hired an instructor from back east to aid the development of their program. However, when the Civil War broke out, the instructor departed to enlist in the army. This First Men's Gymnasium was in use for little more than a year when national events intervened. The building was apparently razed by 1873 (other sources indicate 1867). There was no gymnasium for women until the 1870s. The 1861 date makes it one of

FIGURE 1.4. A stock certificate from the subscription gathered by the students for the first gymnasium in 1861. Three dollars invested provided two years of membership. (Oberlin College Archives)

the earliest such facilities in the western states, but it should be noted that at some institutions portions of existing buildings likely were used for various physical activities. Almost all institutions of higher education had outdoor fields for recreation and exercise.

Beginnings of Physical Training

Efforts to train individuals to become physical educators in the US began by the mid-nineteenth century. Likely the first program was that organized by Dio Lewis (1823–1886) in Boston in 1861. This was followed in 1866 by a similar program in New York City. Founded in 1885, the Training School for the Young Men's Christian Association (YMCA) at Springfield, MA (later Springfield College), was opened. These and other institutions, including Oberlin, played key roles in establishing the importance of physical exercise as part of a complete education.

Throughout the last third of the nineteenth century, there remained proponents of manual labor as inherently superior to gymnastics or the sports and games that soon followed. As noted earlier, there was a very modest beginning for gymnastics at Oberlin, but it soon faltered as numerous students went off to war. Many locals signed on with Company C of the Seventh Ohio Volunteer Infantry Regiment. Recruits often found themselves physically inadequate for the military requirements. Upon their return to campus after the end of hostilities, there was a renewed emphasis on physical activities. In the postwar years, military drill was introduced as a form of exercise, with males engaged for up to two hours per day.

Various types of recreational exercises appeared on Tappan Square (map, fig. 0.4) in the years just after the Civil War. The pattern of student initiation of various activities was predominant in many colleges and universities during this period. Throughout these years, as was true for the first gymnasium, the faculty reluctantly accepted the idea of student participation in various physical activities. However, they provided no support. The general religious convictions eschewed such wicked, sinful activities. The minutes of a faculty meeting of April 9, 1869, record that games on the square were permitted only at restricted hours, 12:00–3:00 and 6:00–8:00 p.m., and that they must be played solely east of the plank walk, which generally cut the square in half. Approval was also given for riding nelocipedes (an early form of the velocipede, now known as a bicycle) east of the plank walk.

Emergence of Athletic Contests

The earliest sports engaged in by Oberlin students were cricket and football (then similar to modern North American soccer), both outdoor sports. The popularity of cricket, which was played on the square and had 8–10 teams by the late 1850s, soon waned as baseball overtook it in popularity. Several teams were organized and participated in local competitions (fig. 1.5). The faculty often voted against requests to play against outside competition. Occasional contests between these early baseball teams and groups from Cleveland and Hudson occurred by the end of the 1860s. Games became more frequent in the 1870s. Baseball diamonds were first laid out on Tappan Square (fig. 1.6) and somewhat later on open areas, located behind Cabinet Hall, which stood

FIGURE 1.5. The 1868 Resolutes baseball team, which followed the Penfield 9 club on the Oberlin scene. The former took their name from a local man who provided them with wagon tongues to use for making bats. (Oberlin College Archives)

FIGURE 1.6. Tappan Square with the College Chapel and a portion of a baseball diamond used in the 1870s. (Oberlin College Archives)

between the current Peters Hall and the King Building. As was true for the appearance of many other sports at the colleges in Ohio, contests took place in eastern states before they spread westward. The first college baseball game occurred in 1859, when Amherst defeated Williams 73–32. It was followed the next day by a chess match between the same schools.

Summary

Physical education and sports took hold initially, with European influences, in the northeastern US. A philosophy that combined physical endeavors with academic engagement remained the foundational concept throughout this period. The Oberlin Collegiate Institute opened with the stated policy of using the manual labor system as a means of providing physical exercise for the students. By the post–Civil War period, a transition began that incorporated calisthenics and various forms of gymnastics for both men and women. The philosophy espoused by John Dewey and others, called pragmatism, which involved direct experience as a key element of the learning process, influenced the later portions of the period 1833–1870 covered in this chapter. Both the participation in various organized physical activities and the development of facilities and playing fields occurred several decades later in the nineteenth century in places like Ohio than in Massachusetts. Male students provided funds for a gymnasium, but that lasted less than two years, in part because of the Civil War. Various recreational activities and the earliest forms of team competitions were held on Tappan Square, with baseball as the first team sport played at the college.

Sources Consulted for Chapter 1

Full citations are found at the end of the book.

Barrows, I. C. *Physical Training: A Full Report of the Papers and Discussions of the Conference Held at Boston in November 1890.*
Bowen, W. G., and S. A. Levin. *Reclaiming the Game: College Sports and Educational Values.*
Bucher, C. A. *Foundations of Physical Education.*
Chessman, G. W. *Denison: The Story of an Ohio College.*
Fairchild, J. H. *Oberlin: The Colony and the College, 1833–1883.*

Fletcher, R. S. *A History of Oberlin College from Its Foundation through the Civil War.*
Goerler, R. E. *The Ohio State University: An Illustrated History.*
Hackensmith, C. W. *History of Physical Education.*
Hubbart, H. C. *Ohio Wesleyan's First Hundred Years.*
Leonard, F. E. *A Guide to the History of Physical Education.*
Lewis, D. *The New Gymnastics for Men, Women, and Children.*
Mechikoff, R. *A History and Philosophy of Sport and Physical Education.*
Putney, C. *Muscular Christianity: Manhood and Sports in Protestant America, 1880–1920.*
Schwendener, N. *A History of Physical Education in the United States.*
Smythe, G. F. *Kenyon College: Its First Century.*
Van Dalen, D. B., and B. L. Bennett. *A World History of Physical Education.*
Wayman, A. R. *A Modern Philosophy of Physical Education.*
Weston, A. *The Making of American Physical Education.*

CHAPTER 2

Gymnastics

1871–1895

Background

The post–Civil War era was a time of expansion in higher education (see Appendix A for timelines). The Morrill Act of 1862, which created the Land Grant Universities, resulted in the emergence of institutions with agricultural and related programs in each state. Normal schools opened for training teachers. A number of small colleges emerged in the eastern and midwestern states during the decades after the war. Notable examples among these taught only one gender, and others were coeducational: Wellesley, Smith, Wabash, Vassar, Wooster, Carleton, Beloit, Swarthmore, Radcliffe, and Bryn Mawr. In the southern states new schools included Berea College and Sophie Newcomb Memorial College, and, for the education of students of color, both Spelman and Morehouse Colleges opened in Atlanta. The period was characterized by reform and innovations in curriculum and scholarship. Against this background physical education came to be dominated by gymnastics, but during the final decade of the nineteenth century seeds germinated for the New Physical Education involving a culture of sports and games.

Several trends characterized the growth of physical culture during the late nineteenth century. One was dominance of the German and Swedish gymnastics, to which were added other programs, among them systems developed by François Delsarte (1811–1891) in France and by Dudley A. Sargent (1849–1924) in Boston. Considerable discussion regarding the benefits of these various methods, along with their introduction and implementation throughout America, became known as the "Battle of the Systems." A seminal gathering in Boston in 1890, attended by representatives of all of the systems, resulted in a report which remains an important document regarding this period (*Physical Training: A Full Report of the Papers and Discussions of the Conference Held in Boston in November 1890*). There was no clear "winner." Depending on the institution, distinct forms predominated, and some locations implemented more than one system. At Oberlin, the men tended to use the German approach and the women the Swedish system mixed with the methods Delphine Hanna (1854–1941) learned with Sargent. Some eastern schools leaned heavily toward one or the other of the two major schemes. The smaller colleges in Ohio tended to have the same sort of dichotomy as at Oberlin.

The basic underlying need to develop and support mind–body harmony remained the primary philosophy and focus; combining academic rigor across all disciplines with regular, daily, physical exercise. By the end of the century, Progressivism was taking hold. Though the pattern of a half day of academics and the other half devoted to labor of various types was no longer the rule, sufficient afternoon time was allotted for physical exercise. The introduction of gymnastics occurred in the eastern states and then spread westward. The shift to gymnastics was gradual, as some programs, first introduced in the 1850s, shifted to games and sports in the 1890s.

Oberlin College incorporated physical education into the curriculum over a twenty-year span, a critical, foundational period. Developments in program availability focused on both training teachers and introducing new approaches to the subject matter. In addition, all students enrolled in physical education classes; this requirement came and went for varying periods until 1970, when it was abolished. Though gymnastics in various forms predominated, other arrangements for physical exercise also developed, particularly by the 1890s. For some students, the required exercise component was met by physical education, while others engaged in games and sports. New avenues for recreation, both outdoors and in gymnasiums, provided opportunities for individual or group exercise. This era is summarized by the fourth president of the college (1891–1896), William G. Ballantine (1848–1937), a strong champion of the mind–body philosophy. Ballantine attempted to shift physical education at Oberlin to a scientific basis by promoting the phrase "Mens sana in corpore sano" [a healthy mind in a healthy body], an ideal now scientifically sought out.

Philosophy

The theory and practice of physical education prevailing from 1871 to 1895 was rooted in thoughts and developments from prior decades using the mind–body paradigm as the central focus, melded with emerging views. Among the more significant of the components for the new philosophy were the following: (1) evolution by natural selection; (2) biological science, including medicine and the new practice of anthropometrics; (3) physical education benefitting both the individual and society and promoting good character development; and (4) the social reform movements of the period. The key underlying philosophy later in this period was pragmatism, for which John Dewey (1859–1952) was the foremost synthesizer and proponent. The progressive approach was a major component of educational and social reform that reached into the twentieth century and will be addressed in more detail in the next chapter.

The ideas put forward by Dewey and others built upon a series of events that happened in the years between 1850 and 1890. These included physical fitness as a primary goal of the different forms of activity, which embodied the need to be physically healthy for proper functioning of the mind. In 1861, Edward Hitchcock, of Amherst College, responding to the generally poor health and inadequate physical fitness of American youth, developed a program with required physical training and lessons on personal health and hygiene. This served as a model for programs at other institutions.

Anthropometrics, the scientific measurement of a wide variety of external body characteristics, was another piece of this thought process. The underlying purpose was that by rigorously evaluating different aspects of the body, specific exercises could be established for attaining the individual's optimum physical fitness. In this country, these assessments originated in the 1860s, pioneered by Dudley A. Sargent in Boston. Near the end of the nineteenth century, he produced a standard chart involving more than fifty measurements used to determine the physical condition of every female and male student. Delphine Hanna, the founder of the physical training program at Oberlin, was a student with Sargent in his summer school at Boston. Vestiges of her programs using anthropometry lasted, in minor form, into the 1960s. Students enrolled in the "Body Mechanics" service class at the middle of the twentieth century at Oberlin College experienced aspects of physical measurement such as walking pattern recorded on film, spinal column alignment, and checking for any foot ailments.

An element of change pivoted on the progression from manual labor to acceptance of programs of gymnastics as the primary focus for achieving physical fitness. By the end of the century, the next steps in this process had commenced, as games and sports became more popular. This did not mean the end of gymnastics. Detractors, including some people at Oberlin, favored a continued focus on manual labor; a few maintained their stance into the early years of the twentieth century. Their objections focused on several arguments: (1) gymnastics was dangerous; (2) it was unnatural; (3) it was unphilosophical; and (4) those who engaged in manual labor as a career were averse to sports and held them in contempt.

Gymnastics

German and Swedish systems dominated nineteenth-century gymnastics. German gymnastics became popular in the US, in part, because of the large number of immigrants from the "old country" who settled in many American cities during the middle decades of the nineteenth century, before and after the Civil War. In Germany, the origins arose from the need for conditioning and skills used by the military during various wars of the first decades of the nineteenth century. This rationale included a large political component, preparing men for the conflicts that would result in German domination. The military drill that became part of college life at many schools in the US after that war contributed to the movement toward this form of exercise. The practice included exercises such as the vaulting horse, balance beams, parallel and horizontal bar apparatus, and a collection of calisthenics and jumping exercises. To this were added rope and pole climbing, stationary and flying rings, and various weight lifting activities.

This gymnastics approach owes some of its growth and popularity to the fact that many public schools originated and expanded during these same decades. The German system was introduced by immigrant groups

FIGURE 2.1. Women engaged in an interpretive dance program at the Memorial Arch on Tappan Square. (Oberlin College Archives)

on the east coast by the 1830s. Annual festivals, called *Turnerbunds,* were held each year from 1850 to 1860 and resumed in 1865. Instruction in this form of gymnastics began in private schools in eastern cities by the 1850s and 1860s, and subsequently in Chicago public schools in 1885 and in Cleveland in 1887.

Swedish gymnastics also originated from a need for physical conditioning and military preparedness, but with different exercises as the foundation. Swedish forms required less physical strength and were thus favored for women. The German forms occasionally occurred in groups and rhythmically, but mostly were done as individuals. This was generally not the case for Swedish gymnastics, which used more group activities, and frequently included musical accompaniment. At Oberlin, records indicate acquisitions of pianos for use during these activities. Swedish gymnastics involved free exercises consisting of movements of arms, legs, and trunks, movements that included thrusting, jumping, and balance, and class exercises like fencing, and dance. Frequently, these movements were performed in unison and had structured, choreographed sequences. Examples from Oberlin illustrate students engaged in expressive, combined arm and leg exercises, and an interpretive dance (fig. 2.1).

Delphine Hanna

Two individuals played prominent roles in the development of physical education at Oberlin: Delphine Hanna and Fred E. Leonard. Their contributions established Oberlin as an incubator for ideas about proper methods for educating future instructors and developing curriculum to fit those needs. The program of physical education at Oberlin College was founded and led by Delphine Hanna starting in the mid-1880s. She was joined, in the next decade, by one of her early pupils, Fred E. Leonard (1866–1922), who helped popularize some of the programs for men that Hanna originated for women. Together, they formed the nexus for launching the prominent, national role of Oberlin in the field of physical education.

Delphine Hanna (fig. 2.2) came to Oberlin in 1885 to direct the new gymnasium and provide training in physical activities. Her background included degrees from the Brockport State Normal School in New York (1874) and training at the Normal School of Dr. Dudley A. Sargent in Boston (1885). Time spent with school children, while teaching in Monroe County, NY and in Kansas, convinced her of the need for better physical exercise regimens for younger people. For her first year at Oberlin, she received no salary but instead was granted $350 for living expenses, and a $350 donation was made for the purchase of equipment for the new gymnasium. Her original title was Instructor in Physical Culture. She completed her education while employed at Oberlin, obtaining the M.D. degree from the University of Michigan (1890). Dr. Hanna served as Director of Physical Training in the Women's Department from 1887 to 1903. Her methodology was the basis for the formal program in physical education begun at Oberlin in 1886. In recognition of her work, in 1931 Delphine Hanna was among the first class voted as Fellows of the American Association for Physical Education; she was also selected for the University of Michigan Hall of Fame. Dr. Hanna was given an honorary A.M. degree from Oberlin in 1901. After retiring in 1921, she moved to Florida, where she resided until her death in 1941.

Women involved in physical education first used the old Music Hall as a gymnasium space (map, fig. 0.4). When it burned in 1881, the college decided to construct a new Second Ladies Gymnasium in a planned annex to the Second Ladies Hall. The first floor of the annex was about 29' by 40'. Shortly, the administration affirmed the idea that, rather than rely solely on students to provide instruction, it would be prudent

FIGURE 2.2. Delphine Hanna in the early twentieth century at the middle of her time at the college. (Oberlin College Archives)

to hire a person to run the gymnasium and provide a program of exercises. The first floor served as a gymnasium, and the upper story was used for housing students and Delphine Hanna.

Hanna was a strong proponent of physical exercise based on scientific principles. Her main efforts at Oberlin centered on working with new students to make anthropomorphic measurements. These enabled individualized instruction for each young woman. Her major interest was in proper posture. In 1893, Hanna published a chart, which, when combined with student measurements, was used to provide an individual program of exercises. The chart was updated in 1895, and a full revision was published in 1915.

She used her well-founded ideas and expertise to begin a one-year training program for young women who wished to enter the physical education field as a teaching career. Students received a certificate from her, but not a degree. In 1892, this was officially listed as a two-year program offered by Oberlin College. Dr. Hanna provided other classes for faculty and children, including one for men who paid her a small fee for each class session. Among those who received instruction in the first men's group were Fred E. Leonard, Thomas D. Wood, and Luther H. Gulick. All three played major roles in the development of physical education as a discipline and profession on the national level. Later, Hanna was the primary mentor for Jesse Feiring Williams, Gertrude Moulton, and Jay Bryan Nash. They too became prominent figures in American physical education.

Delphine Hanna published the results of her successful program for aiding physical development and correcting postural and movement problems for young women. One outcome of her work was acknowledgment of the need for equal treatment for women concerning the mind–body philosophy underlying physical culture. She was arguably the foremost pioneer and innovator for physical education for women in America. On a historical note, Ms. Julia Dickinson was the Sunday School teacher for the young Delphine Hanna at a small village in upstate New York. Ms. Dickinson later became a significant benefactor of the women's physical education program at Oberlin by endowing positions for women administrators. One of the early playing fields for women was named in her honor.

Over her thirty-five years at the college, Delphina Hanna achieved several changes related to the program of physical activities for women. Her well-constructed curriculum followed the trend toward sports as a replacement for some gymnastics by the end of the century. Hanna's students could take short courses of about six weeks' duration in a number of sports including archery, basketball, bicycling, tennis, swimming, skating, modern dance, and others. For many of these, the women could then choose to concentrate on just one activity during a subsequent term or year. When the Rockefeller Skating Rink (map, fig. 0.4) opened in 1896, Hanna was able to use it in the spring, summer, and fall as a covered area for a variety of physical activities, and this expanded to all seasons when the rink was enclosed in 1905 and ice was no longer provided. Dr. Hanna strongly supported formation of the Women's Athletic Association (WAA). Her varied efforts combined working with all of the students, teaching some students the basics of movement, along with introducing new sports. She continued, throughout her time at Oberlin, to advocate for and improve the training of instructors for schools, YWCAs, and other community programs for both youth and adults.

Oberlin and the University of Nebraska were the first institutions to offer four-year training programs for physical educators (1901); the first female to receive a degree in this major graduated from Oberlin in 1902. In 1903, Hanna became the first female in the US appointed as a professor of physical education. She broadened Oberlin's program when she purchased land near Lake Erie (see chapter 5) for a summer camp. Soon, cottages replaced the original tents used for housing, and she introduced aquatic- and camping-based activities. When Oberlin town residents purchased lots and built summer homes at the Lake

Erie site, they formed the Oberlin College Beach Colony, located near Huron, OH. Camp Hanna was used for more than three decades by the women's physical education program. Delphine Hanna spearheaded the drive that resulted in required physical education for men beginning in 1911. She served as a strong advocate for a new women's gymnasium and swimming pool, both of which were built or planned before her death.

To honor Delphine Hanna's many contributions, a group of former students, academic descendants, and friends started the Delphine Hanna Foundation. Collected donations enhanced curricular and extracurricular activities for women in physical education by funding presentations, workshops, and other similar activities. There was also a named lectureship in her honor, which provided for an annual speaker at the meeting of the Society for Health and Physical Educators.

Fred Eugene Leonard

Fred E. Leonard (fig. 2.3) received both the A.B. (1889) and A.M. (1892) degrees from Oberlin College. Except for several years away to obtain an advanced degree, he spent the remainder of his life at the college. He was in the first group of men trained under Delphine Hanna. Leonard worked as an assistant to Dr. Hanna in the early 1890s. He obtained his M.D. from Columbia in 1892, after which time he returned to Oberlin as a faculty member in the Department of Physiology and Hygiene. Leonard played significant roles in both the development of curriculums related to physiology and exercise as well as in physical education. He was a strong proponent of gymnastics and remained so throughout his career, even as games and sports became more prominent in the decades after 1900. Leonard traveled extensively in Europe, where he studied the German and Swedish systems of gymnastics. He returned to campus with many ideas and techniques to incorporate into Oberlin's program.

Leonard was the first Director of the Second Men's Gymnasium (1888–1889; 1892–1922) and Director for the Teachers Course in Physical Education for Men (1906–1922). He played an important role in the planning and design for Warner Gymnasium, completed in 1901. Leonard's name is associated with the history of physical education through two important books: *Pioneers of Modern Physical Training* (1915) and *A Guide to the History of Physical Education* (1923). The latter was published posthumously, as Leonard died at age fifty-six in 1922. He promulgated

FIGURE 2.3. Frederick E. Leonard was a student of Delphine Hanna in the 1880s and then a faculty member at Oberlin for thirty years in the areas of physiology, hygiene, and physical education. Leonard taught classes that were part of the physical education major including anatomy, hygiene, and physiology, several of which also counted as credit toward the major in zoology. (Oberlin College Archives)

his views on physical education through involvement with numerous summer schools and publications in a variety of professional journals. He is respected by many as one of the founders of what is known today as exercise science. A quote provides a summary of his views:

> This department aims, first to find out as accurately as possible the physical condition and tendencies of each new student; second, to recommend special work for the correction of any defects discovered; and third, to provide for all, by means of class drills, exercise which, besides promoting health and furnishing something of recreation, shall be educational in its character, cultivating a correct carriage, symmetrical development, muscular control, a fair degree of strength and endurance, agility and grace. (Shults, 1959, 45)

Physical Education Training Programs

An example of synchronicity, when the right person meets the appropriate circumstances, occurred at Oberlin College in the 1880s and 1890s. The shift from manual labor, as detailed in chapter 1, to gymnastics and related exercises brought about the development of programs like those of Dr. Sargent at Cambridge, MA. Soon, his colleagues collaborated on researching the scientific and practical aspects, and apparatus for systems geared toward physical training; his approach has been called the American system. The underlying philosophy regarding the connections between a healthy body and efficient mind remained as a basis for having academics integrated with physical exercise. The emergence of programs of physical exercise spread to the public school systems in the latter half of the 1880s. Lacking was a curriculum that promoted teacher training so that Dr. Hanna's innovative methods could be implemented in those public schools. Her lifetime goal was to help fill this growing need for instructors in the relatively new field of physical education as a distinct discipline. One key discernment that evolved from the work of Dr. Hanna and others who helped found the programs in instruction for physical education is that there are three types of programs: (1) those designed for primary and secondary schools; (2) those for colleges and universities; and (3) those for playgrounds, youth camps, and organizations like the YMCA and YWCA.

Perhaps the first training program was that started by Dio Lewis in Boston at the Normal Institute for Physical Education in 1861. Another school, devoted to the German gymnastics tradition, started in 1866 and moved from several eastern locations to end up in Milwaukee, WI. During the same period that the teacher training program emerged at Oberlin, there were similar developments at several eastern colleges. One of the early training schools in the US was founded by Dudley A. Sargent (1849–1924), who became director of the Hemenway Gymnasium at Harvard University in 1879, a position he held until 1919. In 1881, he founded a school, with prominent summer sessions, for the training of teachers of physical education. In 1887 the need for trained physical educators to staff the growing number of YMCAs and other gymnasiums around the country led to the opening of the Young Men's Christian Association Training School at Springfield, MA, which later became Springfield College. A program was founded in New Haven, CT, and one at Chautauqua, NY, in 1886, with the latter being a summer school, similar to the arrangement Dudley Sargent had in Boston with Harvard for his separate summer program.

The Physical Education Training Program for Women was officially listed in the 1894–1895 Oberlin College catalogue. Prior to then, Hanna offered private tutoring to interested students. Initially, a one-year course resulted in a certificate she issued to each pupil who successfully completed her program. The new college-sanctioned program was expanded to a two-year curriculum in 1896. Along with Hanna and Leonard, faculty from disparate fields that included chemistry, physiology, philosophy, rhetoric and oratory, and drawing and painting had students from the physical education training program in their classes. For several years prior to this, Leonard had been teaching two courses for the college, one on Human Physiology and the other on Hygiene. Students in the program took required classes in the regular curriculum at the college as well as those in the physical training program. Women who completed the program received diplomas, indicating their achievement. A total of thirty-five women completed the two-year course in its first eight years. The curriculum included:

> First Year: Cat Anatomy, Chemistry, Physics, Human Physiology, Zoology, Elocution, Drawing, Human Anatomy, Exercise Physiology, Histology, Oratory
> Second Year: Psychology, Kinesiology, Anthropometry, Massage, Physical Examination and Diagnosis, History of Physical Training, Hygiene, Emergencies, Medical Gymnastics, Pelvic Anatomy and Physiology, Practical Work and Teaching throughout the year

In 1899–1900, the program expanded to four years, and students wishing to enroll needed to meet the requirements for admission to the college. Thus, Oberlin became the first college in the country to offer a major in physical education as part of the regular liberal arts (A.B.) degree. Further, students were required to be in one of the three pathways to a bachelor's degree: Classical Course, Philosophical Course, or Scientific Course. They completed the plan for that degree, plus the classes necessary to receive a diploma in physical training. The more extensive curriculum involved most of the courses offered for the two-year diploma, but which now were part of a set of classes in one of the three areas offered for the bachelor's degree at the college. It is noteworthy that the general form and many topics of the classes at the outset did not change a great deal over the next nine decades, until the major was discontinued in 1985. What did change was the content of the classes, the introduction of more types of pedagogy, and shifts in terms of dropping classes no longer needed and the addition of new topics. These will be covered in more detail as the narrative progresses into the twentieth century. The training program for men began as a certificate offering in 1892 and was first listed in the college catalogue in 1901. It became available as a four-year degree in 1906.

Religion and Race

Two topics, pertinent to the time period for this chapter and extending into the twentieth century, deserve specific coverage: religion and race. Oberlin was founded by men of fervent religious convictions; evangelism undergirded the college from the beginning. Also, soon after the college opened, students of color were admitted to attend a course of study. Both topics are important to an understanding of the early years of the college and pertain to campus life, including physical activities. This section examines the pathways for both religion and race in connection with physical education and athletics. Other small colleges, though not the state universities, were founded based on religious principles. Students of color were not considered for admission at most of the colleges at their founding. It was not until the later years of the nineteenth century or the early decades of the twentieth century that many institutions opened their doors to African Americans.

In the 1850s in Great Britain and within the next two decades in the US, "Muscular Christianity" arose in response to the belief that male Christians could be more effective with strong, fit, trained physical bodies. Oberlin was among the schools in America to adopt a system that promoted this new form of social relevancy to accompany religion. One Oberlin individual in particular, Luther Halsey Gulick, a prominent figure in this movement, worked with the YMCA at Springfield, MA. He wrote extensively on the need to combine play and recreation with faith and religion.

Protestant evangelism was ingrained in the fabric of daily life at the college from its inception. Chapel was required five days each week, and Sundays were devoted to worship and other religious activities. The fervor involved many revivals on campus. Oberlin's physical activity, primarily during the period of manual labor (ca. 1833–1880 at the college) was certainly influenced by the Muscular Christianity movement. The evangelism continued, albeit with less vigor, until the later years of the nineteenth century and lessened during the first decades of the new century, when Progressivism became the main theme with social reform as a key focus. This shift was more prominent after World War I when the war did not end all wars as many of strong faith had hoped. Muscular Christianity diminished in the 1920s. Oberlin and some other similar institutions became more secular and have remained so up to the present. The Graduate School of Theology, present since the opening of the college, closed in 1965 and merged with the Theology School at Vanderbilt University in Tennessee. At Oberlin, mandated chapel attendance diminished by the post–World War II period and was discontinued as a requirement by 1961. During the decades prior to their elimination, weekly chapel meetings served a more general audience, and the religious emphasis decreased.

Women did not become involved with Muscular Christianity. Dudley A. Sargent in Boston, a mentor for Delphine Hanna, took a position that women, being the weaker sex, should learn about sports in order to appreciate them, but not necessarily to participate in the games. Soon after, in the mid-1870s, however, Sargent agreed to coach some sports at the all-female Wellesley College.

The modern version of Muscular Christianity remains a potent force at some institutions, primarily those which retain the strong religious affiliation of those who established the school. Where the founder's identity diminished, groups of players at various more secular schools choose, for example, to pray together before athletic contests and have Bible study groups. No materials pertaining to Muscular Christianity emerged during an examination of archival materials at the Oberlin College libraries. So, while there were likely important connections between religion and some forms of physical activity, twentieth-century Muscular Christianity does not appear to have been a major influence on athletics at the college. One factor in the exchanges about the involvement of Muscular Christianity at many schools is that it promotes a more dominant role for men. As attitudes and practices concerning the roles of women in our society slowly matured after World War II, this schism became more evident.

In terms of the involvement of people of color in the various athletics at Oberlin, there was little participation, with a few years as exceptions, until the 1970s, after which both male and female students of color engaged in intercollegiate sports in greater numbers. From the founding, with its abolitionist sentiment, the college laid plans to admit students of African American heritage. The first Black student to graduate from Oberlin was granted a degree in 1844. Records show that Middlebury College in Vermont was the first school to grant a baccalaureate degree to a person of color (1823). From 1844 through 1967 a total of 708 African American students (399 men and 309 women) received diplomas. Enrollments at Oberlin in the past five years have included an average of 30% people of color; those numbers include students of Black and Hispanic heritage.

A complete collection of photographs of almost all athletic teams is available for each sport for every year since the inception of baseball as an intercollegiate sport in 1886. Women's sports are included after they became varsity teams in the late 1970s. Participation by students of color as members of athletic teams varied during the years prior to 1970, with numbers ranging between zero and six members of all teams across all intercollegiate sports in any given year, most often involving football, basketball, and track. Since 1970, the record shows that participation by students of color in varsity athletics has increased for men to include a total of 4–12 participants on the football, basketball, and track teams in many years, with 1–2 athletes for a number of the other sports in any selected year. The record for women, which begins in 1977, reveals that from their inception there were Black students on many teams, with a greater number of participants for basketball, volleyball, and track than for other sports. Almost all team rosters for women's athletics included people of color at one time.

From the data above, the overall involvement of Black male students in athletics was quite low for more than eight decades, but has increased in the last fifty years. This pattern fits the overall number of students of color at the college. Beginning in 1871, soon after the Civil War, many decades passed during which various forms of segregation occurred at both the college and in the city of Oberlin. As recently as 1967 the freshman class had fewer than a dozen Black students out of more than 500 who enrolled. This changed beginning in the eighth decade of the twentieth century for both college and city. Today, though disparities certainly remain in the local community, the efforts by the college to attain greater diversity have proven generally successful. Varsity teams at most larger schools have a significant number of people of color, particularly in, but not limited to, the major sports. Many smaller colleges typically followed the pattern observed at Oberlin; more students of color are being admitted. This results in more participation across the available men's and women's intercollegiate teams.

Facilities

The Music Hall served as the First Ladies Gymnasium, beginning in 1874, though prior to that exercise classes had been staged in a room in the Second Ladies Hall (fig. 2.5; map, fig. 0.4). After fire destroyed the Music Hall in 1880, the physical culture program was moved to

FIGURE 2.4. A 1903 view of the exterior of the Second Ladies Gymnasium. The upper floor housed students and, for a time, Dr. Hanna. The lower floor was the gymnasium. It was located southwest of Second Ladies Hall, later replaced by Talcott Hall, a corner of which is visible on the right side. The structures were connected by a short passageway. The building was used for a variety of purposes beginning several years after 1939, when Hales Gymnasium opened. The old structure was removed in 1955. The gate to the left is an entry to an outdoor exercise area, which also had a basketball court. The Rockefeller Skating Rink is in the left background (see fig. 2.6 for an aerial view). (Oberlin College Archives)

an annex (built 1881; fig. 2.4; map, fig. 0.4) of the Second Ladies Hall. Because of cramped quarters, conditions were far from ideal. Over time and with the oversight provided by Delphine Hanna, this became a very functional space for the women. Initially, outside exercise areas extended west and southwest from the gymnasium building. When a fire severely damaged the Second Ladies Hall in 1886, the gymnasium structure was left relatively unscathed. Talcott Hall (map, fig. 0.4) was constructed on the site of the destroyed building in 1887 with a connection to the gymnasium annex. Living quarters occupied the upper floor of the annex. The first floor included a main exercise room, dressing room, massage room, and resting room, as well as the office for Dr. Hanna. From the 1890s into the first decade of the twentieth century, each new female student at the college received a set of instructions during the summer prior to matriculation for sewing their own clothing for physical education classes. This insured appropriate clothing for the nature of the exercises and provided uniformity (fig. 2.1). A view of the interior of the

FIGURE 2.5. A 1910 view of the inside of the Second Ladies Gymnasium showing a group of women dressed in the outfits appropriate for physical exercise. Also shown are a number of items used for particular physical activities including a bicycle, a basketball, a field hockey stick, a fencing foil and mask, a tennis racket, and numerous Indian clubs and dumbbells of various types arrayed along the rear wall. (Oberlin College Archives)

Ladies Gymnasium shows a group of female students holding various items with additional clubs and apparatus in the background (fig. 2.6).

An aerial view (fig. 2.6 and see map, fig. 0.4) of a portion of the north campus shows the locations of structures and outdoor areas associated with the women's program in the early 1920s. In 1895 Mr. John D. Rockefeller, a Cleveland native, provided funds to construct a covered ice skating rink (map, fig. 0.4), which was available initially to the women, and then, at specified times, to the men. The facility was connected to the Second Ladies Gymnasium and open at the ends and sides (map, fig. 0.4, fig. 2.7 right center, and fig. 3.7). When not being used for skating, i.e., in the spring, summer, and fall, the surface was ideal for various sports and games. Maps and written references show that the structure was removed in 1948–1949. In addition to these indoor facilities, there was a fenced area (fig. 2.7 left center) next to the gymnasium and tennis courts in the adjacent field.

A Second Men's Gymnasium (fig. 2.7; map, fig. 0.4), constructed in 1873, was financed by student subscriptions, like its predecessor. The

FIGURE 2.6. An aerial view of the women's sports facilities taken in 1922. Talcott Hall is in the upper center, and the Second Ladies Gymnasium is the smaller, lower structure with a dark roof at the middle of the view, directly below Talcott. The building with the large sloping roof just below the center is the former Rockefeller Skating Rink, by this time enclosed and used as a field house for the women. To the left of the field house is a fenced area for outdoor activities with a softball diamond and tennis courts. (Oberlin College Archives)

interior was modified several times to accommodate new equipment as the exercises changed over the years (fig. 2.8). The newly formed Men's Gymnasium Association ran the program of physical training and sports. When its financial situation became dire in 1877, the college took over control of the finances, the building, and the various programs. In the years following this change, the Men's Gymnasium Association staged several concerts and lectures in order to help raise money to augment their own contributions to pay off the debt incurred for the building construction and furnishing it with apparatus.

As at Oberlin, the initial push for physical activities at some peer institutions came from students, often without wholehearted faculty approval. As years passed, student organizations formed to manage

FIGURE 2.7. The Second Men's Gymnasium as completed in 1873. This 1883 photo shows the structure, which measured 75' by 25' and cost $1,000 to construct. It was located west of North Professor Street, not far from the site of Warner Gymnasium, in the southeast portion of today's Wilder Bowl. This building was moved about 200' north at the time the new (Warner) gymnasium was built, used as a carpenter's shed for a time, and then demolished. The foreground surface may be early tennis courts. (Oberlin College Archives)

FIGURE 2.8. The interior of the Second Men's Gymnasium featured a coal burning stove, an exercise mat, various ropes, weights with pulleys, bar apparatus, an early version of a rowing machine, and a collection of clubs along the wall. (Oberlin College Archives)

these endeavors ran into financial difficulties. At Ohio Wesleyan, students formed a Gymnastics Association in 1864. By the 1880s, the college administration took over the control and finances of the organization. At Denison, the Gymnasium Association formed by students in 1884 became the Athletic Association in 1888, at which time control was ceded to the college officials.

During this period, other colleges and universities constructed new facilities for physical education and sports or, in some instances, repurposed existing buildings. Among these were the YMCA Training School at Springfield, MA (1885), as well as Lasell Gymnasium (1886) at Williams College. The original Harvard structure was replaced in 1879 by the more familiar Hemenway Gymnasium. Among the schools in Ohio, Kenyon College repurposed a portion of a former chapel as a gymnasium in 1884; Ohio State University constructed an armory and gymnasium in 1898; Ohio Wesleyan College opened the Fairbanks Gymnasium in 1888; and at Denison College the Old Frame building was furnished as a gymnasium in 1880. The dates for the structures devoted to physical activities in Ohio are 20–30 years later than similar developments in New England, reflecting, in part, the continuing importance of physical labor as a form of exercise for some colleges until the decades following the Civil War. Designated outdoor playing fields appeared on the campuses by the mid-1880s and were improved with better locations, maintenance, and sometimes with seating for fans.

At Oberlin, in early 1894, the General Faculty voted to approve a recommendation from the Committee on the Men's Gymnasium that a Committee for the Regulation of Athletic Sports be appointed, to include three trustees, three alumni, and three students. An interior view of the Second Men's Gymnasium reveals a stove for heating, a floor mat, several types of equipment positioned along the walls, and some apparatus hanging from the ceiling (fig. 2.8). The pressure to provide modern facilities soon culminated in planning for what became Warner Gymnasium.

Outdoor facilities for men evolved beginning with spaces on Tappan Square and the field behind Cabinet Hall, near the location of the Second Men's Gymnasium. Expansion led to the first facilities at the north end of campus, where the entire athletic campus is located today (map, fig. 0.5). In April 1885, the college authorized the purchase of land "in the suburbs," which became Athletic Park (fig. 2.9; map, fig. 0.5). Students played baseball and football, track and field meets occurred, and

FIGURE 2.9. This 1897 view shows a corner of the baseball field and grandstand at the Athletic Park on North Professor Street. Note the sizeable crowd in the stands and the fans standing to the right dressed in period attire. (Oberlin College Archives)

tennis courts were laid out. Half of the original area of 17+ acres was designated for sports fields; this eventually expanded to the full original land area and to eight additional acres, added in 1913. In late summer each year, the baseball field at Athletic Park was plowed up to provide an even playing surface for the football season. This led to many complaints about mud when it rained and dust in dry weather.

The most consistent refrain noted in the General Faculty Meeting minutes for the ensuing three decades during the last years of the nineteenth century concerned regulations covering ball playing on Tappan Square. Admonitions were directed to the students (males) for regularly disobeying these rules, and mention is made of punishments for teams and individuals who disobeyed. Many entries in the minutes deal with infractions for playing and practicing at times other than those permitted by the authorities. It seems that sports and games were destined to become a part of the physical culture of the college, regardless of what the elders thought was best.

Oberlin College Graduates Play Significant Roles in the Development of Physical Education

One of the rationales for this book is to tell the story of significant roles played by individuals who either worked at Oberlin, received their train-

FIGURE 2.10. Luther Halsey Gulick Jr., M.D. (OC attended), graduated from the Oberlin Preparatory Academy and began school at Oberlin College as the roommate of Thomas D. Wood. (Oberlin College Archives)

ing at the school, or were mentored by Oberlin alumni at other institutions. Glimpses of the work accomplished by Dr. Delphine Hanna and one of her pupils, Dr. Fred E. Leonard, along with two other students from the early Hanna years provided major stimuli for the nascent field of physical education. These two are Luther Halsey Gulick (1865–1918) and Thomas D. Wood (1865–1951), who both participated in the first class that Hanna held for training men in 1885–1886. Her students served as ambassadors, reflecting her views and principles of physical training. Other contributors with Oberlin connections will be introduced in subsequent chapters, as the influence continued to be prominent up until the 1940s and even, through several textbooks, to the second decade of the twenty-first century.

Luther Gulick (fig. 2.10), born in Hawaii, was a member of a family of missionaries and a devout Christian. Though he left Oberlin College early due to health issues, he soon attended Dudley A. Sargent's Normal School for Physical Training in Cambridge, MA, and then completed his medical degree at New York University. During his time at Oberlin, Gulick roomed with Thomas D. Wood, and they enjoyed many stimulating conversations. A portion of what they discussed concerned the scientific bases for physical education. This interest derived, in part, from their training under Hanna. One conversation, about their futures, quoted below, led them to resolve to devote their careers to the exploration and advancement of the interrelationships between healthy bodies, mental training, and good morals. Both men followed through on their joint plan. Luther Gulick describes his own perspective on the development of physical education and his interactions with Wood:

> The advent of one of Dr. Sargent's graduates, Miss Delphine Hanna, now Dr. Hanna, had brought to our minds in a more vivid way than ever before, that there really was such a thing as scientific teaching

of gymnastics, genuine body building. We had, both of us, been very much interested in the gymnastics and athletics of the college, had identified ourselves thoroughly with all of the work that was going on in these lines, and had read as far as we were able to what had been written on the subject at the time. Blackie's "How to Get Strong," particularly the chapters entitled "What a College Gymnasium Might Be and Do," filled us with enthusiasm. One Sunday afternoon we took a long walk out into the woods, and sitting beside a rail fence, I can picture the situation even now), we looked forward to the future of physical training. We spoke of the relation of good bodies to good morals, we thought of the relation of body training to mental training. . . . That day, that hour, was a turning point for both of us, and . . . the glimpses which we secured that day of the future has remained . . . a prophecy of the work which each of us was to do. (Leonard 1915, 130–131)

Gulick's career began with a position at the YMCA Training School (1887–1900) in Springfield, MA, serving as superintendent for most of that time. He maintained that the role of YMCAs involved "working for young men, not simply their bodies, minds and souls, but for the salvation, development and training of the whole man complete as God made him" (Dorgan, 1934, 27). In his position he asked one James Naismith to develop a game that could be played indoors during the winter months between the football and baseball seasons. That new game was an early version of basketball, with peach baskets serving as goals. Further, Gulick played a role in the development of the original pentathlon.

Gulick spent much of his professional career in New York City, in various capacities with several schools and organizations. Additional endeavors included being a founder of all of the following organizations: Playground Association of America; the American Association for the Advancement of Physical Education; the Academy of Physical Education; the Camp Fire Girls; the American Folk Dance Society; and the American School Hygiene Association. His influence on the field was solidified by authorship of six books covering both the philosophy and the instruction of physical education. Many of these volumes provided critical foundations for the development of physical education as a professional discipline. The philosophy underlying his practices and writings was derived, in part, from the work of John Dewey with its emphasis on pragmatism.

FIGURE 2.11. Thomas Denison Wood graduated from Oberlin College, working his last two years in the gymnasium. He enjoyed a distinguished career as the primary developer and proponent of the New Physical Education, which defined the modern program of physical education in American school systems. (Oberlin College Archives)

Throughout his written works, lectures and presentations, and short courses, Gulick emphasized the scientific aspects of the field. He was a strong proponent of and contributor to anthropometrics, used in conjunction with traditional methods, to achieve a balanced body. He integrated studies of therapeutics in the form of physical exercises, notably gymnastics. In 1920, *A Philosophy of Play* was published posthumously. The book was widely acclaimed for bringing together information on children and the role of play in their development. In 1923, the Luther Halsey Gulick Award was established by the Physical Education Society of New York City, and it is given annually for an outstanding career in the field. Today, the award is made by the Society of Health and Physical Educators.

Thomas D. Wood (1865–1951; fig. 2.11), was born in Sycamore, IL, where he spent his early years. He matriculated at Oberlin College in 1884, graduating in 1888. He completed his A.M. and M.D. degrees at Columbia University (1891). His first faculty position was at Stanford University in 1891, where he was instrumental in establishing the school and provided the framework for the program in physical education, which was first offered in 1892–1893. In 1901 he moved to Columbia University, where he spent the rest of his career. Wood authored or co-authored several key books pertaining to physical education, including

Health and Education: A Program for Public Schools and Teaching Institutions and, in 1927, the definitive book, *The New Physical Education*.

Throughout a long career, which continued into the 1930s, Wood's philosophy is best summarized in his own words: "The great thought in physical education is not the education of the physical nature, but the relation of physical training to complete education, and then the effort to make the physical contribute its full share to the life of the individual, in environment, training, and culture" (Dorgan 1934, 27). Like Gulick, Wood remained committed to the underlying concept of mind–body harmony. He was at the forefront of the movement to develop the New Physical Education, which relied much less on gymnastics and more on sports, games, and dance. Wood was a primary leader in the movement to separate physical education and health education. In his philosophy, both the health of the individual and that person's physical condition influenced their ability to think and effectively integrate into society. His work helped to define the curriculums for classes on both topics. Wood is often referred to as the originator of modern physical education. Though classes were specified in some states and cities before 1890, the program Wood developed emerged at the same time as the nationwide adoption of required physical education classes. For his distinguished career, Wood received the third Luther H. Gulick Award in 1925.

Oberlin Athletics

As presented earlier, the transition from gymnastics toward games and sports began in the 1890s, though, as with all such transitions, some locations in the country engaged in this shift a bit earlier. The appearance of the "New Physical Education" involved not so much a full change in philosophy, but rather a redirection in terms of the manner in which students could achieve their physical training goals. The New Physical Education is the primary subject of the next chapter.

Oberlin College's programs exemplified the typical changing patterns across higher education with respect to engagement in team sports. With some variations, most, including some larger universities, followed similar paths. The college administrators engaged in multiple discussions about which students should be required to take regular physical training and which could be considered exempt. Those excused included

FIGURE 2.12. Members of the high wheel bicycle club pose before a ride. (Oberlin College Archives)

individuals performing manual labor or, as time progressed, those involved in team sports. New sports clubs formed according to student interests, as for example tennis and bicycle riding (fig. 2.12). Beginning in the 1870s class teams in baseball and later football competed against each other in a forerunner of intramurals. Physical training classes shifted away from gymnastics and calisthenics to include instruction in game skills and team play.

The change to more sports and games, introduced first at eastern schools, failed to take hold in midwestern schools for at least a decade. College baseball originated in 1859 in Massachusetts with a game between Williams and Amherst. The first football game was in 1869 between Rutgers and New Jersey (now Princeton). The first track meet occurred in the late 1860s in the New York area. Thus, eastern schools led the way and the pattern of physical activities that characterized the westward flow of gymnastics continued with the introduction of intercollegiate athletic events.

For Oberlin, both baseball and football began with teams from the campus, often from each class. The baseball team was the first to engage in competition against local opponents, with a club formed in 1865. Ini-

FIGURE 2.13. The 1890 baseball team with their gear. (Oberlin College Archives)

tially, games were arranged against communities such as Wellington, and then further afield for contests with Hudson Academy and teams from Cleveland (fig. 2.13). The first intercollegiate game, in 1883, was against Western Reserve. By 1892, the team was playing a faculty-approved schedule of eight games each season. Football was the second sport with outside competition. The first external game occurred in 1878 against a team from Wellington. As interest in intercollegiate competitions grew, college teams were chosen from the best players on the class teams. By 1892 there was a regular football season schedule, which expanded over the next decade (fig. 2.14). For early sports, opponents included other small colleges in Ohio and oftentimes schools like Ohio State and Michigan, which had not yet grown in size compared to what they became in the first quarter of the next century.

Tennis and track soon followed baseball and football with teams playing against outside competition. Chronologically, locations for tennis matches included Tappan Square near Council Hall, courts next to the Ladies Gymnasium, and twelve courts located at the Athletic Park area on North Professor Street. The Lawn Tennis Association formed in 1885. Enthusiasm for track meets was an outgrowth of the annual Field

FIGURE 2.14. The 1892 football team. Note the relative lack of padding in the uniforms and the absence of helmets. The latter did not appear in college football until the turn of the century. There is one African American player on this team, an unusual occurrence for the times. The person dressed in a suit in the middle of the photo is likely John Heisman. (Oberlin College Archives)

Day, held each spring, where students celebrated their athletic accomplishments from the school year. Tennis matches were held against Ann Arbor and Toledo in 1887 and Wooster in 1889. The first intercollegiate track meet was held in May 1890, and included events for running, bicycling, sack races, mile walk, tug-of-war, hop, skip, and jump, and boxing.

Lacrosse was played in 1887–1888, on an experimental basis, but then was not part of intercollegiate athletics for sixty-one years. Golf appeared as a sport played by college students just before the end of the century. Women played the first basketball on campus in 1896, and by 1898 class teams of women competed each year. The list of sports played by Oberlin teams, and by the other schools in the region, expanded, as just noted, before the turn of the century and continued to do so up to the 1930s.

In 1890, the Oberlin students' Athletic Association was permitted to join the Ohio College Athletic Association, but only for men's baseball and tennis. This was the first affiliation for Oberlin athletics with other schools; it began a long history of such groups, to be discussed in subsequent chapters. In 1896, participation in the Ohio Inter-Collegiate Athletic Association was approved, but only for track and field. By the late 1890s, a gradual shift in the foundational philosophy underpinning physical training emerged, particularly for athletics. This transition produced a modest diminution of the philosophy of a mind–body connection and heralded a move toward a more competitive and emphasis-on-winning approach to games and sports.

As intercollegiate athletic contests began during the last twenty years of the nineteenth century, General Faculty Meeting minutes record individual decisions made for the scheduling of each specific contest in baseball and football. By the start of the twentieth century, approval was often granted for a series of games covering a particular school year, with limits imposed on how many could be traveling games. During this time, the first concerns were expressed in faculty meetings about betting on the outcomes of athletic contests. This never appeared as a serious problem at Oberlin. In the following decades, as gambling became an issue for bigger schools, the gap between smaller and larger institutions resulted in a great deal of variance in the performance of athletic competitions. This was primarily true for the "major" sports, particularly football. In 1895, regulations for Oberlin College athletics included restrictions forbidding competition against teams other than those from similar colleges, preventing undue concentration of interest in any single game, and concomitant, unwise expenditures for coaches or other purchases pertaining to athletics. However, as will be noted in chapter 4, football games still occurred against teams like Ohio State until 1920.

During the last third of the nineteenth century, most athletic contests involved only men, though early physical activities and contests for women emerged. From 1870 to 1900, women too shifted from a program based strictly on gymnastics to a more inclusive and comprehensive one including sports and games. General Faculty Meeting minutes reflect attention given to female students through increases in Dr. Hanna's salary (up to $700 in 1890 and $1,000 in 1893), the formation of a standing committee for women's physical training, asking Dr. Hanna to join the faculty at their regular meetings, providing tennis for women, and discussions about bowling. Like the men, women engaged

FIGURE 2.15. Women playing field hockey in 1900, most likely on the field west of the Second Ladies Gymnasium. This would be the area of today's Harkness Hall. (Oberlin College Archives)

in class competitions, with their contests being in field hockey and basketball (fig. 2.15). In 1904, the women formed their own Gymnasium and Field Association.

Important Athletes

Two Oberlin-connected men had significant roles in the history of sport in the US. Moses Fleetwood Walker (fig. 2.16) left the college in 1882 to play for the University of Michigan and moved to professional baseball in 1883 with the Toledo Blue Stockings. He is credited with being the first Black professional baseball player in America and, in 1884, the first to play in a major league game. Moses played catcher; he caught barehanded without a mask. He did, however, move back from home plate and caught the ball on the first bounce. In 1990, James Foels, then the Director of Athletics and Physical Education, led a group of Oberlinians that placed a proper, engraved tombstone on the grave of Moses Walker in the cemetery at Steubenville, OH. One of those who enjoyed keeping score for the Oberlin nine in the 1880s was Mary Church Terrell. She

FIGURE 2.16. Moses Fleetwood Walker was a member of the class of 1882; his brother, Weldy, joined the class of 1885. Walker, seated at the left of the second row, gravitated to baseball as a youth and became wholly immersed while at Oberlin. Weldy is standing in the middle of the back row. They played for the college as the era of competition against outside teams was launched in 1881. (Oberlin College Archives)

became an iconic figure in both the nascent Civil Rights Movement and for women's suffrage. The main library at the college was named in her honor in 2017.

John Heisman (fig. 2.17) was known for his czar-like demeanor with his teams and for being an innovator in terms of plays and strategy. The undefeated 1892 football team beat Ohio State and Michigan, though the latter contest is still subject to some disagreement. The team finished with a 7-0 record. Their two victories over Ohio State were by a combined score of 90–0.

Summary

Gymnastics was central to physical training for much of the last third of the nineteenth century, though it began a transition to what became known as the New Physical Education. The major philosophical tenets,

FIGURE 2.17. John Heisman in the classic pose used for the Heisman Trophy. The photo was taken in 1892 during the period when he was both coach and player for the Oberlin College football team and was a student taking classes. Much of his fame came after he left Oberlin to coach at several other institutions, most notably at Georgia Tech. His coaching prowess extended to baseball and basketball. (Oberlin College Archives)

involving integrating the development and nurturance of the mind with the regular exercise of the physical body, remained as a foundation. These thirty years were critical to physical education at Oberlin College. Delphine Hanna and three of her students, Fred E. Leonard, Luther H. Gulick, and Thomas D. Wood, all made significant contributions to programs for training physical education instructors. Dr. Hanna, the first female professor of physical education in the country, founded the first Physical Education Training Program for Women. Both religion and race impacted physical education and athletics at the college, though both waned during the century and into the next. Upgrades and additions to facilities positioned the college to be a leader in terms of both educating instructors and engaging in physical activities. Early forms of what became intramurals, beginning with men's baseball before 1870, became widespread for both men and women, eventually encompassing several sports. The true beginnings of intercollegiate athletics started during the final two decades of the century.

Sources Consulted for Chapter 2

Full citations are found at the end of the book.

Barnard, J. *From Evangelism to Progressivism at Oberlin College, 1866–1917.*

Barrows, I. C. *Physical Training: A Full Report of the Papers and Discussions of the Conference Held at Boston in November 1890.*

Baumann, R. *Constructing Black Education at Oberlin College: A Documentary History.*

Brandt, N. *When Oberlin Was King of the Gridiron.*

Chessman, G. W. *Denison: The Story of an Ohio College.*

Consentino, F. et al. *A History of Physical Education.*

Dorgan, E. J. *Luther Halsey Gulick 1865–1918.*

Fairchild, J. H. *Oberlin: The Colony and the College, 1833–1883.*

Fletcher, R. S. *A History of Oberlin College from Its Foundation through the Civil War.*

Fuess, C. M. *Amherst: The Story of a New England College.*

Gerber, E. W. *Innovators and Institutions in Physical Education.*

Goerler, R. E. *The Ohio State University: An Illustrated History.*

Gulick, L. H. *A Philosophy of Play.*

Hackensmith, C. W. *History of Physical Education.*

Harvey, R. S. (ed.). *Those Fleeting Years: Wabash College, 1832–1982.*

Heisman, J. M., and M. Schlabach. *Heisman: The Man Behind the Trophy.*

Hubbart, H. C. *Ohio Wesleyan's First Hundred Years.*

Keeler, H. L. *The Life of Adelia A. Field Johnston.*

Kinsey, D. C. 1935. *The History of Physical Education in Oberlin College 1833–1890.*

Kornblith, G. J., and C. Lasser. *Elusive Utopia: The Struggle for Racial Equality in Oberlin, Ohio.*

Ladd, T., and J. A. Mathisen. *Muscular Christianity: Evangelical Protestants and the Development of American Sports.*

Lee, M. *A History of Physical Education and Sports in the U.S.A.*

Leonard, F. E. *Pioneers of Modern Physical Training.*

———. *A Guide to the History of Physical Education.*

Lynn, M. *An Historical Analysis of the Professional Career of Delphine Hanna.*

Mechikoff, R. *A History and Philosophy of Sport and Physical Education.*

Morris, J. B. *Oberlin: Hotbed of Abolitionism.*

Putney, C. *Muscular Christianity: Manhood and Sports in Protestant America, 1830–1920.*

Rice, E. A., J. L. Hutchinson, and M. Lee. *A Brief History of Physical Education.*

Rudolph, F. *The American College & University: A History.*

Schwendener, N. *A History of Physical Education in the United States.*

Shults, F. D. *The History and Philosophy of Athletics for Men at Oberlin College.*

Smythe, G. F. *Kenyon College: Its First Century.*

Waite, C. L. *Permission to Remain Among Us: Education for Blacks in Oberlin, Ohio, 1880–1914.*

Wayman, A. R. *A Modern Philosophy of Physical Education.*

Weston, A. *The Making of American Physical Education.*

CHAPTER 3

New Physical Education

1896–1925

Period Events

The New Physical Education dominated the last years of the nineteenth century and first decades of the twentieth century (see Appendix A for timelines). This approach, with Thomas D. Wood as the principal founder, combined a number of elements. Among these were broadening of physical education to include more athletics and intramurals, an increase in the importance of play behavior in development of younger people, and concern about character development and integration into society. Health education, as a component of physical well-being, became an added feature of the curriculum for most programs in physical training. As Mechikoff writes: "Physical education was committed to the whole being, yet had to separate and fragment the various aspects of the individual for analysis and measurement. The problem then became how to achieve reintegration of the whole person" (Mechikoff 2010, 16). This chapter follows the story of the New Physical Education, changes in underlying philosophy, and the people who had Oberlin College connections who forged key aspects of this transition. Comparisons and context are provided by examination of peer institutions during this thirty-year span.

The separation of small and big schools in terms of athletic competition occurred over this same time frame, with major sports competitions restricted to schools of similar size by the early 1920s. Most importantly, physical education instruction became a profession, combining excellent scientific studies, new training programs, and the emergence of professional societies. Graduate studies in physical education, begun in the 1890s, expanded with more institutions offering master's degrees, and some schools added doctoral degrees. New pedagogical approaches and programs were featured at regional and national meetings and then published in a variety of books and journals.

The transitions occurred in the context of significant changes in society, including development of and increasing use of new modes of transportation and communication. A continuing movement to broaden and improve public education, especially at the primary and secondary school levels, prompted expanded teacher preparation programs. World War I, with the need for personnel to serve in the armed forces, demanded high standards of physical preparation and strength training for our country's young men. One outcome was recognition of the appalling lack of physical conditioning among American youth. Some 33% of those tested for military service failed the physical part of the examination. After the war, this disturbing finding led to new approaches to physical education and increased recreational opportunities. In the years leading up to World War I and those immediately following, a day in the life of a typical American underwent dramatic changes. Legislation shortened the work week; inventions facilitated more travel and made it easier to maintain the home. Americans enjoyed more leisure hours, which encouraged greater participation in a variety of physical and recreational activities.

There were a number of other important developments directly pertinent to physical activities. These included the founding of the Playground Association of America (later the National Recreation Association), Camp Fire Girls, Girl Scouts, and Boy Scouts of America in the first decades of the new century. All of these were integral to the development of a social ethic that emphasized physical activity through both individual and group participation in diverse games and sports. Throughout the US, local communities and schools established playgrounds and designated fields for sports and games. A 1906 gathering of representatives from numerous college and universities created the Intercollegiate Athletic Association of the United States, which became the National Collegiate Athletic Association (NCAA) in 1910. The modern Summer Olympic Games were first held in 1896, and the Winter Olympic Games in 1924. These ignited enthusiasm among both the general populace and athletes. Given the widespread appeal of the Olympics, some athletes began to strive to attain elite-level performance.

In 1917, in response to the need for governance and regulation of athletic endeavors, a Committee on Women's Athletics was formed by the American Physical Education Association, followed in 1923 by a Women's Division of the National Amateur Athletic Federation. Men's and women's sports were maintained separately at coeducational schools, often with two departments of physical education and frequently with different facilities and gymnasium directors. The title "Director of Athletics" referred to men who guided the male intercollegiate sports programs at each institution.

Two paths emerged that created a divide between smaller colleges and larger universities, with the latter evolving to include scholarly work and research in areas not readily available to students at the small schools. At the university level, curriculums now included coursework in engineering, applied aspects of physical sciences, agriculture, and others. Smaller schools often retained the classic education paradigm with a shift underway toward what became known as a liberal arts program. While Progressivism dominated the pedagogy of both types of institutions, it was more evident at universities. The earlier physical education curriculum was replaced with a more practical set of classes, and the focus became one of proficiency in teacher training, instead of education as an end in itself. This training shifted from the smaller colleges to the purview of universities, though some colleges—including Oberlin—persisted in the major course offerings for physical education into the later decades of the twentieth century, and several liberal arts colleges retain this major into the twenty-first century.

Athletics charted new territory, in part due to the availability of resources at the larger institutions of higher education. Football, as the new national pastime, became a huge drawing-card at universities, where alumni and corporate sponsors became eager to underwrite winning teams. The smaller schools, with less funding, lacked the finances to compete against the larger schools. As early as the 1920s, the major universities all featured football as the premier sport; it received less emphasis at smaller schools. The larger schools faced issues such as the brutality of the game, along with subsequent injuries and some deaths. Also important on university campuses was the professionalism becoming more evident in the governance and management of athletics. Both alumni support and extensive media coverage enhanced the domination of football. New stadiums and field houses were built for football and other sports that also became a part of the new landscape at bigger schools. In summary, football became a business; it was no longer "just a sport." This continues today, as the revenues from football, and now basketball as well, provide funding for entire athletics programs at bigger schools. Oberlin and many other smaller institutions continue to put much less emphasis on football. In fact, by the 1970s and 1980s, discussions at Oberlin and several other colleges focused on whether to retain football as a part of the athletic program (see chapter 7).

By the 1920s, physical education in colleges remained based on traditional training for teachers and athletes; their mission shifted slightly under the influence of Progressivism. The approach to athletics was muted, compared to larger schools. At the bigger institutions, alumni and fans began to exert a controlling influence on school sports. At smaller schools, the administration still held a tight rein on the structure of the sports culture. At universities and, to a lesser degree at the colleges, many individuals who did not enjoy elite-level abilities became spectators, rather than participants. It was much easier to cheer for one's team than it was to endure the discipline of rigorous physical training. The "spectatoritis" became evident in the lack of fitness and readiness of men recruited for service in World War I.

Changes in Philosophy and New Physical Education

John Dewey was among the preeminent philosophers belonging to the school called "pragmatism," which had its roots in the last quarter of the nineteenth century. A primary tenet was that one needed hands-on experience to achieve the best learning outcomes. This was true for physical activities in addition to classroom subjects. Dewey's approach defined learning as an interactive process, which should be designed to provide youth with the knowledge and skills to attain their potential. To do so required that their education involve both social and experiential components. These practices also fit the mold for social reform, which was prominent at the time. Teachers should guide the process and aid the students in relating what they learned to practical experiences in their lives. Dewey's writings repeatedly return to the notion that both the student and the teacher are participants in the educational enterprise. After Dewey others, such as Edward Thorndike (1874–1939) and G. Stanley

Hall (1846–1924), held that direct experience was necessary for learning and that a need for adequate physical activity for the young could be met through games and sports.

How do these ideas fit with the ongoing changes in physical education and exercise? With the advent of sports and games, beginning to replace gymnastics by the last decade of the nineteenth century, students became more involved in the activities. The somewhat static routines that characterized much of the gymnastics tradition gave way to more improvised activities with rewards for creativity and innovation. These helped usher in the era of the New Physical Education. Indeed, the last decades of the previous century witnessed a number of the student activities at Oberlin centered around sports and games, played both indoors and outside at locations like Tappan Square and Athletic Park. These can be viewed as forms of the Dewey-inspired thinking with application to physical education and exercise.

The philosophy of the New Physical Education was an outgrowth from the earlier emphasis on mind–body connections. The "new" element primarily centered on the combination of the development of physical bodily strength, while acquiring athletic skills through direct participation. An increasing appreciation for aspects of the human body was a key factor in this shift. The resulting philosophy was that physical activity in the form of games and sports fostered more than just individual development. Interpersonal and emotional improvement were realized through teamwork and cooperation, group understanding, character building, and enhanced personal well-being. Students, as amateur athletes, played competitive intercollegiate contests, largely for their own personal enjoyment and the entertainment of spectators. By the second decade of the new century, larger universities were moving toward a higher level of competitive engagement, with athletics programs that included larger budgets and new, specialized facilities. Expanded opportunities became available and attractive for the aspiring athlete, as increased support was devoted to university athletics. Soon, these larger institutions offered financial aid to draw students into their programs. The campus life evolved toward a major time commitment to a training regimen, with the goal of maintaining a winning team in a chosen sport.

Harry A. Scott, in his book *Competitive Sports in Schools and Colleges,* provides insight into the philosophy underlying the New Physical Education:

> A game, when analyzed, is analogous to a cross section of democratic community life in which social activity is governed by rules, regulations, customs, traditions, rewards, and punishments. In the game, however, the tempo of living is tremendously accelerated, thus increasing enormously the opportunity for experience in social living. (Scott 1951, 151)

In addition to Thomas Wood and Luther Gulick, two other Oberlin graduates, Jay Bryan Nash and Jesse Feiring Williams, and also Clark W. Hetherington, a graduate assistant with Wood at Stanford, were leaders in the formation, implementation, and revisions of the New Physical Education. Together, they shifted the common exercises of the early years of the century toward development of the physical body on its own. Physical education now focused on individual needs and served to promote the overall learning for each student. In practice, this meant a combination of some gymnastics exercises, now part of American traditions, with a variety of sports and games, which could be played both indoors and outdoors. Though the Battle of the Systems, which commenced in the last decade of the nineteenth century and continued into the first two decades of the twentieth century, the decline of German and Swedish gymnastics was inevitable with the rise of the New Physical Education. This innovation was not a shift away from the mind–body harmony philosophy, but rather a shift in how it was achieved.

The types and forms of the exercises and games were scientifically based and tailored for individuals and groups of students. Intramurals emerged and grew, effectively an expansion of the class and house teams engaging in baseball, football, and basketball as played in previous decades. Men's sports entered what has been called a "Golden Age." This era, characterized by building large stadiums for college football and professional baseball, included extensive media coverage, and a boom in advertising surrounding sporting events. A class of professional athletes, primarily those playing baseball and football, became well known and served as role models for youngsters. This group included baseball stars like Babe Ruth, Lou Gehrig, and Christy Mathewson, along with football heroes like Red Grange, Jim Thorpe, and Ernie Nevers. Other sports featured athletes such as Johnny Weissmuller (swimming), Jack Dempsey and Joe Lewis (boxing), Jesse Owens (track), and Bobby

Jones (golf). Young men benefitted from sports through character- and body-building, overcoming adversity, and receiving recognition for their efforts.

Which activities comprised this new approach? Clark Hetherington, a protégé of Thomas Wood at Stanford, is credited as the foremost philosopher of physical education in the early twentieth century. Several quotes from his work provide a glimpse into his approach:

> Most children have no homes. Child life and home life have been sacrificed to industry. The home has become a dressing room and refreshment center. Old home functions are shifted to the school. Physical education is one of these, so recently in its new place that it needs interpretation. Physical education is concerned with physical training or big muscle activities as distinct from manual activities, linguistic activities, nature study activities, etc., which are the concern of other special phases of education. These big muscle activities are of three classes: (1) Natural activities or big muscle play, including running and jumping, stunts on the playground or gymnastic apparatus, chasing and fleeing games, swimming and water stunts, boating, tussling and wrestling, athletics, folk games, etc. (2) Formalized or invented activities, including tactics, gymnastic drills, special corrective exercises, etc. (3) Related activities, including gardening, agricultural projects, industrial work—all activities using the big muscles vigorously, but organized for other than physical training purposes, yet having a physical training value. (Hetherington 1921, 520)

Organized games can be added to Hetherington's list, for both individual and team sports, such as golf, tennis, football, and basketball. Between 1880 and 1930, new sports were invented with increasingly complex and formal sets of rules. These guided both the play of the game and established competition standards between individuals and between teams.

Events at Oberlin College

At Oberlin College, events of the thirty-year period included curriculum changes, new facilities, and contributions by individuals who maintained the prominence of the college in the field of physical education. Administrators encouraged the New Physical Education throughout the period from 1896 to 1925. This approach required improved and expanded physical facilities, so construction on campus began in earnest at Oberlin and also at other similar institutions. Warner Gymnasium, along with its later expansion, a new football stadium with a track, and tennis courts in several locations, reflected the enthusiasm of faculty and students alike. New and improved outdoor venues included Galpin Field, Dickinson Field, and Dill Field (maps, figs. 0.4, 0.5).

At Oberlin College, national trends influenced physical education and athletics. Changes involved curricular offerings, reflecting shifts in the structure of physical education and as part of the college experience. "Learning and Labor" as a form of daily manual exercise transitioned to organized calisthenics and gymnastics in the 1860s–1870s. Staid college administrators were at first reluctant to accept the newly developing trends, but ultimately, they pledged their support to the students. When Delphine Hanna was hired (1885), the college accepted gymnastics as the best form of exercise for the students. At the time Charles W. Savage joined the college (1905), he promoted the New Physical Education. Oberlin followed the traditional styles of physical education during this period, while at the same time readily and promptly accepting and implementing some of the new elements. For this transition, the rapidity of acceptance was made possible through advocacy by both students and faculty. Additional information on transitions in training physical educators at Oberlin was covered in chapter 2.

Under the thoughtful, enthusiastic guidance of Delphine Hanna and with Leonard's assistance, the program in physical education instructor training grew to include faculty and coursework from other departments, for example, chemistry, zoology, mathematics, and anatomy. The addition of faculty and instructors from outside the major broadened the educational foundations for majors in the two physical education departments. From 1903 to 1910, 43 women graduated in the major and in the same period 13 men completed the degree requirements. In the ensuing decade, 103 women and 42 men graduated.

By 1910, the courses in the normal college curriculum for a female physical education major involved areas of science and the following classes: Practical Work for Freshman and Sophomores; Theory of Play and Games; Applied and Human Anatomy; Practical Work and Teaching Experience for Juniors and Seniors; Medical Gymnastics; Physical Diagnosis and Examination; and Emergencies. For men, the nearly parallel offerings were the following: Advanced Physical Training; Theory of Games and Athletic Sports; Training; Physical Examination; and the Prescription of Physical Exercise. Joint classes included Theory of Physical Training, and History and Literature of Physical Training.

Changes in curriculum during the first quarter of the twentieth century also occurred at other small colleges. By the first decade of the twentieth century, Denison University offered some classes for students intending to teach physical education. This was expanded to a major in 1924–1925. The classes offered were quite similar to those at Oberlin, though fewer in number until the next decade. These included offerings on the history, theory, and practice of physical training, as well as learning the basics of examination of students and taking physical measurements (anthropometry). Courses for practice teaching were required for those wanting to obtain certification to go to schools in Ohio. Springfield College in Massachusetts, originally the School for Christian Workers, provided a two-year certificate program, like the one at Oberlin, by 1889. By 1909, there was a major with thirty classes on all aspects of physical training, athletics, and health education. This also included practice teaching. By the 1930s, just after the end date for this chapter, the program at Springfield had changed only little with some consolidation of classes. This was the foremost program in training physical educators for schools, YMCAs and YWCAs, and a host of other organizations for more than a century. The program continues today as the Department of Physical Education and Health Education and offers a master's degree.

By the early years of the twentieth century, Oberlin had a well-qualified staff managing and supporting efforts in physical education. The people involved with these events comprise a section later in this chapter. Two separate departments existed, one for men and one for women, each with its own chair. There were also directors for the Ladies Gymnasium and Men's Gymnasium; there was a director of athletics for men's intercollegiate athletics; and there was a director of intramurals. A compilation of all of the individuals who held these various positions at Oberlin from the 1880s to the present is found in Appendix B, which also illustrates the changes in the administrative structure over time.

A four-part mission for physical education emerged, and athletics evolved at many American institutions, including Oberlin. These core areas were driven by different needs and philosophical underpinnings. The first part of the mission, physical training for students (often later called service programs), centered on classes for undergraduates to pro-

FIGURE 3.1. The 1910 seniors of the Women's Physical Education Training Program at Oberlin with a dog, which may have been the class mascot. (Oberlin College Archives)

vide them with healthy bodies through exercise. In many ways, this part of the physical training regimen remained rooted in the philosophy of harmony between mind and body. Incorporated into this regimen, games and sports provided benefits to all students regardless of individual ability and existing physical condition. Required periods for training formed part of the weekly regimen, using the sorts of calisthenics, gymnastics, and weight training described earlier. Students also acquired requisite skills needed for various games along with knowledge of the rules in order to properly engage in those activities. These needs were met by two courses in the freshman year followed by two more in the sophomore year. At varying times in the ensuing seven decades one or both of the first two years of these activities was mandatory or sometimes voluntary. The requirement was often different for women and men. Academic credit and requirements for physical education classes varied over time, and any attempt to assemble these changes would be difficult and not very fruitful.

The second area of the four-part mission consisted of courses of study and practice teaching required for the degree from the Physical Education Training Program (fig. 3.1). This curriculum soon grew to a four-year program for women under Delphine Hanna, resulting in a full college degree, and later for men in 1912. The underlying bases for the major curriculum reflected the need for instructors for physical training programs in the rapidly expanding public school systems and in other venues such as YMCAs and playgrounds. Here the philosophy focused on scientific progress in the understanding of the human body, on how the various muscle groups worked, and the integration of physical conditioning and mental performance. By 1902–1903, Fred Leonard offered a one-semester course on hygiene and physiology. Two years later, this expanded to two sequential classes, with the second course covering advanced aspects of the same material. Practical instruction in aspects of poise, games, gymnastics, fencing, and other activities accompanied the classes. Together the acquired skills provided a strong basis for ready employment upon graduation.

The third part of the mission incorporated intramural athletics, in essence a continuation and expansion of the class teams and individual competitions that characterized the early games and sports dating from the late nineteenth century. Intramurals, which remain today as an embedded fixture of Oberlin and all other small colleges, are designed to provide students with physical exercise, with experiences incorporating cooperation and team spirit, and a modest level of competition. At this time, intramurals were the primary outlet for team and individual competition for women, though this shifted during the period covered in this chapter. A wide variety of sports was available for students of both genders and with new activities added as they became popular.

The fourth and last portion of the mission, intercollegiate athletics, was engaged in solely by men at this time. Baseball games played between teams from Oberlin and other institutions started in 1886. Regular seasons of football games between Oberlin College and teams from other schools began in 1892. This level of competition increased in the twentieth century with expanding schedules and with the addition of other intercollegiate sports. Teams were added between 1900 and 1925 for track and field (1901; fig. 3.2), basketball (1903), tennis (1905), and cross country (1915). Much of this growth occurred under the guidance of Charles W. Savage. Hiring Savage signified the college's commitment to a full program of intercollegiate athletics. Expanding the number

FIGURE 3.2. Men's sprint race (top) and pole vault (bottom) during a 1916 track meet. (Oberlin College Archives)

of sports in the ensuing three decades cemented this process. During the two-year period in 1918 and 1919, when the US was most heavily involved in World War I, athletic teams were maintained, but with limited events; the spring 1918 games schedule was cancelled, and play resumed that fall. This was, in part, because of the presence of fewer coaches and players, but also due to wartime restrictions on travel.

The thirty-year career of Charles W. Savage (OC 1893), commencing in 1905, encompassed major growth. Of special note, he was the first athletic director and first physical educator to receive full faculty status at a US institution of higher education. He summed up his rationale and indeed his philosophy for beginning work at the college:

> The greatest single factor in my decision to enter upon the new work was the frank recognition on the part of Oberlin College that physical activity had a very real and indispensable part to play in the education of youth, and that the fixed purpose of the college was not to restrict and repress intercollegiate athletics but to direct and utilize them in a manner befitting an educational institution, and to conduct them in a right relation, to all the other interests and activities of the life of the campus. (*Oberlin Alumni Magazine* 31:172)

Classes for men and women combined appeared in the course catalogue for the first time in 1929–1930. At the same time, the major was split into two possible routes, one being a general physical education major and the other a teacher's major. Both changes—combining some classes across genders and offering a choice of tracks within the major—reflect shifts both within the college and nationally in terms of needs for training in physical education and the underlying movement toward equal treatment of men and women in this specialty area. Occasional joint meetings of the faculties of the two departments occurred soon after the start of the twentieth century.

This was the era when athletic teams from Oberlin faced opponents from larger schools and often won. Notable victories occurred versus opponents like Ohio State, Michigan, Illinois, and Purdue, all members of today's Big Ten. However, by 1920, the big schools had expanded their programs to the extent that Oberlin was no longer competitive in major sports like football and basketball. The change occurred when larger institutions ventured into recruiting and offering athletic scholarships.

Oberlin College serves as a good example of the pattern of changes in the level of competition for smaller schools as time passed into the 1920s and generally continuing to the present. Many of the smaller colleges that competed with Oberlin and remain as rivals in 2020, inside and outside of the North Coast Athletic Conference, underwent these same transitions. So too did other small schools in organizations like the Ohio Athletic Conference, where Oberlin was a member for much of the twentieth century.

The perceived impetus for Oberlin's continued participation in such contests against larger schools stems from three factors, which remain a part of today's motivation for intercollegiate sports at Oberlin and similar institutions. These are: (1) a continued concern for developing mind–body harmony; (2) the prestige accompanying the scheduling of specific teams in various sports; and (3) the publicity garnered for such contests in terms of media coverage. Of course, attracting alumni support, as fans attending the games, as supporters of the program, and financially through contributions to the college, are important considerations. In a few "minor" sports, such as fencing, lacrosse, and ice hockey, Oberlin teams continued to compete with the larger institutions until the 1960s and later, when the bigger schools still did not recruit heavily or offer large scholarships for certain teams. Today, there are few contests between schools like Oberlin (NCAA Division III) and the larger, or even mid-sized, colleges and universities (NCAA Divisions I and II).

Securing sufficient funds to underwrite intercollegiate athletics is a perennial problem for smaller schools like Oberlin. Initially, for men, the student association managed their budgets and collected needed money via gate charges for contests and events such as outside special speakers or performance groups. In time, the finances were assumed by the college and its treasurer's office. However, students retained a voice via an advisory council and voted to "tax" themselves by requiring a small addition ($3 per term initially) to their term bill to cover the cost of athletics. As football ascended in popularity, gate receipts from those games covered most of the costs of other intercollegiate sports, including track and field, tennis, and basketball (fig. 3.3).

Eventually, the fee was inadequate, and expenditures of general revenues from the college budget were needed to fulfill all of the financial needs of the athletics program. Today, none of the sports is self-supporting, and most resources derive from the college's general budget.

FIGURE 3.3. The 1921 basketball team, which had an 11-1 record, including a victory at Michigan Agricultural College (later Michigan State University). Note the kneepads worn by each player. Coach L. F. Keller is shown at the left of the back row. (Oberlin College Archives)

Charles W. Savage and J. Herbert Nichols, as well as others close to the athletics program along with several Oberlin College presidents, fought hard to avoid the commercialization that became the norm for big-time university athletics programs. Amateur standing for college athletes constituted a "badge of honor."

Women

Among Oberlin's peers, Allegheny College first admitted women as students in 1879, while Kenyon College did not become coeducational until 1969. Wabash College remains an all-male school. At Denison, Shepardson College was a separate female institution until it merged with the male school in 1927, and Monnett Hall was a female seminary that combined with Ohio Wesleyan in 1877. Like Oberlin, the College of Wooster and Earlham College were founded as coeducational schools. At all of the schools except Kenyon, various women's sports activities and recreation commenced by the late 1880s. More organized games, for example, basketball, occurred by the mid- and late-1890s. Similar patterns transpired at this group of schools and many others in the region into the middle of the twentieth century, including Play Days (see chapter 7), wherein groups of women from two or more colleges got together to engage in sports and games. More regularized competition with intercollegiate schedules emerged in the decades after World War II. Oberlin followed a path in line with all of the other schools that had female students and thus can serve as an example both in the early stages, as depicted in this chapter, and in years covered in subsequent chapters.

For women, these decades witnessed new and expanded opportunities in sports such as rowing, soccer, field hockey, fencing, and golf (figs. 3.4, 3.5). Dance in various forms was an important part of the women's program. National and international championships soon were established in tennis, golf, and basketball, though Oberlin athletes did not compete in these events. Women began competing in the Olympics for the first time in 1900 and increased their participation with each recurrence of the quadrennial games. National models for young women included Gertrude Ederle (swimming), Helen Wills (tennis), and Babe Didrikson Zaharias (golf, track and field).

The Second Ladies Gymnasium (fig. 2.5), which expanded to incorporate the former Rockefeller Skating Rink in 1906, underwent several renovations. New equipment was added to accommodate changing thoughts and practices on what exercises best supported development and integration of physical and mental health. One interesting item in the notes of the meetings of the Women's Department for 1926–1927 was that an accounting of the number of women taking showers in the renovated locker rooms was measured by counting the number of towels used.

The Women's Gymnasium and Field Association (GFA) formed in 1904 and continued until 1926 when it was replaced by the Women's Athletic Association (WAA). These groups scheduled and regulated women's sports. Based on the now incorrect assumption that women should not overly exert themselves, the range of activities in which women could engage was limited to sports like tennis, gymnastics, ice skating, and basketball, with the last played without any dribbling. While there was a gradual shift in men's athletics toward a philosophy that included "winning" as a primary goal, women's activities retained the traditional mind–body philosophy of earlier years. Playing for enjoyment

FIGURE 3.4. Woman golfer in 1925. (Oberlin College Archives)

FIGURE 3.5. Two women fencing. (Oberlin College Archives)

and exercise was considered sufficient. One fundraising practice to support the women's department budget involved bringing important individuals to campus to present lectures. Dance performances served as another worthy pursuit for young women, along with pageants to display their skills (fig. 2.2). The Association never received official recognition from the college; however, places like Dickinson House served as a gathering place for the group. These innovative women pioneered the breakdown of old, outdated boundaries that had been inherent in women's physical activities. The new practices supplanted the prevailing notions about "delicate" women and their "inferior" position in society. Even into the 1960s, the Hi-O-Hi yearbook contains photographs of teams and board meetings of the WAA, but none of women's sports in action.

At Oberlin, class teams and individual sports provided the bases for women's intramurals as part of physical education. By the 1920s, women's intramural sports at the college included lawn bowling, archery, golf, field hockey, and softball. The first women's basketball game at Oberlin was played in 1896 on a court normally used for tennis and located in the area behind the Second Ladies Gymnasium. A passage from the May 13, 1896, *Oberlin Review* covers this game:

> One of the weaker points of the game was the wild throwing of the ball, when it went out of bounds. The weakest point was the playing of the forwards. This was because the girls had had no practice playing in the out-of-doors and took no account of the wind. . . . But in spite of the fact that no baskets were won, the game was a decided success. . . . Two young men witnessed the game and they kept at a safe distance—one peering through the vines of the porch across the way; the other snatching occasional glimpses around the corner of Talcott.

The Yale–Princeton women's all-star basketball game originated in 1905 and was contested again in 1907 (fig. 3.6). The names of the teams were chosen to reflect the prestige of the Ivy League institutions. The contest involved only students from Oberlin, chosen from the best players on various class teams. It was played indoors for the first time in the recently converted Rockefeller Skating Rink (fig. 3.7). This event became an annual fixture on the Oberlin sports calendar until it was discontinued in 1981, soon after Title IX brought about full participation by women in intercollegiate athletics. Each team had its own cheerleaders.

FIGURE 3.6. The first women's Yale–Princeton basketball game, played outdoors in 1905. The court seen here was adjacent to the Second Ladies Gymnasium–a tennis court with baskets added. A small corner of Talcott Hall can be seen in the center background to the right and left of the gymnasium. Note both the uniforms of the players and the attire of those attending the contest. (Oberlin College Archives)

FIGURE 3.7. In 1906, the Rockefeller Skating Rink was enclosed as an annex to the Ladies Gymnasium. The interior is shown after its 1906 conversion to full-time use as a venue for indoor physical education and women's athletics. It was then sometimes referred to as the Field House. In later years, after its use for women's physical activities ended, it was commonly referred to as the Eyesore. Removal occurred sometime during 1948-1949. The World War II Navy V-12 unit did some of their drill routines in this venue. (Oberlin College Archives)

Halftime of each game featured stunts and performances, initially by members of the two teams and later, from 1913 onward, by groups of female students from the different dormitories. For a time, beginning by 1930 and lasting for several decades, there was an annual field hockey match of top players from class teams: this event, played at Galpin Field, was the Annapolis–West Point game. An all-star volleyball game played for a period in the 1960s featured the Crimson and Gold contest. Other, similar events for women involved softball (Army vs. Navy) and, much later the soccer match of female all-stars (Oxford vs. Cambridge). The beginning of intercollegiate competition prior to Title IX (1972) is presented in chapter 6.

Facilities

During the thirty-year span covered by this chapter, the buildings and playing fields used for physical education and athletics underwent significant changes, by construction and demolition. Some of these can be seen in an aerial view (fig. 3.8). Field locations for various activities were added and developed. The Second Men's Gymnasium proved to be too small; it was in disrepair by the end of the nineteenth century. Plans for a new structure materialized when Dr. and Mrs. Lucien Warner provided funds for a building, which was named in their honor (fig. 3.9; map, fig. 0.4). The new sandstone building was located behind and to the west of Cabinet Hall, which was torn down in that same year. Warner Gymnasium opened in 1901. The old Men's Second Gymnasium was relocated north, about 200', and used as a carpenter's shop until it burned in 1909 and was demolished.

The main floor of the Warner Gymnasium measured 65' by 110', with a height that arced upward from 22' on the sides to 40' at its apex. Offices, examining rooms, a trophy room, and large locker rooms, for general use and for athletes, occupied the floor below the main gym. There is also a smaller gymnasium on the upper floor. The basement contained a ball cage and courts for indoor games like handball and squash as well as storage areas. In 1912, a second gift from the Warners funded an addition on the north side of the original structure (fig. 3.9, bottom). A running track was suspended around this main floor area, with seventeen laps needed to complete a mile (fig. 3.10). Today, this building serves as the Warner Center, home to the Oberlin College

FIGURE 3.8. An aerial view of the college campus from about 1925 looking south, with east to the left and west to the right. Main Street (Route 58) is shown on the left side. The two reservoirs are visible in the distance on Morgan Street, southwest of town. The first street up from the bottom is Lorain Street. Tappan Square is in the left center with College Street along the south side (top of picture). The Graduate School of Theology (now Bosworth Hall) dominates the north side of the square, with First Church and the Carnegie Library on either side of it. On the west side of the square, along Professor Street, we find (north to south, bottom to top), Finney Chapel, Cox Hall, Peters Hall, and Warner Conservatory. Talcott Hall is on the southwest corner of College and Professor Streets near the center of the photo. Attached to Talcott are (a) the Second Ladies Gymnasium and (b) the Rockefeller-funded structure that was a skating rink, now converted for use as part of the women's athletic facilities. Just southwest of Peters Hall is Warner Gymnasium (fig. 3.9, top) and located between that structure and the Men's Building (now Wilder Hall) are two baseball diamonds. Additional athletics venues were located on the north end of campus (map, fig. O.5). (Oberlin College Archives)

FIGURE 3.9. The east side (front entrance) views of Warner Gymnasium, now the Warner Center. The top photo was taken prior to the 1912 addition, which is visible on the right side of the modern photograph (bottom). (Oberlin College Archives)

FIGURE 3.10. Interior view of the main playing area in the new Warner Gymnasium showing the elevated running track around the perimeter. This was one of the first indoor running tracks of its kind–suspended above the main floor. (Oberlin College Archives)

Dance Program. Warner Gymnasium's functions subsequently transitioned to the Phillips Physical Education Center (1971) and the Heisman Club Field House (1992).

The period 1896–1925 witnessed an expansion of athletics venues at the north end of campus. As a guide to these facilities and anticipating further references to the various playing fields a quick review is in order. The first fields for athletics were on Tappan Square, in an open area behind Cabinet Hall on the main campus, and then at Athletic Park on North Professor Street (map, fig. 0.5). In 1893 an open area located between Lorain and College Streets and bordered on the west by North Cedar Avenue was designated as Dickinson Field to honor Ms. Julia Dickinson for her contributions to the college. Most significantly, she endowed the positions of Dean of Women and Director of the Ladies Gymnasium. The college purchased a structure at 166 W. College St. in 1908, and designated it as Dickinson House (map, fig. 0.4). It was remodeled for use as a clubhouse and social hall for women. Later, those same functions transferred to a Second Dickinson House located at 166 W. Lorain Street just south of Galpin Field. The latter served as a clubhouse and as headquarters for the Women's Athletic Association for some years after Galpin Field was opened for women's athletics.

In 1923, Mr. W. A. Galpin of Buffalo, NY, donated $15,000 to cover the purchase of land behind what is now Mercy Allen Hospital; the college originally acquired the land in 1920. Further, the college bought additional acreage which was added in 1929. The field was prepared for women's athletic teams, and use of Dickinson Field was discontinued. Galpin Field served as a home for a wide range of women's sports. Plans included field hockey, soccer, tennis, archery, obstacle golf, and a bridle path. In reality, the field was used for a number of women's athletics teams and class games. Today the field is home to practice areas for several women's sports and for intramurals. For a time, several tennis courts existed on the area directly behind today's hospital. The current Hunsinger Tennis Courts are located along the east side of the field, just west of Woodland Avenue. A total of 2,000 trees were planted at Galpin Field, some of which, along with their "offspring," are present today on the western boundary.

The earliest football contests were played on the recreation fields north of campus and then at Athletic Park. In 1913 the Cleveland Alumni Club of Oberlin provided funding for a second football field and running track built on land just west of Athletic Park, named Old Dill Field. In 1925 a new, third facility, with a quarter-mile track, was completed on the site of the present stadium (fig. 3.11). This was soon designated Savage Stadium in honor of Charles W. Savage, Oberlin graduate, coach, and longtime director of athletics. A portion of the funding came from subscriptions obtained from alumni, students, and friends of the college who purchased seats in the new structure for $12.50 each. The capacity was initially set for about 1,750, but eventually it expanded to twice that size. Savage Stadium was demolished after the 2013 football season to make room for the new Knowlton Athletics Complex (see chapter 8).

Dill Field (map, fig. 0.5) has a complicated history. In a 2004 filing with the Ohio Historic Inventory, the original Dill Field is described as the football field and includes a portion of Savage Stadium. The original 17.8 acres named Dill Field were acquired in 1884. The 1913 construction plans for the area included tennis courts as well as the football and track facilities noted earlier. The second football grounds remained in use until

FIGURE 3.11. Construction of the new stadium, which opened in 1925, and was later named for Charles W. Savage. (Oberlin College Archives)

Savage Stadium opened in 1925, where the playing surface retained the name Dill Field. Additional land purchased over time created an area of more than twenty-five acres, though it is not clear whether the fields were collectively known as Dill Field. At some point, Dill Field became the designated name for the baseball playing area, which now has seating for fans, a press box, and mature landscaping. The open lands to the north and west of the ballfields are used for practices, intramural sports, and recreation. The cross country team uses the outer portions of these fields and trails in the adjoining woods as well as around the solar power array to achieve running courses of varying distances. Further, in 1952, the college named a portion of the outdoor athletic grounds as Savage Field.

In 1921, college planners designed a recreation center for use by both female and male students. The facility would feature a kitchen and several dining rooms of different sizes, a room for billiards and games, a bowling alley, social parlors, a dance floor, and a moving picture theater. This last was suitable for performances and lectures. Due to the cost and the college's austere financial situation, the building was never constructed.

Major changes occurred for facilities at peer institutions during these decades, some before and others after World War I. A major impetus for these additions came from increased interest by fans—alumni and locals. Several of the facilities from this period were used, with upgrades, for many decades. At Denison, Cleveland Hall and Doane Gymnasium, used for indoor activities and basketball, were both opened in 1905. Deeds Field, home for Denison football, was finished for the 1922 season. Rosse Hall at Kenyon was repurposed for physical activities and athletics in the 1890s, but burned in 1897. A new structure was completed for use beginning in 1900–1901. For Ohio Wesleyan, the earliest basketball was played in the converted Williams Opera House. Then, both Edwards Gymnasium (1906) was finished, and later, Selby Stadium (1929) opened just after the period covered by this chapter. New facilities also appeared at several eastern liberal arts colleges: Lasell Gymnasium at Williams College opened in 1886, and the college began using Weston Field for football that same year. At Amherst College, The Cage, a field house, was completed in 1924, and at Tufts, Cousens Gymnasium opened in 1931.

In addition to the on-campus facilities at Oberlin College, three other locations served as important venues for recreational activities. The first of these, in use primarily by men, was about ten miles northwest of campus, along the banks of Chance Creek, where it meets up with the Vermilion River. Second, the Oberlin Beach Club, was reserved expressly for women. Founded by Delphine Hanna, the undeveloped property was approximately five miles east of Huron, OH, on Lake Erie (fig. 4.13). Hanna's visionary approach was evident, when she purchased the forested area with no paths or roads. The third location was the Ladies Grove part of what is now the College Arboretum, just off south Morgan Street, southeast of the old clubhouse of the Oberlin Golf Club.

Oberlin's Influence on Physical Education

As a prelude to providing synopses of the contributions from Oberlin people, it is important to indicate the roles played by numerous individuals from many other institutions and organizations in the development of physical education. One of these, Dudley A. Sargent (1849–1924) and his training schools, position at Harvard University, and summer sessions for preparing physical educators located at Cambridge, MA, was noted at several earlier junctures in this book. He likely is the most influential US figure in the early history of training for physical education teachers. Edward Hitchcock (1828–1911) of Amherst College, also mentioned earlier, was the forerunner of similar individuals at other institutions of higher education, including Oberlin. He was one of the first two individuals to bring together the disciplines of medicine and physical education. Other notable contributors include the following. Charles Beck (1798–1866) helped introduce German gymnastics to America through his work at the Round Hill School at Northampton, MA. Catherine Beecher (1800–1878) was a proponent of teacher training and the need for women to engage in sufficient exercise. As part of her efforts, she founded both the Hartford Seminary (CT) and the Women's Female Institute at Cincinnati (OH). Dio Lewis (1823–1888) argued strongly for exercise as a major component of the daily school program and was a strong proponent for equal opportunities for women to gain physical activity. Edward M. Hartwell (1850–1922) was a major figure in establishing the discipline of physical education as a profession and held several key administrative and advisory positions pertinent to these efforts.

Ethel Perrin (1871–1962) used her roles as teacher and administrator to further the expansion of physical education in schools and city recreation programs, particularly in the Detroit School System. She was a major figure in the development of sports for women and for the integration of health education with physical education. William G. Anderson (1860–1947) was the organizer for the foundational meeting of what became the American Association for the Advancement of Physical Education in 1885, and Jessie Hubbell Bancroft (1867–1952) was perhaps the strongest advocate for physical education with schools, administrators, camps, and youth associations, meeting with and "proselytizing" to any who would listen about the need for the inclusion of exercise in all organizations. Elizabeth Burchenal (1876–1959) was a major influence on the incorporation of folk dancing as a form of recreational exercise. Through her appointments at Columbia University and with the New York City Public Schools, she was able to both train others to become teachers of the subject and to engage many young people in the benefits of dance as a form of exercise.

Among peer institutions here in Ohio and in the Midwest, there were no major contributors to the actual development of physical education, though there are some notable persons who graduated from these colleges and had careers related to the playing, coaching, and administration of athletics. Among these individuals are Branch Rickey, a major league owner and innovator (Ohio Wesleyan 1904); George Little, a College Football Hall of Fame coach (Ohio Wesleyan 1912); Charles Follis, the earliest recorded Black professional football player (Wooster 1902); Bill Veeck, a baseball executive and innovator (Kenyon attended); and Woody Hayes, famed football coach at Ohio State University (Denison 1935).

Key figures in the history of physical education in the US with Oberlin roots began their work during the last two decades of the nineteenth century. Delphine Hanna, Fred E. Leonard, Luther H. Gulick, and Thomas D. Wood had careers that extended into the third decade of the twentieth century. Their accomplishments helped lay the groundwork for the advancement of physical education both as a professional discipline with scientific bases, and as a career pathway for teaching children, students, and adults about fitness and exercise. Together with other pioneers who emerged during the early twentieth century, Oberlin continued to exert a significant influence on physical education, its philosophy, its scientific bases and practice, its history, and the growth of national professional societies. The eleven individuals chronicled briefly here are collectively a very influential cadre who helped to shape American physical education. Several have been noted earlier; collecting these summaries provides a comprehensive look at the totality of their combined careers.

It is fair to say, given their extended list of contributions, that no other institution produced more graduates who had a greater influence on this discipline over the period from 1885 to 1950 than Oberlin. Five of the first eight Gulick Awards were made to individuals with Oberlin connections; eight of the first thirty awards honored people connected with the college.

One common thread among these individuals is that most, though not all, obtained medical degrees as part of their training. This pattern shifted during the ensuing decades into the post–World War II era. Many of these individuals authored groundbreaking, highly influential books across various aspects of physical education involving basic principles and textbooks, history of the field, and particular subjects like play behavior, diagnosis, and individual sports. As a group, these scholars were important figures in national professional organizations and sports' governing bodies. Together, they spanned four periods in this history with different philosophies and means of achieving the objectives generated by those conceptual frameworks. These carefully considered guiding principles evolved from gymnastics to the New Physical Education (sports and games), and to the rise of intercollegiate athletics.

Delphine Hanna (fig. 2.2) founded the Women's Department of Physical Education (1904), among the first of its kind in the country. She helped organize and was a charter member of the American Society for Research in Physical Education (1904), a landmark in the professionalization of this field. She managed the construction of the Rockefeller Skating Rink, its later renovation as part of the Ladies Gymnasium, and the development of Dickinson Field. She initiated the purchase of what became the Oberlin Beach Colony at Lake Erie. Hanna retired in 1920 after thirty-five years of service, well recognized by peers everywhere for her significant efforts to organize the preparation of women (and eventually men) for teaching physical education.

Fred E. Leonard (fig. 2.3) is best known for his two books, *Pioneers of Modern Physical Training* (1915) and *A Guide to the History of Physical Education* (1923). They both broke new ground, extensively documenting the early years of the field and setting the stage for others to follow. Leonard was considered the "father" of studies of the history of physical education. He was an early proponent of what is now called exercise physiology, both in terms of his classroom efforts teaching physiology and hygiene, and in his scientific work on the underlying muscle and body processes involved in physical exercise. He was among the founders of the American Society of Physical Education. At Oberlin he applied his expertise to the design and construction of Warner Gymnasium, which was used for physical education and athletics for more than seven decades.

Luther Halsey Gulick (fig. 2.10) authored a number of influential books on aspects of physical training. Among these were *A Philosophy of Play, The Healthful Art of Dancing, The Efficient Life, Physical Education by Muscular Exercise,* and at least a dozen more, including the *Gulick Hygiene Series.* In addition to publishing, Gulick was heavily involved with the YMCA and other recreational organizations. He held leadership roles in six professional societies and was perhaps the most significant figure in physical education during the first twenty years of the twentieth century. He, in partnership with Dudley A. Sargent and Henry Curtis, founded the Playground Association of America in 1906. Gulick helped develop and manage boys' and girls' summer camps in Maine. His legacy is honored annually with the presentation of the Luther Halsey Gulick Award made by what is now the Society of Health and Physical Educators (SHAPE).

Thomas Denison Wood (fig. 2.11) helped found Stanford University (1885) in California. He developed that school's physical education program beginning in 1891, with a full training program by the mid-1890s. Sports, games, and dance formed the core of his program. He coauthored *The New Physical Education,* which became the standard for the field for several decades. His major contribution was the push to emphasize not just the "physical" part of the program, but also the "educational" portion. He wrote books on various aspects of health education, including *A Program for Public Schools and Teacher Training Institutions* and *The Child in School Care.* Wood received the Gulick Award in 1925.

Three individuals with Oberlin connections emerged during the period 1896–1925. Each had a major influence on a variety of aspects of physical education and athletics on a national scale. Clark W. Hetherington was a protégé of Wood, completing both his undergraduate and graduate studies at Stanford. While at the University of Missouri, he became one of the first administrators to have control over both the physical education program and athletics. He emphasized the importance of play behavior for young people. He authored *The School Program in Physical Education,* which was a standard textbook for many years. Selected as the first Fellow of the American Academy of Physical Education, he later received the Gulick Award (1928). The annual Clark W. Hetherington Award is currently given in his honor, by the American Academy of Kinesiology, to an individual who has provided great service.

Jay Bryan Nash (OC 1911), mentored by Delphine Hanna, earned a Ph.D. from New York University under the tutelage of Clark Hetherington. He extolled the idea that play was a means to attaining individual happiness and as an aid to discovering one's place in life. He was a major proponent of integrating physical exercise with recreation and camping. Together these activities would help fill the newfound leisure time experienced by many Americans. Like several of his contemporaries, Nash's interests centered on the youth in primary and secondary schools. In addition to numerous published articles, his works included books on *Philosophy of Recreation and Leisure, Physical Education: Its Interpretations and Objectives, Spectatoritis, Teachable Moments,* and as editor of the five-volume collection on *Interpretations of Physical Education.* Nash was a prominent figure in many professional organizations, serving as president of several of them. His work as Superintendent of

Recreation and Director of Physical Education for the city of Oakland, CA, provided a model system, soon emulated by other growing metropolitan areas of the US.

His work on "spectatoritis" drew attention to a key trend that emerged during this period, involving the growth of crowds of people gathering to watch athletic contests. As just noted earlier in this chapter, many schools and colleges constructed stadiums and indoor arenas so an ever-growing number of spectators could watch athletic events. In the early 1930s, Nash chaired a committee to develop a set of standards for assessing and regulating college and university programs for teacher training in physical education. He received both the Gulick and Hetherington Awards from the American Association for Health, Physical Education, and Recreation. Consistent with his beliefs and his teaching, he maintained that physical education was designed to (1) provide for physical fitness; (2) generate good physical health; (3) nurture social and moral values; and (4) facilitate the acquisition of lifelong leisure time activities. A quote summarizes his views on this subject:

> The four objectives (of physical education): organic power, neuromuscular development leading to skill in performance, the ability to do interpretive thinking and the guiding of the emotional urges essential to group living provide a sense of wholeness for the individual. (Nash 1948, 77)

Jesse Feiring Williams (fig. 3.12) was the most prolific author of this group, producing more than forty books over the course of more than forty years. He was a dominating figure during his career in physical education (1916–1964). Williams (OC 1909) achieved his M.D. degree at Columbia in 1915. He devoted his career to work at Columbia as a faculty member and leader. He believed that through exercise, sports, and games, individuals could learn self-discipline, leadership, cooperation, how to work in a group, and within societal norms, to keep their bodies healthy and fit. He believed that students learned best by active involvement and not by sitting through lectures and lessons. His philosophy incorporated the wholeness of the person, dependent on an integration of mind and body. An eloquent quote from one of his books reflects Williams' views:

> When mind and body were thought of as two separate entities, physical education was obviously an education of the physical; in similar

FIGURE 3.12. Jesse Feiring Williams. (Oberlin College Archives)

fashion, mental education made its own exclusive demands. But with new understanding of the nature of the human organism in which wholeness of the individual is the outstanding fact, physical education becomes education through the physical. With this view operative, physical education has concern for and with emotional responses, personal relationships, group behaviors, mental learning, and other intellectual, social, emotional, and esthetic outcomes. Although important and not to be neglected it is quite insufficient to develop strength of muscles, bones, and ligaments, to acquire motor skills, and to secure physical endurance. (Williams 1932, 1)

While at Oberlin as an undergraduate, Williams served as the athletic director for the Oberlin Preparatory Academy. His books include *Principles of Physical Education* (eight editions), *Manual of Elementary Physical Diagnosis,* and *The Administration of Health and Physical Education.* He mentored many well-known students, among them Norma Schwendener, a noted historian of physical education. Williams was involved with professional organizations, including presidencies of the American Physical Education Association and College Physical Education Association. He received the Gulick Award in 1939 and an honorary degree from Oberlin College in 1956.

In addition to the individuals just noted, four other people made important contributions to (1) the discipline of physical education and athletics at the college; (2) various national organizations; and (3) the continuing development of this field. These were Charles W. Sav-

FIGURE 3.13. Charles W. Savage. (Oberlin College Archives

FIGURE 3.14. The Four Horsemen of Oberlin College football. The 1891 team featured Carl Semple, Carl Williams, Howie Regal, and Charles Savage. This was the first year for intercollegiate football competition at the college. Note the uniforms, lack of sufficient padding, and absence of any head protection. (Oberlin College Archives)

age, John Herbert Nichols, Whitelaw Reid Morrison, and Gertrude Moulton. All were Oberlin graduates who returned to their alma mater for major portions of their professional careers.

Charles Winfred Savage (fig. 3.13) graduated from Oberlin in 1893, where he starred in baseball and football (fig. 3.14). He obtained an A.M. degree from Harvard (1898) and taught briefly at several locations before returning to the college, where he served first as a faculty member in the men's physical education department and then as director of athletics. Using that platform, he was a strong advocate for sports as an opportunity for all students and not just a few with great talents.

Savage consistently campaigned against the growing tendency toward commercialization of and professionalism in college sports and for the need to retain high standards for amateur athletes. At Oberlin he held the athletic directorship from 1906 (some sources give 1905) to 1935, with a period when he was away (1918–1920) and T. Nelson Metcalf was in charge of athletics, during which time, six men's intercollegiate sports teams were added. He is a member of the Heisman Club Hall of Fame. Delphine Hanna had secured college appointments for members of both the men's and women's physical education departments from the college. Savage was responsible for elevating the coaches to faculty status, which they retained until the 1970s. To achieve faculty status, physical educators were required to (1) teach in the service class program; (2) qualify to teach academic classes in the physical education major program; and (3) coach one or more sports. In addition, faculty members helped administer the intramurals program. Savage Stadium was named in his honor, as also were portions of the college's athletic fields for a period of time.

When the college sought a nickname for its sports teams, one suggestion was to call the athletes the "Savages" in honor of Charles Savage. This moniker lost out to "Yeoman," a shortened form of Ye Oberlin (O) Men and not, as is often assumed, a reference to the English Yeomen of the Guard (Beefeaters). Accordingly, as women became more involved with intercollegiate athletics, the term "Yeowomen" was adopted as their nickname. Savage was president of athletics organizations in Ohio, and the American Association for Health, Physical Education, and Recreation as well as of the College Physical Education Society. He was elected to the American Academy of Physical Education and received the Gulick Award recognizing his extensive contributions to physical education and athletics. His expertise and mindfulness about the purposes of intercollegiate sports resulted in service on the NCAA Committee on Football Rules from 1905 to 1928 and on the US Olympic Committee for both 1924 and 1928.

John Herbert Nichols (OC 1911) (fig. 3.15) was a standout football and basketball player who obtained his M.D. at the University of Chicago (1916). He helped establish the physical education program at Ohio State University before returning to Oberlin in 1928. He was in charge of the intramurals program, expanding its scope and including upwards of 80% of the male students in various sports programs for some years. When Savage retired, Nichols was chosen to serve as director of athletics. Like Savage, Nichols was a strong opponent of commercialization, insisting that funds for intercollegiate sports be allocated from the general college budget. Nichols is a member of the Heisman Club Hall of Fame.

He became well known for the leadership role he took in establishing and managing Camp Pemigewassett in Wentworth, NH. A number of

FIGURE 3.15. John Herbert Nichols. (Oberlin College Archives)

Oberlin students attended or served as counselors at this camp; among them were Fred Shults, Norman Craig, and Robert Kretchmar. During his lifetime, Nichols published more than 100 papers in physical education journals, covering a variety of topics. He served as a referee for Big Ten football (twenty-three years) and basketball (fifteen years). The gateway to the athletic complex at the college is named in his honor. The inscription on one of the two side pillars describes his good work:

> Erected by friends of a man who as a student, teacher, and director of athletics, lived taught, and fostered for over forty-five years this ideal of a wholesome athletic program for all Oberlin men.

Whitelaw Reid Morrison (fig. 3.16) completed both the A.B. and A.M. degrees at Oberlin (1910) and his M.D. at Columbia (1914). He held a position at Columbia in the Department of Physical Education before returning to Oberlin in 1923, shortly after the death of Frederick E. Leonard. He served as director of the men's gymnasium for twenty-eight years and, as a professor, taught classes in physiology and hygiene as part of the program in physical education. He was a prolific author and exerted a strong influence on the field through a number of books: *Physical Diagnosis* (co-authored with Jesse Feiring Williams), *A Text-book of*

FIGURE 3.16. Whitelaw Reid Morrison. (Oberlin College Archives)

Physical Education, and textbooks with Laurence Chenoweth, including *Community Health, Normal and Elementary Physical Diagnosis,* and *Community Hygiene: A Textbook in the Control of Communicable Diseases*. Several of these books went through multiple editions and thus influenced a generation of students intending to pursue careers in physical education and hygiene. Later, Morrison co-authored *Basketball: A Handbook for Coaches and Players,* which served as the standard reference for the sport across many decades. He returned to teach in Columbia's summer school for several years. Professionally, Morrison was active in the Association for Health, Physical Education, and Recreation, the American Academy of Physical Education, and other organizations. He served as chair of the Lorain County Health Board for twenty years.

Gertrude E. Moulton (OC 1903) (fig. 3.17) was a student with Delphine Hanna; she later completed an M.D. degree at the University of Illinois in Chicago (1919). Following teaching and leadership roles at several institutions, most notably the University of Illinois in Urbana-Champaign, Moulton returned to her alma mater in 1923 to chair the Women's Physical Education Department. Moulton held the position until her own retirement in 1946. Nationally, she was a primary figure in women's physical education with regard to establishing standards for training students intending to become instructors in physical and

FIGURE 3.17. Gertrude E. Moulton. (Oberlin College Archives)

health education in primary and secondary schools. She was known for her unbounded physical energy and enthusiasm for outdoor recreation activities, as well as her mentorship of hundreds of Oberlin female undergraduates. Under Moulton's guidance, the physical plant for women's athletics expanded to include Galpin Field, Crane Pool, Hales Gymnasium, and the full use of the Hanna Camp at Lake Erie. She wrote many articles for professional journals, covering topics like war and physical education, the postwar programs for physical exercise, and the relationships between sports and world citizenship. Her professional efforts included serving as president of the National Association of Directors of Physical Education for Women in Colleges and Universities and as an editor for the *Research Quarterly*. Moulton was one of the first women elected to the American Academy of Physical Education. A passage from her writings offers insight into her philosophy concerning competition in women's athletics and the benefits from these activities:

> If there is any value in the experience of winning and losing with equanimity—of playing one's own part without trying to do the work for the whole team—of having the joyous experience of working your best, for the fun of the game against friendly opponents, who test your

mettle, so that experience should not be saved for the ones who have already had the most of it. Each will have the opportunity to try herself out in social relationships under stress, to develop her strength and skill and endurance, and to increase her margin of safety. Each will have a rich background of experience that will make for force and enthusiasm and with the understanding to win or lose with courage and turn the loss to a richer gain. (Moulton 1930, 197)

In the administrative files for the Men's Department of Physical Education for the year 1923–1924, there is a list of individuals trained at Oberlin in the first two decades of the twentieth century who, at the time, held prominent administrative positions with physical education departments around the country. The influence of Oberlin, with its underlying philosophy relating to physical education and its views on larger issues in this field, was quite widespread by 1925. That influence continued to expand during the ensuing twenty-five years as the second generation of Oberlin graduates pursued their own careers, mentoring yet another generation of teachers and scholars. This list included the following names:

Dr. Dudley S. Reid, University of Chicago
Dr. Thomas D. Wood, Columbia University—Teacher's College
Dr. Jesse F. Williams, Columbia University—Teacher's College
Dr. Edwin Fauver, University of Rochester
Dr. Edgar Fauver, Wesleyan University (Connecticut)
Dr. J. E. Nichols, Ohio State University
Prof. T. N. Metcalf, Iowa Agricultural College (Iowa State University)
Prof. C. C. Bird, Ohio University
Prof. O. N. Mikiloff, University of Cincinnati
Prof. C. D. Giaque, Ohio University
Mr. Roy E. Tillotson, Miami University (Ohio)
Mr. Fred J. Martin, Wesleyan University (Connecticut)
Dr. J. Bryan Nash, New York University
Mr. Thomas A. Neill, Western Reserve University (Case Western Reserve University)
Mr. Warren E. Stellar, Bowling Green Normal School (Bowling Green State University)
Mr. Arthur E. Winters, Case School of Applied Science (Case Western Reserve University)

Mr. Willis O. Hunter, University of Southern California
Mr. F. E. Yocum, Western Reserve University (Case Western Reserve University)

Summary

The period 1896–1925 encompassed major transitions and key events, on both the national and international stages and for practices and advances in physical education and athletics. The events of the pre-World War I era, the growth in public education, the trauma of war, and the glamor and high spirits of the 1920s served, over time, as backdrops for enhancements in the educational enterprise. The physical education curriculum split into four areas, covering service classes, courses for majors, intramurals, and intercollegiate athletics. In the early years of the twentieth century, physical education changed from gymnastics to the New Physical Education and, by the 1920s, the emphasis shifted again, this time toward competitive athletics. Eleven individuals with strong Oberlin College connections, including four whose careers began in the final decades of the nineteenth century and seven more who played significant roles in the advancement and professionalization of American Physical Education through the first five decades of the twentieth century, are exemplars of the enormous influence the college exerted on these changes. Many other people made significant contributions over this same time period, including both men and women who shared the progress that resulted in the emergence of a new, comprehensive discipline. Women's programs now included more contests against other schools across a number of sports. The curriculum for training physical educators, led by places like Springfield College, expanded to include a range of courses connecting physical activity, biology, and health education. The physical plant at the college was augmented by structures that included Warner Gymnasium and Savage Stadium. Galpin and Dill Fields were developed for female and male physical activities programs. A similar pattern of new buildings and playing fields occurred at other colleges and universities, spurred in part by the increase in the public to attend athletic contests. College athletics shifted from competition that often included games against larger institutions to schedules that included only schools similar in size and caliber to Oberlin.

Sources Consulted for Chapter 3

Full citations are found at the end of the book.

Brandt, L. J. *The Evolution of Women's Intercollegiate Athletics at Oberlin College.*

Cohen, A. M., and C. B. Kisker. *The Shaping of American Higher Education: Experience and Growth of the Contemporary System.*

Dewey, J. "The New Psychology." *Andover Review* 2:278–289.

———. *Democracy and Education: An Introduction to the Philosophy of Education.*

Gerber, E. W. *Innovators and Institutions in Physical Education.*

Gulick, L. H. *A Philosophy of Play.*

Hackensmith, C. W. *History of Physical Education.*

Hetherington, C. W. *American Journal of Public Health.*

Horger, M. "Basketball and Athletic Control at Oberlin College, 1896–1915." *Journal of Sport History* 23:256–283.

Lee, M. *A History of Physical Education and Sports in the U.S.A.*

Leonard, F. E. *A Guide to the History of Physical Education.*

———. *Pioneers of Modern Physical Training.*

Moulton, G. "The Scientific Development of Physical Education." *Oberlin Alumni Magazine,* 26:197.

Nash. J. B. *Philosophy of Recreation and Leisure.*

———. *Physical Education: Interpretations and Objectives.*

Pollard, J. E. *Ohio State Athletics, 1879–1959.*

Rice, E. A., J. L. Hutchinson, and M. Lee. *A Brief History of Physical Education.*

Rudolph, F. *The American College and University: A History.*

Schwendener, N. *A History of Physical Education in the United States.*

Scott, H. A. *Competitive Sports in Schools and Colleges.*

Shults, F. D. *The Life of Fred Eugene Leonard, M.D.*

———. *The History and Philosophy of Athletics for Men at Oberlin College.*

Smith, R. A. *Sports & Freedom: The Rise of Big-Time College Athletics.*

Trekell, M. *Gertrude Evelyn Moulton, M.D.: Her Life and Professional Career in Health and Physical Education.* Ph.D. Dissertation. Columbus: Ohio State University.

Wayman, A. R. *A Modern Philosophy of Physical Education.*

Weston, W. *The Making of American Physical Education.*

Williams, J. F. *The Organization and Administration of Physical Education.*

———. *The Principles of Physical Education.*

Williams, J. F., and W. R. Morrison. *A Text-book of Physical Education.*

CHAPTER 4

Sports as a Cultural Phenomenon
1926–1950

Period Events and Context

This chapter examines a period when physical education and athletics shifted only moderately from what they were in the 1920s (see Appendix A for timelines). In the US, the quarter century from 1926 to 1950 involved the Great Depression, World War II, and the beginning of a period of economic and population growth in the years after that conflict. The educational enterprise expanded as returning veterans and others who had worked through the war were now anxious to get an education and move onward with their lives. Government support helped sustain students and colleges during the Great Depression and continued after the war through programs like the GI Bill. Educational institutions added programs, both baccalaureate and graduate degrees.

Initially, the tenor of higher education remained much as it was prior to 1925, with an emphasis on earlier concepts and principles. Students, however, were not satisfied with the status quo and demonstrated in protest to stimulate curricular changes. New courses offered included topics ranging from diverse views on political science and sociology, along with varied economic systems encompassing Marxism and an enhanced capitalism. Science and engineering curriculums were expanded to incorporate many advances in knowledge and technology.

As the US moved forward, sports assumed a new, higher place in terms of the focus of many Americans. The characteristics of American football, strength, agility, combativeness, and strategy, which gained in importance in a postwar environment, made it the predominant sport for males. This trend grew stronger as the decades passed, gaining more adherents to the football culture. The only other major sport at the time was baseball, then still considered the American pastime. Culture was a primary influence on what sports became popular in particular regions of the country: soccer was the sport most often played by those in communities of recent immigrants; car racing predominated in southern states; the emerging sport of basketball was an urban game; and rodeos were prominent in the southwest and Rocky Mountain states. While these patterns still are visible in many areas, the general predominance of football at both collegiate and professional levels is the one constant focus across the US.

Accompanying these changes in society and education was an expanded emphasis on intercollegiate athletics. In particular the American desire for entertainment resulted in larger crowds at many sporting events; hence the chapter title. A culmination of factors contributed to this increase. Competition, particularly in major sports, resulted in intense contests and a desire to win, though there was usually a gentlemanly approach to these contests—a system of friendly, oftentimes traditional, rivalries. The biggest state schools came to dominate in major sports like football, basketball, and baseball, with large stadiums and arenas. Media coverage now included radio broadcasts, and print media coverage by reporters for each sport at the larger newspapers. Many people became fans of sports at large schools and professional squads, devoting their free time to following the exploits of these teams.

Between 1926 and 1950, various professional sports leagues formed and expanded. Baseball added new stadiums. Professional football, involving up to twenty-two teams, many from small towns, changed by the 1940s; franchises moved to larger cities and what became the National Football League (NFL) organized. The National Basketball Association (NBA), formed from several earlier professional basketball organizations, emerged in 1949. A key to all three of these professional-level sports, but especially football and basketball, was recruiting, drafting, and hiring college players. Sports programs at bigger universities realized that their athletic programs could function as "feeders" to the "big" leagues. Professional baseball did this to some extent, though it had a tradition of drafting younger players, many of whom did not attend college. Smaller schools, like Oberlin, were not really part of this pattern, though, on occasion, athletes from liberal arts colleges "graduated" to careers with professional teams.

The expansion of sports and teams at the collegiate level included many so-called "minor" sports beyond the big three, such as golf, tennis, track and field, wrestling, and skiing at appropriate locations. The quadrennial Olympics, both summer and winter, after a hiatus for the war, continued to grow as new sports became part of the games. The number of national championships, both those sponsored by college and university organizations like the National Collegiate Athletic Association (NCAA) and National Association for Intercollegiate Athletics (NAIA—formed in 1945), and others such as the Amateur Athletic Union (AAU), expanded. The differentiation between large and small institutions' sports programs became increasingly evident, and soon the "playing field" would need to be leveled in order to maintain appropriate contests. Organizations like the NCAA instituted regulations to govern recruitment and any possible forms of compensation to college athletes.

The increased emphasis on competition for males meant that athletes continued to pursue the benefits of daily exercise, cooperative team efforts, and competition. There were intramural sports and the development of a few club sports for those who were interested, but these involved only a modest proportion of students at the larger schools and, over time, diminishing numbers at smaller institutions. Required physical education classes continued at many schools, though often taking the form of three one-hour class meetings per week. This frequently constituted the total exercise commitment for many students.

Changes in Philosophy and Control

The predominant underlying philosophy at the outset of this period followed the tenets of John Dewey. Pragmatic ideas based on practical experience and learning by doing were the central focus. This was not only the impetus behind varsity athletics, but, by the late 1920s, the renewed emphasis on intramurals and recreation as a means for obtaining physical exercise fit the same paradigm. In the years after World War II and continuing into the 1950s, there was a trend away from both the mind–body connection and the playing of athletic contests as an opportunity for competition and camaraderie. Spectator interest increased, as did the need to win as a major consideration.

It is noteworthy that, over the course of 100 years, students provided much of the impetus to alter the focus of the physical activities. The Oberlin College administration instituted the manual labor movement in the first half of the nineteenth century. However, college leadership often declined to support gymnastics and then games and sports despite mounting student enthusiasm for shifting to new avenues of physical exercise. For many schools, the pattern shifted with college administrations taking charge of athletics, both for financial reasons and to control tendencies toward professionalism. By the second quarter of the twentieth century, this pattern shifted when larger schools began to realize the potential revenue generation from big team sports. Ticket sales and money from merchandise offerings, later coupled with corporate sponsorships and alumni contributions, enabled larger schools to use that revenue to support other aspects of their athletic programs. Meanwhile, at smaller institutions, students continued to express their strong interest in sports through their enthusiastic participation and commitment. Such avid involvement proved critical for sustaining athletics departments at schools with fewer students.

War Years

Several changes, some of a temporary nature and others more long-lasting, occurred during World War II. In 1942, a US Navy V-12 unit was assigned to the campus (fig. 4.1). The presence of veterans just after the war extended to about 1950. The V-12 unit used the Second Ladies Gymnasium and the adjoining enclosed structure that was originally the Rockefeller Skating Rink. These two venues housed indoor drill sessions, and many of the exercises and other activities for the military personnel. Men from the V-12 unit and later veterans were eligible to participate on the athletic teams. This was also true for some schools against whom Oberlin competed. The presence of these somewhat older and generally better conditioned men changed the nature of the contests, both for intramurals and intercollegiate athletics. Oberlin especially benefitted from the effects of the influx of V-12 athletes, because the person assigning the men to specific institutions was himself an Oberlin graduate, who played football with Lysle Butler as the coach.

During the course of the early years of Oberlin's physical education and intercollegiate athletic teams, students served as managers and

FIGURE 4.1. Beginning in 1942 and until shortly after the conclusion of World War II, a Navy V-12 unit trained on the Oberlin campus. V-12 units were located on many college and university campuses. The primary goal was to produce commissioned officers for naval service. Members of V-12 units took classes on campus and participated in campus activities, including athletics. (Oberlin College Archives)

coaches. Over several decades, these students continued to serve as managers, but no longer were directly involved in coaching. Beginning in the 1940s and continuing until today, coaching responsibilities have occasionally been filled by personnel from outside the physical education and athletics department. Both head and assistant coaching by these "outsiders" customarily occurred on a voluntary basis. In addition to faculty and staff at the college, capable and qualified coaches from Oberlin High School served with the college athletics program.

One curious phenomenon occurred during the war, when travel for off-campus events was at a premium and often restricted. Sports contests could be limited to just the home venues. Sanctioned swim meets occurred between opponents with competitors remaining on their home campuses, using a specified time and format. Times and scores for performances were transmitted via telegraph to the other competing institution(s) so that winners and other placements could be determined.

The same novel solution was used for bowling in 1941 and perhaps for track and field and cross country.

Physical Education and Athletics at Oberlin

Throughout the years, support for the facilities and athletics teams came almost entirely from the general college budget. New construction was largely dependent on contributions from donors such as alumni and friends of Oberlin. All students had free use of all facilities. The general activity fee at the college was set at $16.40 per semester, with just $4.25 of that going to sports activities, including intercollegiate athletics. The amount allocated for sports from these fees was considerably less at Oberlin than at peer institutions.

Among the faculty who joined the men's and women's departments, several played prominent roles during the period 1925–1950 and continued into the 1950s and 1960s. These included Lera B. Curtis (fig. 4.2), whose primary influence was in physical education; Guy C. Throner (fig. 4.3), who taught in the curriculum and served as a coach; Helen Domonkos (fig. 4.4), who created a full dance program; and Katherine von Wenck (fig. 4.5), who established the aquatics program.

Lera Curtis served on the faculty during the war years and into the period of changes that followed. She taught classes in the physical education major and the service courses. Her efforts were important for transitioning between the programs that were suitable prior to the war, and what was needed by the late 1940s and early 1950s. Curtis served as Director of the Ladies Gymnasium from 1946 to 1954, at which time she retired.

In his early career, Guy Throner (OC 1924; fig. 4.3) coached at several high schools and was supervisor of physical education for the State of Virginia. He coached at his alma mater from 1924 until 1954, when he retired holding the all-time record for most victories by an Oberlin College baseball coach. He also assisted with football and several other sports at different times during those thirty years. For much of his time at the college, Throner was the individual who managed all of the intramurals for men. He also taught classes in physical education. He is a member of the Heisman Club Hall of Fame.

Helen Domonkos (fig. 4.4) received her B.A. from Ohio Wesleyan College (1920) and an M.A. from Wellesley (1922). She trained for dance

FIGURE 4.2. Lera B. Curtis came to Oberlin in 1935 after teaching for many years in public schools, often in rural areas. She obtained a B.S. at what is now Michigan State University and her A.M. from Columbia University. (Oberlin College Archives)

FIGURE 4.3. Guy C. Throner possessed a set of skills, as coach and mentor, which made him among the most beloved members of the Men's Department of Physical Education during his career at Oberlin. (Oberlin College Archives)

with Martha Graham, both in New York City and Germany. Domonkos increased the number of participants, broadened the varieties of dance included in the program, and added more exhibitions and performances by visiting groups. After retirement in 1965, she continued to teach dance classes. Her enthusiastic leadership led to the formation of the Delphine Hanna Foundation.

Katherine von Wenck (fig. 4.5) obtained her bachelor's degree at Queens College in North Carolina (1917) and later an M.A. degree from New York University (1934). She was the first person to run a full swimming and aquatics program for women at Oberlin. Von Wenck served in several administrative roles including acting Dean of Women and Associate Dean for Women, and as Acting Director and then Director of the Recreation Program.

Appendix B has a comprehensive list of the various positions and the people who filled those roles in the administration of physical education and athletics, including for the period covered in this chapter. In 1935, this list included a Director of the Ladies Gymnasium (Ger-

FIGURE 4.4. Helen Edwards Domonkos joined the Oberlin faculty in 1922 and soon became a respected teacher and was responsible for fostering the growth of the dance program over the next forty-three years. (Oberlin College Archives)

FIGURE 4.5. Katherine S. von Wenck joined the college faculty in 1925 as an instructor and became an assistant professor in 1937. (Oberlin College Archives)

trude Moulton); Director of the Teachers Course in Physical Education for Women (Gertrude Moulton); Director of the Men's Gymnasium (Whitelaw Reid Morrison); Director of the Teachers Course in Physical Education for Men (Charles W. Savage); Director of Athletics (Charles W. Savage and then John Herbert Nichols); and Director, Intramural Athletics (John Herbert Nichols). In later years, as the list in Appendix B illustrates, the number of positions was diminished when the consolidation of responsibilities occurred.

Between 1926 and 1950, the underlying philosophy for women remained more in concert with the mind–body harmony of earlier decades than was occurring for men. Both the internal and external sports activities were regulated through the Women's Athletic Association (WAA). Women learned various skills, while also enjoying camaraderie, teamwork, and exercise. The sports offered in the service classes for women covered a broad range of electives: basketball, field hockey, archery, tumbling, running, lifesaving, synchronized swimming, golf, tennis, soccer, softball, and others. The Yale–Princeton basketball game continued as an annual fixture. As part of the contest, the halftime break now consisted of singing performances or skit exhibitions among groups from various houses and dormitories.

While some sports involved team competition, many were on the individual level. For all sports, it was the sheer enjoyment of playing the game—and not necessarily the outcome—that was important. For the physical education major at larger schools, much of the responsibility for teaching subject classes fell to the women in the department, while the men began to concentrate more on coaching. This was particularly true for larger institutions. At Oberlin, these changes in duties occurred a bit later, into the 1960s.

The four distinct areas of responsibility for the Men's and Women's Departments of Physical Education remained similar to those presented in an earlier chapter and included (1) general physical education (also called service classes); (2) a major in the discipline; (3) intramural sports; and (4) intercollegiate athletics. From 1935 and continuing, with exceptions, through the 1950s, individuals hired by the Men's Department of Physical Education at Oberlin were selected based on their ability to participate in all four of these activities. Examination of annual catalogues from similar institutions (e.g., Kenyon, Denison, Ohio Wesleyan) reveals the same basic framework for the division of the activities by personnel in the physical education programs.

In the period from 1926 to 1950, many schools, both small and large, offered degrees in physical education (1) for those who planned careers as teachers in public schools and at recreational facilities, and (2) for those intending to obtain advanced degrees in higher education or administration. Oberlin typified this pattern. In 1940, the curriculum in physical education consisted of required classes for freshman and sophomores, with additional, optional activities for juniors and seniors. Those planning to major in physical education took the following classes as part of their curriculum, with the last three in particular geared to students who planned to go into teaching at primary and secondary schools:

Anatomy and Physiology
General Hygiene
Individual Hygiene
First Aid and Massage

Methods and Practice of Teaching Physical Education Activities
History and Principles of Physical Education
Normal Diagnosis and Gymnastics
Theory and Practice of Play
Organization and Administration of Intramural Sports (men only)
Methods and Practice in Teaching Intramural Sports (women only)
Health Education and School Hygiene
Organization and Administration
Observation and Practice Teaching

It was during this quarter century that academic credentials for being part of the physical education and athletics programs shifted. Prior to the 1940s, most of the faculty in the department held medical degrees and a few had doctorates. Over the next several decades this transitioned. By the 1970s, there were no medical doctors and only a limited number with doctorates among physical education faculty at Oberlin. Today, there are no doctorally prepared members of the faculty; some have master's degrees and others, often assistant coaches, have only a bachelor's degree. Why did this shift occur? First, as the discipline of physical education developed, many aspects involved an understanding of the human body and its functioning. Anthropometrics and other assessment techniques were conducted with a clinical perspective. Second, as the use of such techniques declined, other related areas such as kinesiology, exercise science, and sports medicine developed to take on these functions in a more up-to-date manner. Third, the skills needed to conduct service classes, coaching, and ancillary activities such as intramurals did not require the specialized knowledge that was previously needed. Teaching courses for the major in physical education is an exception. However, at schools where majors in physical education, health education, kinesiology, and related academic disciplines in various forms are currently offered, most faculty have doctoral training. At larger schools, athletics and coaching form a separate unit from the physical education program, with its own administration.

During the quarter century covered by this chapter, several intercollegiate sports were added for men at Oberlin. These included both golf and swimming and diving in 1933, fencing in 1934, and lacrosse in 1949. Of these, two, swimming and diving and lacrosse remain part of the men's athletics program in 2021.

Athletics Policy

Policies governing athletics at Oberlin College began by the 1880s. To provide a continuum of understanding of these important documents, they are collected here as they were formalized, beginning in the 1920s. As early as 1869, athletics were regulated by the faculty when various sports were played on the College Green (Tappan Square). In 1885 the faculty created the first standing committee on athletics. A separate committee was assigned to make decisions concerning the relationship between the college and the Second Men's Gymnasium. In 1891, these were merged to form the Men's Gymnasium and Athletic Committee. This was followed, in 1894, by the formation of the Athletics Advisory Committee. It consisted of three faculty, three alumni, and three students. The mission of this committee, as recorded in the minutes from the Faculty Meeting of January 8, 1894, read: "This Committee shall have entire supervision and control of all athletic exercise within and without the precincts of the College, subject to the authority of the General Faculty. It shall report annually to the President." Later, a Committee for the Regulation of Athletic Sports maintained the oversight and management into the twentieth century. In 1958 the Educational Policy Committee (EPC—now the Educational Plans and Policies Committee, or EPPC) began to exercise control over some aspects of athletics.

During the early years of Charles W. Savage's tenure at Oberlin (1905–1935), he put forward several key principles that can be viewed as the foundation for future iterations of the college's athletic policy:

1. Physical education is an essential part of the college work.
2. All athletics are under the direction of the Department of Physical Education.
3. The Athletics Advisory Committee (1894) retains its important functions.
4. The daily college schedule should provide time for recreation for all students and faculty.
5. The required program in physical education should be supplemented by intramurals and intercollegiate athletics.
6. The college should work with the other schools in the Ohio Athletic Conference to provide a scheme of intercollegiate athletics that is dedicated to the interests and welfare of the students.

7. Funds should be sought to endow the maintenance of athletic facilities and fields, and for the purchase of equipment and supplies.
8. All monies associated with intercollegiate athletics should be routed through a special account.

The 1930s policy, also formulated under the guidance of Charles W. Savage, had the following major points:

1. All personnel, including students, faculty, administrators, and alumni accept that athletics is a fundamental part of the educational program, not a money-making enterprise or for publicity.
2. Athletics should be financed through the college budget with funds for equipment, travel, and guarantees to visiting teams should be paid through the student activity fees.
3. The entire Men's Department of Physical Education faculty should be considered as part of the college regular faculty and should be held to the same standards.
4. A broadening of the physical education and intercollegiate athletics programs should be considered.
   Physical education should be required for all four years.
   Attempts should be made to increase the number of intercollegiate sports teams.
   Intramurals should expand to include all students who wish to participate.
   Physical education is the broad base of the pyramid, then intramurals form the middle, and intercollegiate athletics is at the top (see fig. 1.3).
5. Eligibility rules must be simplified.
6. The college should be part of a conference with like-minded schools, but also one where playing all other schools is not required.
7. It is desirable that there be a gradual elimination of the emphasis on gate receipts.
8. Adopt the guest-host friendly atmosphere now in place for sports where individuals compete to team sports.

Twenty years later, in 1950, under the direction of J. Herbert Nichols, the Athletic Policy for Oberlin College contained both similarities to and differences from those of previous versions. The 1954 policy revision, presented here, was quite similar to the one from 1950, with small modifications in wording and a new point added about intercollegiate competition.

1. The Men's Physical Education Department offers (a) service courses and activities; (b) a major with classes and appropriate training; (c) a program of intramurals for all students; and (d) a program of intercollegiate athletics.
2. The intercollegiate athletics budget is controlled by the department but managed through the Office of the Treasurer of the college.
3. The Athletics Advisory Committee retains its important functions.
4. Academics come first for all students; they are selected based on their academic record and there are no favored scholarships for athletes.
5. A broad program of intramurals supports the development of both the mind and body; recreation and intramurals go together.
6. There should be an emphasis on sports that can be played in adult years.
7. The college should offer as many intercollegiate sports as possible.
   This will decrease the pressure on any one sport.
   Going for high winning percentages could elevate a sport or two, but at the cost of others.
8. The college should endeavor to play intercollegiate contests with schools that have a similar philosophy.
9. Further discussion is needed on matters pertaining to conference championships in both team and individual sports.
10. All members of the department staff should share in all four aspects of the program.
11. All forms of media should be used to convey these principles and ways of operating to all students and others.

There are some common threads in the policies over the first half of the twentieth century. Consistent among the listings is the recognition that physical education and athletics are an integral part of the overall college experience; budgetary control being within the department but managed by the college; attempting to play athletic contests against like-minded institutions; providing for physical education and intramurals for all students; and the importance of academics ahead of sports with the absence of any special scholarships. Some unique features include the provision that students' daily schedules include time for recreation and physical activity (1920), the emphasis on sports for the adult years (1950), and increasing the number of intercollegiate sports (1954).

Changes in the athletics policies and practices within the Department of Physical Education will form a part of the discussion in subsequent chapters. Until the 1970s some of these policies applied primarily to the men's intercollegiate athletics teams. After Title IX was passed in 1972, the policies and procedures became more inclusive and pertained to both men's and women's physical education and athletics.

Facilities

In keeping with Oberlin's prominence in physical education at the time and with the ever-increasing need for larger and better venues for athletics, the college added several structures during the period 1926–1950. At Oberlin, the new venues including Crane Pool, Hales Gymnasium, and George Jones Field House. Among the other liberal arts colleges in Ohio, Ohio Wesleyan added Selby Field for football and other sports in 1929. Post–World War II construction included Wertheimer Fieldhouse at Kenyon and Livingston Gymnasium at Denison. Playing fields for some of the outdoor sports—soccer, lacrosse, field hockey—were added or revamped at these schools just as at Oberlin.

For decades, Delphine Hanna and others lobbied arduously for a swimming facility on campus. The students used the pool at the YMCA in Elyria for many years, traveling there by bus. The Oberlin Beach Colony at Lake Erie (see later in this section) provided a short summertime opportunity for women's swimming. The need for instructors trained and certified to teach others how to swim and to provide training in water safety procedures made it highly desirable for Oberlin to build its own pool. This dream was finally realized in 1931 when the Crane family of Dalton, MA, provided the needed capital for construction of Crane Pool (fig. 4.6; map, fig. 0.4). The earth excavated to create the pool site became known as "Oberlin Mountain," and remains on the western side of Galpin Field today. About the time the mound was created, the women needed something to stop errant arrows during archery practice.

FIGURE 4.6. Crane Pool opened in 1931 and is seen here looking southwest, showing the side and back of the structure. There were two pools in the larger section of the building. The smaller portion of the building, to the left, housed offices, locker rooms and showers, and a game room. (Oberlin College Archives)

The mountain worked well for this purpose. Men were permitted to use Crane Pool at specified times, sometimes with a required nominal payment. When some of the men broke a marble bench at the pool area, they agreed to pay for a replacement. The advent of Crane Pool brought about a full aquatics program for women, which was organized and run by Katherine von Wenck (fig. 4.5). As a side note: The YMCA pool at Elyria was again used by Oberlin swimmers during the 2017–2018 academic year; students commuted to Elyria while the Carr Pool on campus was rebuilt.

At the outset of this twenty-five-year period, the Ladies Second Gymnasium was over fifty years old and in poor condition. It originally connected with Talcott Hall and remained in use as home for locker rooms, an exercise space, offices, and the library. The converted Rockefeller Skating Rink, operated year-round for all types of sports activities and other events, was used until shortly after World War II, then was razed in 1948 or 1949. Harkness Hall, a women's dormitory, was opened in 1950 on the west side of this area; the Second Ladies Gymnasium was removed from behind Talcott Hall. The area now called the Harkness Bowl, which previously included two softball diamonds, was no longer used by women for sports activities.

FIGURE 4.7. Hales Memorial Gymnasium in the 1940s. Bicycle racks, reminders of long-standing Oberlin usage of this mode of transportation, are seen along the entry walkway. Air conditioners have been added to several offices on the front of the building. (Oberlin College Archives)

By 1937, long-delayed plans dating back to 1924 for a new Ladies Gymnasium were revisited. In 1939, Hales Memorial Gymnasium was opened (fig. 4.7; map, fig. 0.5), though the structure was not fully completed until after World War II. Funds for construction were donated by G. Willard Hales (OC 1900); it was built in memory of his mother, Lina Rosa Hales. The new structure, sited near Galpin Field, had a large gymnasium with seating, locker rooms, a dance studio, offices, a library (fig. 4.8), and some rest areas. Today this structure has proven very versatile, and has been used for dance, recreation, yoga, fitness classes, physical education activities, club sports, music and concerts, studio art classes, and art exhibitions. It is currently home to the OCircus, a student group engaged in acrobatics and similar performances.

Galpin Field (map, fig. 0.5) was developed in the 1920s. Further work on this large area to the north of Hales Gymnasium and Allen Memorial Hospital continued in the ensuing decades. Some of the original plans were realized while others were not. Field hockey was the primary activity on Galpin Field for the fall season, until the recent development of the Knowlton Athletics Complex, where the sport now shares Bailey Field with the football team. Women's intramurals also used the field throughout this time period and continues to do so today. The annual Annapolis–West Point field hockey game, with teams selected from the top women's intramural players, was staged here for a number of decades.

FIGURE 4.8. For several decades, there was a Physical Education Library which was considered one of the best in the country. Located first in the Second Ladies Gymnasium, the collection moved to Hales Gymnasium (shown here) by the 1940s. Eventually, it was melded into the larger collection of the Oberlin College Mary Church Terrell Library, located in the Mudd Center. (Oberlin College Archives)

In 1947, the college negotiated to have a war surplus building moved from Camp Perry, VA, to the Oberlin campus. After removing tennis courts that occupied the space, the new facility was reconstructed and, with several modifications, became the George M. Jones Field House (fig. 4.9; map, fig. 0.5), named in honor of the longtime secretary of the college (fig. 4.10). It formally opened in the late fall of 1948 with a basketball game. A set of locker rooms, a lobby and a connector to Savage Stadium were subsequently added. The seating capacity was 1,800. A portable wooden floor was installed over the dirt surface for basketball and several other sports. This could be removed when not in use to use the dirt surface for other activities, including track and field. Jones Field House remained in use until 2008, when structural damage necessitated its permanent closure. It was demolished in 2009. During the six decades that it was in use, the facility served as a multipurpose venue for many activities in addition to sporting events. Jones Field House was used for the quadrennial Oberlin Mock Conventions, for concerts

FIGURE 4.9. George M. Jones Field House as it looked in 1948, soon after it was moved to the Oberlin College campus. A portion of the seating for Savage Stadium is visible on the right side of the photo. The vintage automobiles and team bus provide indications of the timing of the photograph. (Oberlin College Archives)

FIGURE 4.10. George M. Jones (OC 1894) assisted the college as a graduate student manager for the athletics teams and the Athletic Association. He served as the College Secretary for nearly forty years (1899–1938). His role included being the secretary and recordkeeper for the Board of Trustees, the College Faculty, and several committees, as well as overseeing the catalogues for each year and running the admissions office. (Oberlin College Archives)

FIGURE 4.11. An aerial view of the athletic complex at the north end of campus in 1950, looking to the northeast. A portion of Galpin Field is to the lower right. In the center left is the baseball diamond, and just below that are a set of clay tennis courts. Savage Stadium and the George Jones Field House are in the center of the photograph. Below them, the open area is what was then known as Dill Field. It contained playing areas for intramurals. Note the four baseball/softball diamonds used for intramurals. (Oberlin College Archives)

and performances, alumni reunion and commencement events, dances, preseason track and field and baseball practice in the spring, and more.

Two views of the athletics facilities on north campus from about 1950 provide perspectives on what the facilities for men's athletics and intramurals looked like. An aerial view (fig. 4.11) shows both the structures and playing fields. Another view (fig. 4.12) displays the tennis courts, with the baseball field behind them, and additional playing fields in the distance.

Dill Field (fig. 4.12) was named for Judge James Brook Dill, who attended Oberlin and then became a lawyer. He made many significant contributions to the college, particularly in the first decade of the twentieth century.

Camp Hanna, created in 1917 through the efforts of Delphine Hanna, began with the purchase of land that is located within what

FIGURE 4.12. This view, looking to the northeast, shows the clay tennis courts and the baseball diamond in the 1950s. (Oberlin College Archives)

FIGURE 4.13. Oberlin undergraduates on a foraging trip along the shore of Lake Erie in search of driftwood for campfires. (Oberlin College Archives)

became known as the Oberlin Beach Colony near Huron, OH. The camp operated until the late 1940s (fig. 4.13). The facilities were used, during the summer months, for a women's retreat prior to the beginning of the fall term each year, and also for reunions of physical education majors. Two camp rules are noteworthy: (1) Garbage may be buried on the beach in front of your own cottage. (2) Rubbish, glass, tin cans, and other trash may be thrown into the swamp at the west end of the camp. In her honor, one of the cottages was named for Delphine Hanna. In 1952, the college discontinued its connection with this area and the Oberlin Beach Association was formed. Today, there are homes along West Lake Road and Colony Lane, between US Route 6 and Lake Erie, just east of the city of Huron, OH.

Oberlin's Influence on Physical Education

During the period 1926–1950, individuals with direct connections to Oberlin College continued to have a sustained influence on the theory and practice of physical education as a discipline. Though the field itself expanded greatly during the first third of the twentieth century, it truly flourished during the middle years of the century. Some institutions of higher education now offered doctoral degrees, and helped advance knowledge for all aspects of physical education and athletics. The overall role of Oberlin College in these developments served a lesser, but still critically important, influence in the period from 1926 to 1950. Numerous books, supplemented by journal publications, authored by the individuals mentioned in several earlier chapters, continued to affect the approach to the teaching of physical education. This pioneering work, evident in the policies and practices of the Oberlin faculty and graduates, remained a potent force in the field. The solid foundation that formed the basis of the early tenets of exercises and games at Oberlin had enduring effects throughout the decades. The ensuing "ripple" effect was widespread, as Oberlin students continued their education with graduate studies, or as they sought employment and served in volunteer positions following graduation. The well-qualified faculty worked diligently to create a meaningful curriculum for the maximum benefit of the students throughout the time period covered by this chapter.

There were some noteworthy, outstanding individuals whose importance for the field began prior to 1935 and whose influence continued into the first 25–30 years of the twentieth century. Among these, we have previously noted Jay B. Nash, Fred E. Leonard, Jesse Feiring Williams, Gertrude E. Moulton, and Whitelaw Reid Morrison. Their impact stemmed mainly from books and articles they published that were available in multiple editions for a period continuing into the 1950s and later. A few examples include *The Principles of Physical Education* (Williams), *A Guide to the History of Physical Education* (Leonard), *Interpretations of Physical Education* and *Spectatoritis* (Nash), and *Health Education in Schools* and *Athletics in Education* (Morrison). Some of these publications were textbooks that went through multiple editions; others included co-authors who took on the revisions for multiple editions. These scholars also provided numerous oral presentations at national meetings of various professional organizations in physical education and recreation. Several generations of students of physical education and academics working in this discipline benefitted from the efforts of these pioneers.

The list below shows the continuous, overlapping generations of individuals who either (1) worked at Oberlin College in physical education, (2) were alumni from the college, or (3) were mentored by Oberlin graduates who became faculty members at other institutions. This provides a long-term perspective which includes more than a century of individuals who exerted varying levels of influence on the development and maturation of many facets of physical education. Of this group ten have been elected to the National Academy of Kinesiology, and six have received the Gulick Award from the Society of Health and Physical Education. The compilation covers approximately six generations of scholars and mentors. Together, they published more than 100 scholarly books, ranging from textbooks with multiple editions helping to educate several generations, to important monographs on aspects of physical education, and manuals for teaching and coaching. During its first two decades, the Society of Directors of Physical Education had five presidents with Oberlin College connections. There are many more academic descendants of those named here who played sports or continue to contribute to the study of physical education and athletics. It is noteworthy that there are only four women on this list. A primary reason for that is the continued male dominance of the physical education profession, in terms of scholarship up until the 1960s. The vast field of academic study of physical education, recreation, exercise science, and kinesiology still has many descendants with direct or indirect Oberlin connections.

While several women at Oberlin were recognized with various awards, it is their highly dedicated work as teachers and mentors which also must be recognized. They provided generations of female students with life skills in terms of exercise, teamwork, and a full sense of the mind–body connection. (*Note that * indicates membership in the National Academy of Kinesiology and + indicates recipients of the Gulick Award from the Society of Health and Physical Education.*)

> Delphine Hanna—at Oberlin 1885–1922; founder of the program
> Fred Eugene Leonard—OC 1889; at Oberlin 1892–1922
> Luther Halsey Gulick*+—Attended Oberlin
> Thomas D. Wood*+—OC 1888
> Charles W. Savage*+—OC 1893; at Oberlin 1905–1935
> Gertrude E. Moulton*—OC 1903; at Oberlin 1923–1926
> Charles Hetherington*+—trained by Thomas Wood at Stanford
> John Herbert Nichols—OC 1911
> Jesse Feiring Williams*+—OC 1909
> Louise Martin—OC 1910
> Jay Bryan Nash*+—OC 1911
> Whitelaw Reed Morrison—OC 1910; at Oberlin 1923–1951
> Lucy T. Brown—OC 1916
> Lysle K. Butler—OC 1925; at Oberlin 1928–1970
> Robert Kretchmar—OC 1940; at Oberlin 1953–1961
> Fred D. Shults—OC 1954; at Oberlin 1957–1959, 1961–1993
> R. Scott Kretchmar*—OC 1966
> Hal Lawson*—OC 1966
> Donald Chu—OC 1971

Summary

For physical education and athletics, the second quarter of the twentieth century may be best characterized as a gradual shift from the earlier games and sports to the beginning of heightened interest in intercollegiate and pre-professional competition. As with World War I, the poor condition of male Americans, with high proportions failing physical examinations for military service in World War II, led to changes in programs for physical education in the schools and additional emphasis on recreation for adults. The underlying philosophy for physical activity also shifted. For men's athletics, the mind–body harmony connection was splitting, particularly at larger colleges and universities, toward an emphasis on competition. There was a shift toward more people becoming spectators and therefore engaging less in their own physical activity. Small colleges, like Oberlin, attempted to maintain the earlier perspective with an academic education combined with opportunities for physical activities and sports. At Oberlin, more athletic teams were added, women engaged in more inter-institutional competition, and intramurals continued to flourish. The facilities for physical education and athletics were enhanced by the completion of Hales Gymnasium for women and the George M. Jones Field House. Oberlin alumni and their descendants continued to influence the growing field of physical education through the middle of the century.

Sources Consulted for Chapter 4

Full citations are found at the end of the book.

Brandt, L. J. *The Evolution of Women's Intercollegiate Athletics at Oberlin College.*
Bucher, C. A. *Foundations of Physical Education.*
Coakley, J. *Sports in Society: Issues and Controversies.*
Dewey, J. *Democracy and Education: An Introduction to the Philosophy of Education.*
Gerber, E. W. *Innovators and Institutions in Physical Education.*
Guttmann, A. *A Whole New Ballgame: An Interpretation of American Sports.*
Hackensmith, C. W. *History of Physical Education.*
Hayes, W. *The Progressive Education Movement: Is It Still a Factor in Today's Schools?*
Horger, M. "Basketball and Athletic Control at Oberlin College, 1896–1915." *Journal of Sport History* 23:256–283.
Lee, M. *A History of Physical Education and Sports in the U.S.A.*
Leonard, F. E. *A Guide to the History of Physical Education.*
Lucas, C. J. *American Higher Education: A History.*
Mechikoff, R. *A History and Philosophy of Sport and Physical Education.*
Nash, J. B. *Physical Education: Interpretations and Objectives.*
Rice, E. A., J. L. Hutchinson, and M. Lee. *A Brief History of Physical Education.*
Rudolph, F. *The American College & University: A History.*
Schwendener, N. *A History of Physical Education in the United States.*
Shepardson, F. W. *Denison University, 1831–1931: A Centennial History.*
Shults, F. D. *The Life of Fred Eugene Leonard, M.D.*

———. *The History and Philosophy of Athletics for Men at Oberlin College.*

Smith, R. A. *Sports & Freedom: The Rise of Big-Time College Athletics.*

Thelin, J. R. *A History of American Higher Education.*

Wayman, A. R. *A Modern Philosophy of Physical Education.*

Weston, W. *The Making of American Physical Education.*

Williams, J. F., and W. R. Morrison. *A Text-book of Physical Education.*

Zeigler, E. F. *A History of Physical Education & Sport in the United States and Canada.*

CHAPTER 5

Athletics as Competition

1951–1974

Context and Philosophy

During the interval from 1951 to 1974, the Cold War and the Vietnam War predominated on the international scene (see Appendix A for timelines). Within our country, two major social issues, Civil Rights and the Vietnam War, resulted in protests, conflicts, and changes in society. The total number of academic institutions for post-secondary education rose from just over 1,700 to more than 3,000, and enrollments increased from 1.7 million to about 11.2 million. A significant portion of these increases happened at the state level as campuses expanded and new, often more regional campuses, were added. At Oberlin, this twenty-four-year span includes both changes in athletics and a significant sequence of events that occurred at the end of the period affecting the administration of the college and the athletics program. In addition, important moves toward equality for women intensified. The reader will notice that chapters 6 and 7 cover several years that overlap in the early 1970s. This allows for the coverage of the Jack Scott story and the advent of Title IX in separate chapters. Jack Scott was a controversial figure, primarily in the 1970s, both for his radical ideas on education and his strong stands on issues like the Vietnam War.

The prevailing philosophy in American higher education during this period was to combine and integrate information across a broad spectrum of disciplines, with increased specialization of materials. This latter included the creation of new subareas within disciplines as diverse as English, history, and the sciences. It was no longer sufficient to learn basic chemistry; there were now subareas such as biochemistry, and history was subdivided further along geographical and ethnic perspectives. Also among the changes was the introduction of new technologies, which involved expanded use of television in the 1950s and led, eventually, to the computer age, starting in the late 1960s. These developments meant greater availability of information and fundamentally changed the educational enterprise.

As time passed, further divergence from the mind–body duality occurred within academics; development of the mind became more separated from physical activity. This shift was more pronounced for male than for female athletes, who continued with an underlying philosophy more in concert with the mind–body harmony of earlier decades. The aforementioned shifts in curriculum and scholarship dominated the mind portion of the duality. However, for men the career track consisted of a range of possibilities extending from physical education service classes to intramurals and club sports, and then to the top of the pyramid (fig. 0.3) with intercollegiate athletics. By contrast, the women's intercollegiate athletics program would lag behind the men's until the late 1970s.

The flow of this chapter deviates slightly from previous ones. This is partially because of the sequence of events occasioned by the hiring of a new president and new athletic director at Oberlin in the early 1970s. For the narrative, the sequence begins with coverage of changes in athletics involving greater competition, and including events at Oberlin. Next is a section on physical education at the college and at other similar institutions. The penultimate segment deals with the aforementioned sequence of events at Oberlin College that changed the face of both physical education and athletics. The last section, as in most previous chapters, deals with changes in facilities.

Athletics

By the 1960s, the gap between large and small schools grew considerably, specifically relating to sports participation and regulation. Policies among schools now varied widely, prompting the formation of conferences among like-minded schools. For bigger institutions, winning began to dominate. Long-standing rivalries often remained the focus in terms of annual contests for bragging rights. The spirit of competition was upgraded even at some smaller colleges, though they remained steadfast in their adherence to the need for enjoyment and participation.

At the larger schools, the three major sports—football, basketball, and baseball—overshadowed the so-called "minor" sports, such as soccer, swimming, lacrosse, tennis, wrestling, and golf. Among the minor sports, school size was less a determinant for fair play, with contests involving small colleges still scheduled against schools with larger enrollments. However, with the "big three" sports, the divergence became evident, when universities were able to recruit elite athletes and to hire specialized coaching staffs. Full-time recruiters were enlisted as part of the personnel for athletics programs. For the "minor" sports, strong recruiting and athletic scholarships for the athletes were not yet fully implemented at the big institutions. At bigger institutions, dormitories for athletes, separate dining facilities, more scholarship aid directed to students in particular sports, and construction of more specialized practice and competition facilities all became part of the recruitment and performance process, particularly for football and basketball. Winning and garnering fan support were paramount for the big schools. Funding was augmented at these institutions by local businesses participating through sponsorships and significant growth in alumni support directed to athletics.

For small colleges, the pattern was different. The NCAA divisional classification was adopted in 1973. Prior to that most small colleges had already designed their athletics programs to compete against similar institutions in all but a few sports. Oberlin was a member of Division III, which comprises schools that do not offer athletic scholarships. The largest schools were placed in Division I, including many state universities, and the mid-sized institutions constituted Division II. As a side note, Oberlin does have one scholarship, named after an early football player, Glen Gray. However, this is awarded to a student who participates in more than one sport and who is admitted to the college based on rigorous academic standards. Financial aid is based on need only and not on athletic ability. Aid is offered only after admission and not as an inducement to come to Oberlin to be an athlete. The same set of rules that governs admission to Oberlin is characteristic of other small colleges with whom the college competes, including Denison, Kenyon, Ohio Wesleyan, Wabash, and Wooster. Joining an athletic conference is

FIGURE 5.1. Betty F. McCue came to Oberlin in 1955 from a position at the University of Nebraska. She received a B.A. (1943) from the University of Pittsburgh and later a Ph.D. from Iowa State University. In 1969, she compiled a book, *Physical Education for Women*, with contributions from her Oberlin colleagues. (Oberlin College Archives)

dependent on adherence to these same principles, thus leveling the playing field with respect to recruitment and competing against athletes of similar abilities and mindset.

Women's athletics continued to grow, and while still based largely on intramurals, more sports were added, and there were more intercollegiate contests. Sports offered for women included basketball, field hockey, archery, tumbling, running, synchronized swimming, golf, tennis, soccer, softball, track, dance, and others. Due to the relative informality of those events, written records are scant, so it is difficult to judge the level of participation. There were Sports Days (see also chapter 7), with invitational events where teams from two or more schools got together, frequently involving contests in several sports. Teams played round-robin games against each other, often followed by some form of social event, such as a picnic or tea in a social environment. Recreation and enjoyment were the main goals, with competition as a secondary consideration. Many alumnae have fond memories of these events, which lasted until the early 1960s.

Betty F. McCue (fig. 5.1) was instrumental in advancing several facets of women's physical education and athletics. McCue chaired the Department of Physical Education for Women from 1955 to 1964 and was Director of the Ladies Gymnasium in 1954–1955. She started her new position at the same time that longtime faculty member Lysle Butler became chair of the men's department. Together they made innovative changes in the physical education major and introduced a number of coeducational classes. McCue was responsible for increasing the extent of intercollegiate play for women through Sports Days, often with multiple outside teams gathering at one school for all-day competitions in several sports.

Continuing a long-standing tradition, an annual highlight of the women's intramural program was the Yale–Princeton women's basketball game. During this period, both internal and external sports activities were regulated through the Women's Athletic Association (WAA). At the national level, the Association on Intercollegiate Athletics for Women (AIAW) was formed in 1972 to replace the Commission on Intercollegiate Athletics for Women (CIAW), founded in 1967 to provide a standardized, regulated basis for inter-institutional competition. National championships were staged by the AIAW in several women's sports. A clash between the AIAW and the NCAA is covered in the next chapter.

Physical Education

The physical education major at Oberlin continued to graduate students progressing to teaching careers at various school levels and organizations, with some students selecting advanced degrees as the next step to a career path. By the mid-1950s, changes occurred in the curriculum: courses were added in Adapted Physical Education (for women only); Recreational Leadership; Methods of Supervision of Athletics; Prevention and Care of Athletic Injuries; Dance in Education; and Camp Counseling and Recreational Leadership. Several of these reflect the post–World War II shift to engage more people in outdoor activities as part of improving the level of physical fitness of Americans. Other offerings replaced or modified existing courses, and some were eliminated in areas involving play and gymnastics.

After World War II, as happened at the conclusion of World War I, people who had measured the physical condition of Americans were appalled at the high rejection rate of men for service in the military because they failed the physical examination (33% of ca. 9 million tested). In 1953, a large international study revealed that US children exhibited much poorer physical condition than those in Europe. In an attempt to remedy this deficit, the President's Commission on Physical Fitness was established in 1956. This program could be easily implemented in primary and secondary schools, and token awards or certificates of completion were presented to successful students. Further, in 1967, an innovative law provided for physical education for students with disabilities. The combined effects of these and other new initiatives was to get more children involved in physical activity on a daily basis. In turn, more instructors were needed to teach the classes. Thus, the physical education major at schools like Oberlin exhibited modest expansion for undergraduate teacher training to provide a more practical curriculum within the four-year program.

The major was organized into four areas: (1) body mechanics; (2) team activity; (3) individual activity; and (4) dance—modern, square, folk. Students were required to take courses in each of these areas. The curriculum for majors now involved about one-third of their courses to fulfill liberal arts requirements at the college, one-third as classes for the major, and one-third as electives. This program of requirements for the major is quite similar to those at other Ohio liberal arts colleges during this interval: Denison, Wooster, Kenyon, and Ohio Wesleyan.

During his years as an administrator of physical education and athletics, Lysle Butler (fig. 5.2) attempted to: (a) include as many students as possible in sports activities; (b) have the goal of using physical training and athletics as part of the overall educational mission of Oberlin; and (c) like his predecessors at the college, avoid using sports for raising money and refrain from awarding athletic scholarships. Some of the tenets of his philosophy originated through Charles W. Savage in the first decades of the twentieth century and were passed on to John Herbert Nichols, and then to Butler. In 1955, Butler became the first person to hold simultaneously the positions of Chair of the Department of Physical Education for Men, Director of Intramurals, and Director of Intercollegiate Athletics. One of Butler's contemporaries, Guy C. Throner (fig. 4.3), exemplified the mentor and faculty member roles through his work as a physical educator, coach, and member of the college and local communities.

Lysle Butler (OC 1925), played football, basketball, and tennis. After obtaining his A.M. degree from Columbia University (1928), Butler joined the Oberlin faculty as an Assistant Professor of Physical Education and head football coach. During his career he completed his Ph.D. at Ohio State University (1947). He coached football for

FIGURE 5.2. Lysle Butler. (Oberlin College Archives)

twenty-eight years and served in the same capacity for basketball and tennis for portions of his time at the college. As Athletic Director from 1955 to 1970, he championed programs like Oberlin's and eschewed what he called "promotional athletics," which he contrasted with the "educational athletics" he had both administered and fostered at Oberlin. Butler is a member of the Heisman Club Hall of Fame.

A surge of change characterized the department hiring in the mid-1960s. No longer were academic qualifications utilized as a primary consideration in the hiring process: rather, coaches specific to a single sport were given preference over candidates who could teach the service classes, the major classes, and assist the intramurals program. The previously strict vetting for new hires that required advanced degrees was relaxed. For men, coaching became paramount, and the divergence from the founding philosophy was complete. Coaching responsibilities for the women, however, were of less concern, as there was no regular intercollegiate athletics program yet for women. Faculty in the Women's Department of Physical Education were expected to be engaged equally in the other three areas—service classes, major classes, and intramurals. When male faculty were not assigned to teach major classes, the women became the instructors for most of the academic offerings.

In a memorandum from the mid-1960s Lysle Butler, incorporating thoughts from Jesse F. Williams and others, summarized the major aspects of the program in physical education as follows: (1) It is a major source for the development of vitality, particularly through childhood growth and maturation. (2) It is required for proper neuromuscular skills and essential functioning as motor organisms. (3) It sets attitudes about play, fights sedentary life and its evils; recreation should become an important part of daily life. (4) It sets the standards for sportsmanship. (5) It is a way of living. (6) It serves as an integrator of school life. He goes on to list a total of seventeen positive aspects of physical education. Among these are that it is a part of general education, provides leadership training, is an indispensable pairing with mental development, and is based on human needs.

Though this rather complex structure served well for a number of years, by the mid-1960s it became readily apparent that significant updates were necessary, in both the organization and mission of the programs in both men's and women's physical education and athletics. A visiting committee appointed in the spring of 1968 was tasked with assessing, evaluating, and presenting their recommendations for the program prior to the end of the year. Throughout 1969 the committee's findings were discussed at great length and in depth by the faculty and administration, prior to implementation, which commenced in 1970. One major outcome of the recommendations was to combine the men's and women's departments into a single Department of Physical Education and Athletics. Each department felt somewhat threatened with such a merger, in that they lost their autonomous, separate existence. Billy Tidwell (fig. 5.3) was appointed interim acting chair.

After much discussion and some strong resistance, the recommendation for a combined department was implemented in the summer of 1970 with Billy Tidwell (fig. 5.3), then a member of the Department of Physical Education for Men, chosen as the first chair. Julian Smith (fig. 5.4) would continue in his role as acting Director of Athletics, and Bill Grice (fig. 5.5) would continue to coach football. Tidwell's selection involved a full search that caused some concern among various department faculty and other members of the college. There was strong sentiment for bringing in an outside person to oversee the many changes associated with the merger because such an individual would not be constrained by long-term involvement with the varied personalities and issues. A fresh perspective was needed. But there was also concern about such an arrangement, with members of the faculty worried about too much change happening too quickly and without full discussion. When Tidwell moved to Kansas, Julian Smith was given the chair position on an

FIGURE 5.3. Bill Tidwell, a former international track star, joined the Oberlin faculty in 1959 as a coach for cross country and track and field. After serving as chair of the new combined department for just a year (1970-1971), he returned to his native Kansas to do coaching and administration. (Oberlin College Archives)

FIGURE 5.4. Julian Smith came to Oberlin in 1959 and later obtained his Ph.D. in Physical Education from The Ohio State University. He coached basketball and golf and served as the Director of Athletics and as interim Chair of the Department of Physical Education. (Oberlin College Archives)

FIGURE 5.5. J. William Grice joined the Department of Physical Education for Men in 1954. He coached football for fifteen years (1958-1972). Grice completed his Ph.D. at The Ohio State University in 1971. When he left Oberlin in 1972, soon after the arrival of Jack Scott, he went to Case Tech, later Case Western Reserve University, where he was athletic director from 1974 to 1985. (Oberlin College Archives)

interim basis. These three individuals, Bill Tidwell, Julian Smith, and J. William Grice, all eventually departed Oberlin; the latter two as part of the fallout from hiring Jack Scott.

Other recommendations from the 1969 report included having common areas for interactions among department faculty and housing all faculty, from both departments, in the new Philips Center. However, failure to complete construction of office space on the second floor of the new structure negated this recommendation. The facility was designed to house only men. The male faculty's attitude was a bit about payback, since their activities were housed in the aging Warner Gymnasium beginning in the first decade of the twentieth century. The women, on the other hand, enjoyed the more "recently" constructed Hales Gymnasium and Crane Pool. Another suggestion involved the development of new classes for the major curriculum. The physical education service class requirement should be retained, with a few exceptions, but it could be waived via a proficiency examination.

Sound foundations for the pioneering physical education program, beginning in the 1880s at Oberlin and continuing through the 1960s, were beginning to falter. Men and women faculty, accustomed to operating with autonomy in their own departments, were now facing an abrupt, rapid alteration in their academic lives. Beginning with the inception of the departments at Oberlin in 1892, joint meetings between men and women in the physical education departments were only held infrequently. Each separate department had its own facilities, with budgets for maintenance and management. While men used Warner Gym and women occupied Crane Pool and Hales Gym, the division also was apparent in the assignment of practice fields. Men's access to Crane Pool was generally limited to the varsity swimming and diving team. Careful scheduling of the practice fields was implemented, so as to avoid "turf wars" between men and women faculty and teams.

Any outside candidate for the position of Chair of Physical Education and Athletics would be met with this unrest among existing faculty members on these issues: (1) the newly combined men's and women's departments; (2) the assignment of collaborative office space; (3) the scheduling of the physical facilities; (4) the proposed alterations in classes for the major; and (5) a suggested revised grading system for service classes. Indeed, this would be a major challenge for someone new to the campus. This set the stage for the most difficult period in the history of the physical education and athletics program at Oberlin College.

The Jack Scott Story

Robert K. Carr served as Oberlin's ninth president from 1960 to 1969. He led the college during a time of great unrest; both the Vietnam War and the Civil Rights Movement were in full bloom during the latter half of his years at the helm. Campus protests, participation by Oberlin students and faculty in national demonstrations, and early beginnings of curricular changes on campus to reflect a more diverse student population were significant features of the educational and social enterprise. The push for change continued into the 1970s and forms the background for the progression of college presidents and shifts in the physical education and athletics programs noted here and in the next two chapters.

Upon Carr's retirement in 1969, and following a brief period with interim leadership, Robert W. Fuller (fig. 5.6), then just 33 years of age, became the tenth Oberlin College president in 1970. He attended Oberlin but did not complete his degree at the college. A physicist by training and profession with a Ph.D. from Princeton, Fuller was a strong advocate for radical change in the education profession. His tenure, which lasted less than four years, was somewhat tumultuous, occasioned in part by his philosophy of education and desire to facilitate rapid modifications. Fuller was most interested in reform, a process that was percolating in American colleges and universities at this time. Among the changes that went into effect during his tenure at Oberlin were a threefold increase in the enrollment of students from minority backgrounds and the shift to coeducational dormitories. He envisioned the challenges facing higher education as an impetus for conceiving and implementing creative, new patterns for learning. Oberlin College, he felt, with its rich history of innovation and openness to change, was an ideal gestational environment for the birth of such changes. Fuller's hiring of Jack Scott (fig. 5.7) as Chair of the Department of Physical Education in 1972 was consistent with his goals for the institution.

Even prior to Scott's hiring, a number of issues existed in the newly formed department. One internal disagreement dealt with "the hair rule" for athletes in men's varsity sports programs. The majority of the department faculty wanted to ban from competition all athletes who had long hair or beards. Fred Shults, of the men's faculty, indicated he would no longer enforce that unwritten rule. He maintained that long hair or beards had no connection with preparation or performance in

FIGURE 5.6. Robert W. Fuller became the youngest president in the history of Oberlin College when he assumed the position in 1970. He strongly advocated for educational reform at American colleges and universities. (Oberlin College Archives)

FIGURE 5.7. Jack Scott, hired in 1972, remained at Oberlin for only eighteen months of his four-year contract. His time at the college was characterized by discord and clashes between what he originally planned to accomplish and the actions he took to implement those ideas as expressed in his 1971 book, *The Athletic Revolution*. Among his various activities was serving as the faculty advisor to the nascent Oberlin Gay Liberation student organization. (Oberlin College Archives)

athletic contests, just as they had no connection with preparation or performance in the classroom. Athletes should not be isolated from the larger academic community; that is why they were called student athletes. With no discussion as to the merits of the hair rule, a suggestion was made that either Shults should depart from Oberlin or, perhaps, the other men's department faculty should leave. After consultations involving members of the college administration, the hair rule was dropped.

Tensions also arose from a shift in the hiring practices within the two departments. As noted earlier, new hires in the men's department were often made with coaching as a principal criterion, and the requirement that all faculty be capable of teaching classes in the program for majors was no longer a primary consideration. This meant that many of the classes intended for both men and women majoring in physical education were taught by the faculty of the women's department or male faculty who had been hired under the earlier pattern. Another factor that played into the growing unrest was the reality that physical education faculty were socially and professionally isolated from their colleagues on campus. Salaries for physical education faculty remained lower than those for their counterparts at the college. Without competitive athletic programs, the school was unable to attract outstanding scholar athletes. These disparities, combined with changes occurring at similar institutions, signaled the need for a careful review. As Dean Reich noted in his summary report, there was a lack of leadership within the Oberlin physical education community to foster and manage the necessary changes.

A full external search resulted in the hiring of Jack Scott, then at the University of California at Berkeley, where he founded the Institute for Study of Sport and Society. He advocated social activism and was a strong proponent of the need for change in athletics, particularly regarding participation of women and minorities. In his book, *The Athletic Revolution*, which appeared in 1971, he pushed for significant shifts in the culture of college athletics, advocating greater integration of the sports culture with the larger educational enterprise. He began his tenure at Oberlin, at age twenty-eight, in the late summer of 1972. The combination of Fuller and Scott initially promised excitement as an avant-garde experiment, railing against the long-held and time-worn tenets of the physical education department and introducing radically new policies in college education.

Jack Scott's hiring was not without controversy. The faculty of the Department of Physical Education, with the exception of Fred Shults, opposed the candidate. Shults felt that Scott offered hope for reinvigorating the academic major and promoting greater acceptance of and respect for women and Black athletes. Scott's visionary plans seemed to coincide with the recommendations of the visiting committee regarding enhancement of the major and improvement of relations within the department. Throughout the interviews and as part of his expressed philosophy, Scott proposed that more minorities and women should become part of the Oberlin College community, both as students and as department faculty, which, in turn, would lead to increased minority participation in athletics. Scott, despite the lack of faculty support, was hired as an associate professor, Chair of the Department of Physical Education, and Director of Athletics, and given a four-year contract beginning in the fall of 1972.

FIGURE 5.8. Cass Jackson was hired as the football coach after being selected as an All-American while playing at San Jose State University and a short stint in professional football. He was just the second African American football coach at a predominately white college or university in the NCAA. Jackson also coached the baseball team. He remained at Oberlin for three years and then took a position at Morris Brown College in Atlanta. (Oberlin College Archives)

FIGURE 5.9. Patrick Penn, hired to coach basketball in 1973, was one of the earliest African Americans to hold that title in the US. He later held several administrative roles at the college, including the final eight years of his career (1987–1995) as Dean of Student Life and Services. He was inducted into the Hall of Honor in 2018. (Oberlin College Archives)

Scott's lofty ideals and intentions were instrumental during his hiring interviews. Where most people anticipated an evolutionary, well-planned, gradual change over time, Scott instead moved at a revolutionary pace. He immediately insisted on frequent department meetings and committees, with both having student representation. This extended to the committees formed to make hiring decisions; for example, students' voices were heard during the search for new coaches and to replace faculty members. Scott often made dictatorial decisions that, in previous times, involved faculty meeting discussions and votes.

Scott indicated he wanted to employ more women for the department faculty. However, one of his earliest actions was to hire more African American, male coaches. He hired three Black coaches, Cass Jackson (fig. 5.8), Patrick Penn (fig. 5.9), and Tommie Smith (fig. 5.10), to coach football, basketball, and track and field, respectively. The contracts of

FIGURE 5.10. Tommie Smith was hired to coach track and field. He is best remembered for the raised-fist protest he and John Carlos staged at the medal ceremony at the 1968 Mexico City Olympics after winning the 200-meter race. He too was a graduate of San Jose State and played a short time in the American Football League. He remained at Oberlin for six years and then moved to Santa Monica College in California. (Oberlin College Archives)

FIGURE 5.11. Joe Horn (OC 1960) won three letters each in football, basketball, and lacrosse. For the last of these, he was the leading scorer in the US for 1960. Horn earned his M.A. at Penn State (1962) and returned to Oberlin as coach for hockey and lacrosse and as an assistant for football. He received his Ph.D. from Ohio State (1976) after leaving Oberlin, and, after a stint at Ohio Wesleyan University, he coached high school sports for the remainder of his career. (Oberlin College Archives)

FIGURE 5.12. Sara Houston earned both bachelor's (1934) and master's (1935) degrees from Wellesley College. She taught at Denison University (1935–1950) and then joined the Oberlin Department of Physical Education for Women, where she remained until 1973. While at Oberlin, she received a Ph.D. from The Ohio State University (1967). She was a renowned scholar in the area of body movement and mentored twenty female Oberlin undergraduates. These studies related body styles, performance movements, and personality. (Oberlin College Archives)

two current faculty members were scheduled for renewal at this same time. Following the unrest and angst within the department, Don Hunsinger left Oberlin. He returned to the college a few years later, where he remained for the rest of his distinguished career. The other, Dick Michaels, stayed at the college, where he coached successful swimming and diving teams from 1970 to 2006 and men's and women's cross country teams. Another faculty member, Joe Horn (OC 1960; fig. 5.11), who coached ice hockey and lacrosse from 1963 to 1972, left the college at this time. One individual adversely affected by Jack Scott was Sara Houston (fig. 5.12), who died in 1973; she felt that her health conditions were impaired, in part, by the manner in which Scott treated faculty and that this led to her fatal illness.

Curricular alterations occurred during 1972–1974 following up on some of Scott's intentions, but only a portion of those changes outlasted his time at the college. Classes were added for Socio-Cultural Aspects of Sport; The Competitive Ethic; International Sports and Physical Education; Women in Sport; and Sports and Games: A Cross Cultural Analysis. Several of these offerings were dropped over the next few years, while others remained, but in revised form.

During his interview, Scott professed a strong interest in advancing the status of women in sports. He did accomplish a few things to implement this goal while at the college. He increased the funding for the women's program threefold. He rearranged locker rooms in the Philips Physical Education Center to provide space for the women, moving the faculty men to another location. He initiated steps which made the Philips Center more coeducational. He arranged equal treatment for women's teams with respect to travel to away games and furnishing training meals for athletes. The next chapter covers changes that occurred for women's intercollegiate athletics after Scott's departure.

Immediately upon his arrival on campus there were conflicts involving Jack Scott, as he clashed with faculty, with administrators, and with students. His preference was to work outside the system, rather than within it. He often seemed visionary when speaking from an outsider's perspective, but he was incapable of sharing governance or implementing his ideas once he was on board. He brought assistant coaches to campus, many of them friends and acquaintances, who were not subject to the requisite formal review by appropriate committees or administrators. He clashed with members of his own department, most notably with one of his predecessors, Lysle Butler. The latter took issue with

Scott's push to dismiss and replace existing coaches, some of whom had enjoyed longtime affiliations with the college. Also expressing concerns and displeasure were alumni and students. More than 200 students, most of them athletes and some physical education majors, filed a petition in the spring of 1973 questioning Scott's methods for changing the department and the heavy emphasis on intercollegiate athletics, while ignoring the major and service class programs. They criticized the content of the "academic" classes as being superficial and lacking in intellectual rigor. Students felt that the new faculty, hired as coaches, were not professionally qualified to teach various subjects in the department curriculum.

Where most people anticipated an evolutionary, well-planned, gradual change over time, Scott instead moved at warp speed. New to Oberlin's tradition was the advent of student voices in such critical realms as contract renewal and hiring practices. Scott developed a reputation for making mercurial, unilateral decisions that effectively prevented faculty participation in any form.

Also, during the hiring process, Scott had boasted about his newly published book, and his ideas seemed timely for launching the physical education department into the next decade, despite the lack of confidence exhibited by the existing faculty. However, his comportment after being hired came nowhere near the professionalism he had exhibited in the vetting process. Tensions festered regarding an abrupt change in the hiring practices within the department. New hires in the men's department were now not expected to uphold the traditional requirement of teaching the service and major classes, and to assist with intramurals. Coaching became the principal criterion, with added consideration being given to those candidates who had played their sport professionally.

As part of his move to Oberlin from California, Scott brought the Institute for Study of Sport and Society with him. It was housed in Hales Gymnasium where Scott had his own office. Several people passed through Oberlin to work on projects and writing related to the institute. One of these, Dave Megyessy, a former professional football player, became a writer and union organizer. His book, *Out of Their League*, details his NFL experiences. George Sauer, a former professional football player, also joined the staff at the institute for a time.

A quote from Jack Scott explains part of his philosophy on sports and society:

> Today, the issue is not whether or not sport has an important role to play in society, but to determine what the nature of that role will be. Those of us actively involved in sport as athletes, coaches, and athletic directors know the joyous, meaningful experience sport can be, and we are attempting to preserve the excellence and beauty that has existed in sport throughout history. But at the same time, we are attempting to preserve the best from the past, we are also trying to get rid of those destructive qualities that are preventing sport from becoming the kind of activity we know it can be. (Scott 1971, 173)

Scott was regularly at odds with the College Faculty Council. Nearly every meeting of that body contained at least one agenda item dealing with Scott's influence on the physical education and athletics programs. Scott seemed to thrive on generating conflicts. Slowly, support for Scott's style and approach began to erode, and those who initially favored his hiring withdrew their approval. These included Dean Donald Reich, Fred Shults, the College Faculty Council, and others. A review of the department commenced in August 1973, just one year after Scott started in his position. The report suggested that the program, including the major and intercollegiate athletics, was in serious danger if remedies did not receive immediate attention: (1) improved relationships among people regarding a lack of democracy within his department and (2) moving away from the sense that winning was the major focus of intercollegiate contests. Scott, too frequently, seemed to be arguing for major societal changes, convinced that he could use the Oberlin College program as a model to promote his views. In short, his authoritarian, strong-arm tactics, despite his oratory to the contrary, soured his colleagues, who anticipated a more democratic system.

Scott's practices were frequently abrasive and demanding. He could and would not tolerate criticism. Howard Cosell visited Oberlin early in Scott's time at the college and provided national exposure. In the fall of 1973 two incidents occurred in close succession that exemplified his problems. One occurred when Scott wanted to use his leverage to obtain a recommendation for admission to Oberlin for a transfer student from Pittsburgh, PA, who would lend support for his agenda. He approached Fred Shults to demand that he write the needed letter. When Shults declined, Scott exploded in a loss of self-control. He used bullying and demeaning language and physically threatened Shults. Scott finally left Fred's office and violently slammed the door. Colleagues with offices near Fred's could not help but overhear the verbal abuse. Visibly shaken,

Shults walked to the nearby offices and made sure his colleagues had witnessed the outburst. With their support, he documented the unprofessional conduct exhibited by Scott and submitted his report to the Dean of the College.

A second incident occurred a few days later, when Shults happened to be in the department office. A student arrived with a final term paper in hand, to turn in for one of Scott's requirements in an academic course. The surprised secretary indicated that Scott had already turned in all his semester grades. The next day, Shults asked the secretary if he could see Scott's grades; they were all As. Apparently, some of the students had received these high marks without even submitting the required term paper for the class. This too was reported to the college dean. Most of the faculty in the department viewed Scott's tactics as "you are either with me or against me; if you're against me, I won't support you." This attitude flew in the face of the democratic procedures previously enjoyed by long-term faculty members. Such incidents and attitudes, coupled with others of a similar nature and a growing dissatisfaction within the department and college concerning his performance, led to an agreement whereby the college paid out the remainder of Scott's four-year contract, and he departed at the end of January 1974. His short tenure was to have significant negative and lasting effects on physical education and athletics at Oberlin, extending well into the next decade. Many of Scott's colleagues were unhappy with the $42,000 buyout that Scott received from the college for the time remaining on his contract. This would amount to about $250,000 in 2020 funds.

Very soon after Scott's early departure, on February 2, 1974, the college also parted ways with Robert W. Fuller. While both he and Jack Scott shared the same fervor for radical change in higher education, their impatience with any delays in the immediate implementation of those ideals led to disruptive tensions among the rank-and-file on campus. The anxiety created by their too-rapid push for reform led to similar fates, and Oberlin College was faced with hiring both a new college president and leaders for the Department of Physical Education and for Athletics.

Facilities

An aerial view of part of the athletics facilities, looking to the southeast, shows the college campus and town in the background as seen in the early 1950s (fig. 5.13; see also fig. 4.11; map, fig. 0.5). This provides an ori-

FIGURE 5.13. An aerial photograph shows portions of the north campus athletic fields in the 1950s. This view was taken to the southeast across Galpin Field. Tennis courts are on the east side of the playing area and Crane Pool, Hales Gymnasium with Hales Annex, and the Allen Memorial Hospital are seen in the right center area of the photo. The bottom center is a portion of some practice and intramural fields. The main campus is at the left and center of the photograph. (Oberlin College Archives)

entation to the changes that occurred during the previous several decades to the women's portion of the venues used by physical education, intramurals, and athletics. These included the addition of Crane Pool, Hales Gymnasium, and Hales Gymnasium Annex, as well as improvements for Galpin Field and adding tennis courts on the eastern side of that area.

The Hales Gymnasium Annex (fig. 5.14; map, fig. 0.5), opened in 1959. It housed the Department of Zoology until the early 1960s, when the Kettering Hall of Science was completed. The structure was used for a variety of purposes in the ensuing decades. Today it houses a bowling alley and coffee house.

In 1963, the Williams Ice Rink (fig. 5.15; map, fig. 0.5) opened. Interestingly, a portion of the funding for the structure was provided by the same Rockefeller family, with Cleveland origins, who had funded the original ice rink behind Talcott Hall. The new rink was named in honor

FIGURE 5.14. Hales Gymnasium Annex shown in 2017. The Cat in the Cream Coffeehouse is on the left and the College Bowling Lanes are on the right. (Lee C. Drickamer)

of Beatty B. Williams (OC 1899), a longtime donor to the college and former president and general manager of the Cooper Bessemer Corporation. It provided a home to both intercollegiate and intramural ice hockey teams for fifteen years and then for a club team until the spring of 2000. During the first year, the hockey team won the Midwest Conference Championship at the Williams Rink; many of the teams in the league were from larger schools like Bowling Green and Ohio State.

The rink was also used for public skating and physical education classes. During portions of the year, when it was not covered with ice, the concrete floor served as a venue for events that included social gatherings and as a location for commencement in inclement weather. Because of the expenses involved in all aspects of offering ice hockey as an intercollegiate sport and the funds needed to repair and maintain a rink for other activities, the rink closed in 2001. Few small liberal arts colleges in the Midwest followed Oberlin's path with regard to having an ice rink. They never attempted, in most cases, to offer ice hockey as an intercollegiate sport. In 2008, the rink at Oberlin was converted to the Williams Field House, which features an artificial turf surface. It

FIGURE 5.15. A view of the Williams Ice Rink (later Field House) in the mid-1960s, soon after it was completed. Jones Field House is visible to the right in this photograph. This picture was taken when the ice rink was still open on the ends, facing north and south. (Oberlin College Archives)

serves as a year-round home for indoor sports activities and as a practice facility.

After many years of discussion, the college committed to constructing a golf facility on the north campus. The plan included a three-hole course, a practice range, and a putting green. These were constructed north of the current baseball diamond in an open area, on a portion of what is now called the North Fields (see map, fig. 0.5). Today the fields are used for intramural and club sports and as a practice area for several teams. The golf holes were completed in 1966, but the setup remained in use for less than five years. The area was returned to the prior grassy field conditions.

Beginning in the mid-1960s, plans were developed to construct what became the Jesse Philips Physical Education Center. This major addition to the Oberlin physical education, sports, and recreation facilities was completed in 1971 and is presented in the next chapter.

Throughout the period from 1951 to 1973, the functions of the various playing and practice fields at the north end of the athletics complex were modified and underwent changes in assignments. The college expanded its use of land to the north, altering the layout to provide for a soccer field and practice areas for several sports as well as intramural contests. Originally, the soccer field was located north of the clay tennis courts and west of the baseball field, while the football team practiced on grounds west of Jones Field House. By the late 1950s, these two were switched, so that soccer was now west of Jones Field House, and intramural ball diamonds and football practice areas moved north. Over several decades, the cross country course used the athletic fields and lands to the west and north, and the wooded areas nearby. Courses of varying lengths for men, and later for women, are laid out involving 5–8-kilometer distances. For a period of time in the 1970s, the cross country teams used a new course laid out in the Oberlin College Arboretum, located at the south end of the campus along Plum Creek and south of Morgan Street (map, fig. 0.4).

Summary

One major event along with several interconnected, smaller, but significant events occurred during the period from 1951 to 1974 which impacted physical education and athletics at Oberlin College. In 1970 the men's and women's departments of physical education were merged. A number of personnel changes related both to the merger and to the hiring of a president and physical education chair and athletics director led to considerable tensions in the department. Some curricular changes followed first the changing environment with regard to the needs of those planning careers in teaching and then from the new changes in administration. The hiring of Robert W. Fuller in 1970 and then Jack Scott's arrival at Oberlin in the fall of 1972 resulted in what is often referred to as the "Oberlin Experiment." In the span of about eighteen months, when the two were both at the college, there were considerable discord, discomfort, and growing pains. Scott, with Fuller's consistent support, instituted major alterations in terms of philosophy, hiring of coaches, departmental procedures, and an overall approach to the meshing of athletics and physical education within the collegiate environment. He and Fuller, working under a cloud of problems, largely of their own making, left the college within weeks of each other in early 1974.

Sources Consulted for Chapter 5

Full citations are found at the end of the book.

Brandt, L. J. *The Evolution of Women's Intercollegiate Athletics at Oberlin College.*

Cohen, A. M., and C. B. Kisker. *The Shaping of American Higher Education: Experience and Growth of the Contemporary System.*

Costa, D. M., and S. R. Guthrie (eds.). *Women and Sport: Interdisciplinary Perspectives.*

Elcombe, T. "Reformist America: 'The Oberlin Experiment'—The Limits of Jack Scott's 'Athletic Revolution' in Post-1960s America." *International Journal of the History of Sport* 22:1060–1085.

Footlick, J. K. *An Adventure in Education: The College of Wooster from Howard Lowry to the Twenty-First Century.*

Galasso, P. J. (ed.). *Philosophy of Sport and Physical Activity: Issues and Concepts.*

Gerber, E. W. *Innovators and Institutions in Physical Education.*

Guttmann, A. *A Whole New Ballgame: An Interpretation of American Sports.*

Kretchmar, R. S., M. Dyerson, M. P. Llewellyn, and J. Gleaves. *History and Philosophy of Sport and Physical Activity.*

Lucas, C. J. *American Higher Education: A History.*

Reich, D. *Rebuilding Physical Education.*

Rudolph, F. *The American College & University: A History.*

Scott, J. *The Athletic Revolution.*

Thelin, J. R. *A History of American Higher Education.*

CHAPTER 6

Title IX, Inclusion of Women, and Sports as Entertainment
1972–1990

Context

On the international and national stages, events during the 1970s and 1980s included the end of the Vietnam War, continued tensions from the Cold War, and the economy moving past the post–World War II economic boom. The 1970s were a time of fiscal concern with a weaker economy, but this shifted to a more positive financial outlook in the 1980s. Activism concerning both women's and gay rights replaced the anti-war and Civil Rights protests of the period 1965–1972. In 1972, Pell Grants began providing support for students in higher education. Federal funding for science-based research increased greatly. Both of these benefitted colleges and universities.

Major changes in demographics occurred during this period. The balance shifted between students at smaller, mostly private colleges and those at bigger, primarily state schools. In 1950 the numbers revealed about 50% of students enrolled at each type of institution. By the 1970s this had shifted to almost 80% of students matriculating at the larger schools. Community colleges and technology schools proliferated, providing evermore opportunities for younger people to obtain a post-secondary education or trade. By 1990 there were 3,231 post-secondary colleges and universities; this number stood at 2,556 in 1979. The 1990 figures include 1,665 four-year institutions, with the remainder as two-year schools. The proportion of women attending college continued the increase begun after World War II and reached a time when more females than males were attending institutions of higher learning. So too, there was a steady rise in the number of students of color matriculating at small and large colleges and universities. An upswing in older, non-traditional students, and in more part-time enrollees provided additional perspectives.

Against that background, three events had major influences on the programs for physical education and athletics in the country and at Oberlin: (1) passage of Title IX of the Educational Amendments of 1972; (2) further shifts in the athletic program that mirrored progressive changes in society and education; and (3) transformations in, and the eventual dropping of, the major in physical education at the college. Athletics continued on a trajectory that, during this period, included intercollegiate sports as entertainment, but with increasing emphasis on winning, particularly at larger schools. These three foci serve as the bases for the major sections of this chapter. The first two topics impacted all colleges and universities, while the third was particular to Oberlin.

Philosophy

Educational philosophy diverged considerably from the traditional mind–body tenets of earlier periods. Though some schools maintained their founders' strong religious affiliations, much of higher education at large institutions and also at many smaller, private schools became more secular in nature following World War II. This was certainly the case for Oberlin, originally steeped in Congregationalism. The predominant philosophy at Oberlin underwent a transformational period, lasting into the 1960s, of severing that connection. A sizeable number of colleges in New England and the Midwest also veered away from their religious heritage. Included in this were several of Oberlin's peer schools in Ohio, among them Denison, Wooster, and Ohio Wesleyan.

Several features characterized education during these decades. A salient theme in the culture of the times was ready access to post-secondary education. A second theme, brought about through a need for individuals with various skills for particular jobs and professions, was training in more specialized and career-ready pathways, rather than just a liberal arts education. Third, a major force in curricular changes, coupled with student admissions, involved broadening multiculturalism and diversity.

For many schools like Oberlin, this resulted in new subject majors, additional courses, and broader perspectives on life and the world.

Pedagogy at the liberal arts colleges was driven by a desire to instill traits like skepticism, critical and logical thinking, and intellectual curiosity in students through asking questions. This replaced long-standing methods that relied on memorization and simple problem solving. Additional hands-on education included more student exercises with active participation and research as part of the curriculum. More specialization of thinking processes and associated skills became a major tenet in higher education. Several disciplines developed into majors on their own, evolving a distinct philosophy of education. Examples include environmental studies, African American studies, and neuroscience. In addition, to accommodate student desires, many institutions provided for self-designed and cross-disciplinary majors, or pre-professional curriculums, among others.

Lastly, the social fabric was changing. Attitudes about some moral precepts shifted for a portion of the population. On campus, mandatory curfews for women, restricting their evening time away from the dormitories, were dropped. Coeducational dormitory living was now possible. Dining became almost entirely cafeteria style, shifting away from earlier practices such as family-style meals. The number of student organizations proliferated, mirroring diverse sets of student interests.

Women's Athletics and Title IX

For many centuries, women were deemed to be of a more delicate constitution than men, and thus should be restricted in terms of all-out physical exertion. This belief overlooked the fact that significant benefits accrued, both in psychological and physical strength, when women competed against each other in organized individual and team activities. The suffrage movement and passage of the Nineteenth Amendment in 1920 stimulated some far-reaching changes in society's approach to the roles of women. Portions of those positive effects were dampened by the Great Depression of the 1930s. The war in the 1940s and its aftermath left matters much as before, with the noteworthy exception of women involved in manufacturing industries, where they replaced men who went off to fight the war. Women also assumed new roles in the military fields. By the 1960s, traditional views toward women again began to expand. One outcome of this was increased participation of women in a greater variety of sports.

For most of the nineteenth century, women engaged in recreation, consisting of walking, for example, at the Ladies Grove in the College Arboretum in Oberlin, or participating in some forms of dancing and gymnastic exercises as part of the physical education program. Through the latter, women could learn about their own strengths and weaknesses and increase their confidence and poise, along with improved self-esteem. The limited opportunities for women to compete were consistent with aspects of the mind–body duality of the early twentieth century. Women engaging in any competitive exercise was frowned upon; only men should express their aggression through such activities. Slowly, in the latter decades of the nineteenth century and into the early twentieth century, women began to play intramural contests in sports like basketball and tennis. Teams organized by class or housing units competed against each other. At Oberlin, women from the Conservatory of Music, both students and faculty, also fielded teams in some sports. Play Days were organized, with games staged among various teams. Play Days usually involved two or more institutions, with teams often chosen across school boundaries. Organized games were often followed by informal refreshments and conviviality. Play Days were modified over time and were also called Sports Days, wherein women from different schools got together, but now played on teams from their home schools. Play Days were still part of the landscape for women into the 1950s. In 1953 a Play Day was held with Hiram College. This included an outdoor picnic as part of the day's events. There was a similar event involving Kent State University. Other Play Days in the late 1950s involved Bowling Green State University and Lake Erie College for Women. For some years, an annual invitational Play Day happened on campus for students from Ohio high schools.

Exhibitions of gymnastics and dance were organized by the Women's Athletic Association and presented to the public. At the intercollegiate level, the first tennis tournament and women's basketball games occurred in the 1890s, though Oberlin was not yet a participant. Throughout, the underlying philosophy remained a duality of mind and body, effectively meshing the academic pursuits with the physical development. Women engaged in sports and games for exercise and enjoyment.

Ongoing national events of the 1950s and early 1960s led to the Civil Rights Act of 1964, which ignited the push for women's equality across many disciplines, including athletics. The Equal Rights Amendment, passed by Congress in 1972, became a focus, but as of 2021, it has not garnered sufficient state approvals to amend the US Constitution. More specifically for women's athletics, the Division for Girl's and Women's Sports was formed within the American Association for Health, Physical Education, and Recreation in 1941. Committees on this subject were formed in 1956 and 1957. These groups served to promote women's intercollegiate athletics by organizing games between institutions and by staging some national championships.

Several events happened in the same time period that foreshadowed the influence of Title IX. Recognizing a growing need for expanded competitive opportunities, the Association for Intercollegiate Athletics for Women (AIAW) formed in 1971. Beginning with 280 schools, it grew to nearly 1,000 members by the late 1970s, including numerous institutions which joined following the passage of Title IX. The AIAW first sponsored national championships in several major sports, most notably basketball and softball. They also held tournaments in a variety of sports that included volleyball, field hockey, tennis, cross country, golf, and others. There was a lengthy and contentious battle between the AIAW and the men's NCAA organization, until the NCAA assumed control of the main AIAW functions, with 1981–1982 as a transition year. This change was not without its entanglements and threats of legal actions, though the NCAA prevailed.

In November 1972, the Ohio Association for Intercollegiate Sports for Women (OAISW) was formed from the Women's Section of the Ohio College Association. The new group's focus was similar to that of the earlier organization—to promote and coordinate statewide intercollegiate competition for women. The group was significant for its role in advancing women's athletics prior to and in the period just after the passage of Title IX.

One of the most momentous, paradigm-shifting events in modern sports history involved the 1972 passage of Title IX, which introduced major changes in women's athletics. Oberlin College serves as a good example of the events following the passage of this law and the myriad aspects of its implementation with particular note for liberal arts colleges. The timing of the transition to coeducation among a group of peer schools illustrates a cluster which occurred both before and after the implementation of Title IX. These schools include Kenyon (1969), Vassar (1969), Williams (1970), Skidmore (1971), and Amherst (1976).

Oberlin, Earlham, and Wooster were all coeducational from their founding in the nineteenth century. Ohio Wesleyan combined a women's program with the college in 1877, and Denison combined women and men in 1927. Similar issues were faced at all of the institutions, though the details of their transitions are sometimes difficult to discern.

Title IX of the Educational Amendments Act was passed by Congress in June 1972 and signed by President Nixon. The following quote summarizes the legislation: "No person in the US shall, on the basis of sex, be excluded from participation in, be denied the benefits of, or be subjected to discrimination under any education program activity receiving Federal financial assistance" (1972, Title IX of the Educational Amendments of 1972). The new law contained multiple provisions, some of which clearly applied to the equality of women in intercollegiate athletics. The Federal Office of Compliance issued a set of twelve guidelines enumerating the areas of Title IX that affected intercollegiate athletics. These provisions can be synopsized as: (1) accommodation for the interests and abilities of both sexes with respect to choices of sports and levels of competition; (2) provisions for equality with regard to locker rooms, travel and per diem allowances for away competitions, medical and training services and facilities, housing and dining services and facilities, and maintenance of equipment and supplies; (3) full access to coaching and tutoring services, with equality in terms of assignment and compensation for coaches and tutors; and (4) equal treatment of both sexes for recruitment, financial aid, publicity, and scheduling. The full list is quite comprehensive, covering all aspects of athletic programs. Most institutions, including Oberlin College, faced years of grappling with the guidelines. The regulations laid out based on the new law required that programs for women's intercollegiate athletics be in compliance and fully operational by the 1978–1979 academic year.

Oberlin, as in the past, was a pioneer in terms of women's participation in several intercollegiate sports. In the fall of 1972, the council of the Ohio Athletic Conference (OAC), of which Oberlin was then a member, soundly defeated a motion adding competitions for women on an equal footing with men. In the fall of 1973, Coach Dick Michaels had women runners compete as a non-sanctioned exhibition during a men's cross country meet. A grievance was filed by the opponents with the OAC, and the college was requested to cease such activities. In January 1974, in defiance of the OAC ruling, Coach Michaels added an exhibition event with women during a men's sanctioned swim meet. Much discussion ensued within the conference council, and the OAC schools called upon Athletic Director Jack Scott to explain Coach Michaels' actions. Though no penalties were assessed, the coach and school were admonished for their behavior. The early stages of a legal battle were brewing. But, by the summer of 1974, the OAC revised its bylaws to treat women on an equal basis with men for athletic competitions.

At about the same time that Title IX became law, a Women's Sports Committee was formed at Oberlin. A key goal of this group was to increase participation by women in intercollegiate athletics. Their constitution advocated for equality and expansion of the women's program, maintaining parity in terms of coaching and facilities, and providing opportunities for students from all levels of proficiency. The committee included representatives from each team, faculty from the department, and at-large members from student and faculty groups. This body played an integral role in the growth of women's sports at Oberlin and in the implementation of Title IX's regulations. Among the goals for which they advocated was the addition of sport-specific female coaches. By 1973 the number of female members of the physical education department had dwindled to just four, compared to eight male faculty. Female numbers were diminished by retirements and resignations. Only with the passage of time was the goal of gender balance restored. Jack Scott initially backed this effort to achieve gender parity among the coaching staff, but eventually abandoned his support in favor of hiring more men's coaches.

In many respects Oberlin serves as an example of the changes, trials, and tribulations that accompanied the implementation of Title IX over the course of the 1970s and into the 1980s. At the college, progress under Title IX moved forward at a modest pace. Somewhat predictably and consistent around the country at schools of all sizes, the women's programs were controlled by men who made most of the decisions. Several schools began the compliance process by combining the men's and women's physical education departments and reorganizing athletics programs under one administrative structure. Oberlin began this transition in 1970, two years prior to Title IX. Nationally, and at Oberlin, the coaching of women's sports, which was exclusively handled by women prior to this change, gradually added men's coaches if qualified women's coaches could not be found. A bias toward male coaches took hold, in part, because there were far fewer women with appropriate levels of training or coaching experience than men at the beginning of the Title

FIGURE 6.1. Mary J. Culhane. (Oberlin College Archives)

IX period. Older women faculty had been hired to teach service classes and courses for the major, and not necessarily to coach intercollegiate athletics. They faced the twin issues of the diminishing size of the major and the new emphasis on coaching competitive sports. At Oberlin, several well-qualified, respected women provided thoughtful, strong input in the changes that were happening. When new sports were added to the program, both men and women were hired in sport-specific coaching positions.

Five women faculty members, whose careers spanned the era from separate departments for men's and women's physical education and athletics into the post–Title IX era, were Mary Jane Culhane, Ruth Brunner, Barbara Calmer, Janet Wignall, and Claudia Coville. Culhane (fig. 6.1) came to Oberlin in 1956 and remained for the final thirty years of her career. She obtained bachelor's (1943) and master's degrees (1956) from the University of Iowa. She served as Coordinator of Women's Sports (1977–1980) and Director of Women's Athletics (1980–1989). She helped found the North Coast Athletic Conference. Her specialty was aquatics, including coaching both swimming and diving, and synchronized swimming. She also did some coaching for field hockey, volleyball, and track and field. She was a competitive swimmer into her mid-70s, winning medals at state and national competitions. The softball field was named in her honor as Culhane Field in 2010.

FIGURE 6.2. Ruth Brunner. (Oberlin College Archives)

FIGURE 6.3. Barbara Calmer. (Oberlin College Archives)

Ruth Brunner (fig. 6.2) taught at Oberlin for twenty years from 1965 to 1985. Her educational background included M.A.s in English Literature and Physical Education, plus the course work for a doctoral degree. She obtained her A.B. degree from George Washington University and an M.S. degree from Wellesley (1943—awarded in 1998). She came to the college as Chair of the Women's Physical Education Department, remaining in that position until the 1970 merger of the Physical Education Departments. Brunner chaired the joint department in 1974–1975. She was both a teacher for the physical education major's courses and a coach for the women's basketball team. Her class offerings included History and Philosophy of Sport, and Women in Sport. She further served Oberlin as a dormitory housemother, which was in addition to raising five children with her husband. Brunner fervently advocated for women's athletics, especially to secure sufficient resources for that cause. She exemplified the dilemma for the other women in the department; she was not professionally qualified for coaching basketball, but was eager to attempt this new challenge.

Barbara Calmer (fig. 6.3) joined the Women's Department of Physical Education in 1950 and remained at the college until her retirement in 1988. She was one of the women dissatisfied with being asked to coach

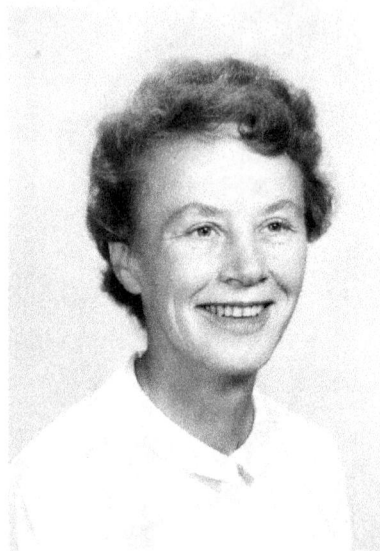 

FIGURE 6.4. Janet Wignall. (Oberlin College Archives)

FIGURE 6.5. Claudia Coville. (Oberlin College Archives)

women's intercollegiate sports. By contrast, she was a superb classroom instructor and scholar, offering classes in dance, outdoor education and recreation, motor learning, and first aid. She worked for many years with handicapped children at the Lucy Stone School. She was a pioneer in elucidating relationships between early childhood movements and the acquisition of initial reading skills.

Janet Wignall (fig. 6.4) came to Oberlin in 1954. In addition to service classes and several courses for the major, she coached field hockey and led the program in modern dance. Wignall played key roles in some of the events of the Jack Scott era and during the period when the major in physical education was dropped. She retired in 1988.

Claudia Coville (fig. 6.5) joined the physical education faculty in 1973 and remained until 1977, at which time she left to pursue a doctoral degree. She was an important stabilizing influence in the department during the mid-1970s and served as Athletic Director for Women during the initial implementation of the changes mandated by the provisions of Title IX.

Initial, incremental steps in terms of implementation of Title IX were carried out under new leadership when Jack Scott was hired in 1972 as both Chair of the Department of Physical Education and Director of Athletics. One of Scott's goals was to provide expanded opportunities for women's participation in intercollegiate athletics. Construction of the Philips Physical Education Center, designed only for men, provided a big step forward, but ignored the needs of women. Women were still using Crane Pool and Hales Gymnasium, both more than thirty years old and in need of renovations. Eventually, women were given use of what was until then the men's faculty locker room at the Philips Center so they could use the new facility for some sports; the faculty men were moved to another location.

In terms of philosophy, Jack Scott supported adding new teams, increasing and adjusting the budget, and making changes in the facilities to accommodate the women athletes. If Oberlin was to continue promoting the mind–body duality, by this time characterized as educating the whole person, these updates were necessary. By his second year, however, Scott switched from supporting both Black and women athletes to concentrating on just male Black athletes and male coaches.

Soon after Scott's departure in early 1974, the leadership consisted of Department Chair Patrick Penn, Director of Women's Athletics Claudia Coville, and Director of Men's Athletics Joseph Gurtis. Lengthy discussions followed that set the stage for future departmental events (see Appendix B). One critical issue was the challenge of requiring women, who trained as teachers and scholars in selected topics covering aspects of history and methodologies as well as service class obligations, to redirect a portion of their time to coaching. How would they acquire the skills needed to coach specific sports? Retaining the current women faculty and shifting their duties could result in individuals who were unfamiliar with their assigned team sports, creating problems both in terms of motivation and skill sets, and the ensuing lack of proper coaching for student athletes. One outcome was that the number of courses offered for physical education majors dropped nearly 61% from twenty-three to just nine. Portending the future, there was also discussion about the consequences of these shifts for the major program. Was it appropriate to envision a future without a major in physical education?

As of 1973–1974, academic credit was finally awarded for women participating in sports including basketball, swimming, field hockey, cross country, volleyball, lacrosse, tennis, synchronized swimming, and fencing. In cases where there were insufficient numbers for a full team, women played with men's club teams. Most of the women's sports program up to this point was managed by the Women's Athletic Association (WAA), which was renamed the Women's Recreation Association (WRA) in 1972. This group often had a student manager or coordinator, with only a small contingent of faculty coaching, and minimal funding. Some forged onward, meeting the challenge, and working with one or more teams, while reluctantly devoting time to learning the appropriate techniques and coaching strategies for their specific sports. Beginning in 1980, one of the requirements for being hired in the department was some prior coaching experience. Another element of the transition concerned the female student athletes. At least initially, a number of them were hesitant to shift the focus of their athletic endeavors to a level similar to that for men, with competitive intercollegiate contests. As new classes of students enrolled, for whom high school athletics had also undergone changes under Title IX, the female student population became enthusiastic about the new opportunities.

When Claudia Coville was hired by Jack Scott in 1973 to coach swimming, her management approach blended the rapidly increasing desire among female students for intercollegiate competition across all sports with the less enthusiastic interest from many of the female faculty. A gradual process was initiated which, over time, proved effective. When Coville left Oberlin in 1977, Mary Culhane stepped in as the new Coordinator of Women's Athletics (in 1980, the title changed to Director of Women's Athletics). She fostered and enhanced the women's portion of the combined program along the path set by Coville.

The first varsity teams competed at the official intercollegiate level in 1977–1978, though numerous contests had occurred in prior years in some sports. During the first years, teams competed in field hockey, basketball, outdoor and indoor track and field, volleyball, cross country, swimming and diving, lacrosse, and tennis. Synchronized swimming was one of the sports offered at Oberlin during this period, but it was dropped within a few years as an intercollegiate team. In 1985–1986 soccer was added; softball became a varsity sport in 2000.

During the first years, Oberlin's women's teams competed in the Ohio Athletic Conference (OAC). After a brief time playing in the Centennial Athletic Conference (1982–1984), they joined the men in the North Coast Athletic Conference (NCAC), founded in 1984, where they remain today. A key reason for the formation of the NCAC was that some schools, like Oberlin, Kenyon, Wooster, and others, were facing small college teams from Ohio and neighboring states that were geared to play football on a bigger stage, guaranteeing that Oberlin and others would lose to those schools almost every year. The new conference's rules made off-campus recruiting for athletes easier for both women and men. Prior to that, coaches could only contact athletes who had already applied for admission to and attained the high standards of the college. Now they could approach students earlier to tell them about the college and encourage them to apply. For individual faculty in the department, this change shifted the emphasis away from teaching in the academic major and service class programs to full-time coaching and recruiting.

Providing an athletic program for women equal to that offered to men required significant budgetary changes. Regulations in Title IX stipulated that the allocation of funds for male and female athletes should be proportional to their representation in the school's student population. In 1972, Oberlin College's athletics budget was $68,000, of which just $1,000 (about 1.5%) was allocated for women's activities. Addressing this imbalance was a hot topic for several years, beginning under Jack Scott's leadership. As with the discussions of coaching, some female faculty were hesitant to push for the significant funding increases needed to meet the regulations. Periodic debates centered on possibly discontinuing the disproportionally large expenses for the football program, redirecting those funds to support both women's and men's teams. Other solutions involved reallocating funds from various men's sports teams to support women's teams or gaining a larger allocation from the college's general budget. By Scott's second year, he succeeded in raising the budget for women's teams to between $7,000 and $10,000. Additional increases occurred in subsequent years, reaching just over $17,000 in 1975–1976. However, throughout these years, in the early-to-mid 1970s, Oberlin College was in the midst of a financial crisis. The college's expenses were higher than its income. By 1976–1977, these shortfalls were moving toward resolution, and the budget was once again becoming balanced.

As women at Oberlin began playing intercollegiate contests, a special committee, charged with examining the department and major, produced important conclusions. First, there was great need for both more coaches and individuals with appropriate expertise in specific sports. Other recommendations involved strengthening recruitment efforts for female scholar athletes and funding increases for both women and men. Parity in expenditures across gender was not fully realized until sometime in the 1980s. The single biggest athletics expenditure continued to be for the football program; this will be covered in the next chapter.

As the Title IX era dawned, Oberlin had just opened the Philips Physical Education Center (map, fig. 0.5) at the north end of Woodland Street. The building was designed to house men's physical education and athletics as a state-of-the-art replacement for the obsolete facilities in Warner Gymnasium on the central campus, which opened in 1901. The women were housed in Hales Gymnasium (1939) and had primary use of Crane Pool (1931). The men were principal occupants of Jones Field House (1947), though it was used on a few occasions for extramural women's basketball. Williams Ice Rink (1964) was available for use by everyone, but the only intercollegiate athletic team using this facility was the men's ice hockey team. Outdoor fields were divided into the football and baseball complex used by men, the softball field for women, soccer fields shared across men's and women's teams, the Galpin field used for field hockey, and assorted fields, mostly at the north end of the athletics complex, as practice areas for various teams, intramurals, and club sports.

Locker rooms in the Philips Center clearly were one issue for concern. Built only for men, there was no provision for women's locker room space. In fact, even after minor accommodations, noted above, there were times when women using the new Carr Pool in the Philips Center had to change into swimwear at Hales Gym and walk a city block to Philips. This is reminiscent of the time, in the early twentieth century, when men on many teams, including football and baseball, changed at Warner Gymnasium and made their way to north campus—often as far as Athletic Park on North Professor Street. Jack Scott raised this issue of equality for men and women in terms of locker rooms, but it was not until 1987 that modifications to the Philips Center created sufficient locker room space for women, resulting in real parity. Today, facilities like the Knowlton Complex, and including the Bailey Field, Heisman Field House, Carr Pool, Williams Field House (see map, fig. 0.5), and other venues, are shared by both men and women, often with scheduled practice times arranged to give each team, regardless of gender, equal opportunities to prepare for games.

Oberlin was a microcosm of what happened on the national level with Title IX actions. With respect to women's college athletics, the 1970s witnessed both a culmination of several decades of changes and the launching of further, dramatic transformations resulting in more equal division of resources and opportunities for women. The philosophy for physical education and athletics had already shifted in the previous forty years for men, moving toward a more competitive model. Women, by contrast, held to the earlier mind–body harmony. However, events leading up to and resulting from Title IX altered this pattern. Women's athletics now became more focused on competition and less about enjoyment of the sport. By 1980, women's teams moved in the direction of men's athletics with efforts for recruitment, training, coaching, and scheduling. Coaches had fewer obligations to the physical education major courses and service classes. Oberlin and other similar institutions followed this pattern, though as NCAA Division III schools, they still did not employ large-scale, formal recruiting practices or provide athletic scholarships.

Transitions like the ones that occurred under Title IX often led to problems. In the case of Oberlin, many issues were resolved internally, but there are two instances of external compliance reviews. The first problem encountered was achieving equality in terms of facilities. Problems with locker rooms and associated spaces were resolved eventually by redesigning the Philips Center to convert a large storage area into locker rooms and showers. Over time, the entire women's program was shifted from Hales Gymnasium to the Philips Center. Increased budgeting, starting in the early 1970s and continuing into the 1980s, insured parity for equipment, training, and other important facets of the women's program. Yet, by the late 1970s it appeared to some that the college administration was not fully addressing certain concerns that arose with the implementation of Title IX.

A group of female student athletes submitted a formal complaint to the US Office of Civil Rights (OCR) in September 1981 regarding what they felt were violations of regulations stipulated in Title IX. The primary bases for this action related to the locker rooms, the disparity whereby most male coaches were tenured and those for women's teams held annual contracts, possible issues with unequal resources for recruiting, and unequal scheduling of the training facilities. A two-year sequence of events transpired involving Oberlin's submission of materials to the OCR, followed by lengthy exchanges of correspondence, resulting in a formal site visit to Oberlin by a team of investigators in March 1983. (See pp. 74–87 of Leland Brandt's 1992 History Honors thesis for a complete explanation of this process.) The report from the OCR visit questioned the coaching for lacrosse and soccer but did not feel this constituted a violation of Title IX. The concern about locker rooms and its solution were noted above.

A second complaint to the Office of Civil Rights (OCR) involving Title IX matters was made in 1993–1994. The issues concerned the equipment needs for women's athletics teams, improved transport for women's teams, and the need for a new gender equity committee. In response to the OCR findings, all of these problems were resolved satisfactorily. In the settlement agreement, the college provided funding for increased bus and transportation to away contests, the purchase of travel bags and uniforms, and the formation of the committee on gender equity, which remains a part of the college procedures in 2021.

Oberlin Physical Education in Transition

By the early 1970s, before Title IX went fully into effect and the major was still intact, the curriculum at Oberlin consisted of the following classes:

- Required Physical Education (first two years)—Activities in more than twenty areas were offered
- The Competitive Ethic (Sport in American Society)
- International Sports and Physical Education
- Women in Sport
- Sports and Games: A Cross-Cultural Analysis
- Philosophy of Physical Education
- Being in the Body
- Human Anatomy—Kinesiology
- Human Anatomy—Physiology
- Motor Behavior in the Atypical Child
- Games, Gymnastics and Self-Testing Activities for Children (grades K–6)
- Sports Leadership (grades 7–12)
- Creative Play for Children
- Separate classes for Teaching Coaching for Football, Baseball, Basketball, Track & Field, Swimming
- First Aid and the Treatment of Athletic Injuries
- Administration of Physical Education and Athletics
- Methods and Directed Teaching

These changes are dramatic relative to the offerings in the 1950s, and reflect a shift in emphases in society during this time period. There are

TABLE 6.1. A compilation of majors in physical education at five-year intervals from 1900 to 1985

GRADUATION YEAR	WOMEN MAJORS	MEN MAJORS
1900	1	0
1905	6	3
1910	0	1
1915	12	3
1920	13	7
1925	14	4
1930	9	5
1935	9	3
1940	5	0
1945	8	5
1950	4	1
1955	4	3
1960	0	0
1965	1	0
1970	1	1
1975	2	0
1980	2	4
1985	1	0

several more classes targeting the need for teachers trained for K–12 students. Newly introduced courses included the incorporation of women and cross-cultural perspectives in sports, and an emphasis on coaching techniques. Many of the subject classes that were part of the major, originally designed to prepare students for graduate study in physical education, were dropped from the curriculum prior to 1970.

A complex sequence of events, taking place over almost twenty years, resulted in the decision to discontinue the physical education major program at Oberlin, effective in 1985. At the college, the number of physical education majors went into an overall decline with most years after about 1960 having fewer than five or six majors (see table 6.1). Two parts of the program from the 1960s are noteworthy. First, the annual sets of physical examinations of students, which began back before the start of the twentieth century and continued to the mid-1970s. On the upper floor of Warner Gymnasium, students removed their clothing and were photographed, measured, and assessed for possible problems. This could lead to recommended physical training to address the condition. These are the data that Sara Houston of the department faculty was using for her analyses—large sets of information that remain, under restricted conditions, in the College Archives. A second practice that remained in place for women up to the 1950s was a course in Health Fundamentals. This class was dropped before the mid-1960s. Some sources indicate that this was required of all students, while others claim that the class was required for females, but not males.

The hiring of Robert Fuller as president was a key factor in the hiring, two years later, of Jack Scott to run the physical education and athletics programs. Both men had envisioned revolutionary changes for education and athletics, respectively. Their visions, formed from external perspectives, proved much more difficult to implement than either had anticipated. Their very progressive ideas, superimposed onto the traditional college community, and their methods for the implementation of their desired changes resulted in long-lasting friction, dissention, and subsequent disruptions among both the departmental and college faculty. For several years after the coincident departures of both Fuller and Scott early in 1974, the college, and particularly the personnel in the Department of Physical Education, suffered from what we might today call PTSD (post-traumatic stress disorder). Issues of leadership, curriculum, and athletic programs required some years to resolve. Fortunately, good people were on hand in both the department and the college administration. With discussion, cautious cooperation, and an improved spirit, engendered by both women and men, a renewed, more vigorous program emerged by the early 1980s, albeit with a much different view of physical education and the concept of mind–body harmony. An analysis of the number of female and male majors in physical education reveals the changes over a century in terms of student interest in this field. A general decline in majors began in the decade after World War II, and the numbers remained low, generally at five or fewer, until the degree was discontinued in 1985.

In 1978, Emil Danenberg, then president of Oberlin, established a President's Committee for the Study of Athletics Policy to examine all aspects of physical education and intercollegiate athletics. The group had at its disposal: (a) the 1968–1969 external departmental review; (b) the Frank Committee report on the football program; and (c) Dean Reich's 1972 report to the Educational Plans and Polices Committee (EPPC). The ad hoc committee operated against a backdrop of changes during the previous decade that affected the programs that were the subject of its charge. These included dropping letter grades for physical education service program classes, shifts in priorities brought about by Title IX, the recently recovered finances of the college, and various ongoing campus events. Student interest in physical education and athletics waned during this period. Strong interest in and time devoted to protest activities associated with the Vietnam War and Civil Rights waned, but some of that energy was now directed to Women's Rights and later to support for Lesbian, Gay, Bisexual, and Transgender (LGBT) students.

A key factor in the decision to drop grades arose with the observation by students that different teachers awarded different letter grades for the same service class. Evaluation by various instructors in some classes was based on student performance relative to normative standards. Others graded based on improvement in skill level exhibited by individual students over the course of the semester. These contrasts were evident when students enrolled in different sections of the same course were issued disparate grades by separate instructors. The inconsistent grading that resulted was cause for student concerns. Dropping letter grades helped resolve this matter. The service classes became pass-fail or credit-no credit.

The report from the President's Committee contained several key recommendations. The first was to retain and emphasize physical education activities, intramurals, and intercollegiate athletics. The academic major was to be deemphasized. At the time, only one faculty member in the department held a doctoral degree, and none had a medical degree. Until this time, most department faculty had, at a minimum, attained a master's degree. Academic offerings had been reduced in number and the overall quality was less than optimal. Just seven courses were offered in the 1978–1979 academic year. The number of majors in the prior six years varied from one to nine, with half of those students pursuing double majors combining physical education with another discipline.

The committee voted to abolish the physical education major with the provision that if there were sufficient student interest and a faculty member with appropriate expertise, classes in specific topics could be offered. However, the General Faculty of the college, following a vote from the EPPC, decided that, at least for now, the major should remain. Discussion ensued regarding certification of students planning to teach physical education in the schools. This process was dependent on classes from the Department of Education at the college. At the conclusion of the discussion, a separate split vote of 5–5 occurred regarding elimination of the football program (see chapter 8).

The second recommendation was to provide increased support for women's intercollegiate teams, taking the form of better efforts to recruit female scholar athletes and, as appropriate, to host state and national championships in women's athletics. Budget increases for women's sports would provide for additional equipment and uniforms. Opportunities for club sports and possible additional women's intercollegiate teams should be advanced.

A third set of recommendations pertained to staffing needs. Several additional non-continuing appointments should be made, generally of one to three years. Students should be included in the evaluation process for individuals teaching activity classes and coaching team sports.

A final set of recommendations concerned budgetary matters. A key part of this was to maintain better control over all expenditures within the purview of the department. Additional funds were needed for equipment, a van for travel, and to maintain better hours of opening for use of the Philips Center for recreation. During Jack Scott's tenure, admission charges for all athletic events were eliminated. The committee wished to see this policy revisited.

Some significant changes occurred in response to these recommendations. The physical education requirement was eliminated. A critical blow to the major occurred at the end of the 1979–1980 academic year, when the Department of Education was dissolved. Gone was the pathway of coursework that led to the K–12 public-school teaching certification in health, physical education, and recreation. Noticeable throughout this period was the attrition of several faculty members from the Department of Physical Education and Athletics via retirement and departure. The substantial loss of long-term faculty led to the lack of year-to-year continuity in program offerings and curriculum changes. The department experienced increasing angst with the lack of community cohesiveness. These feelings prompted the invitation extended to a pair of outside consultants for an on-campus review of the department in 1985. One of the experts called in was Bill Grice, a former department member, who was then Director of Athletics at Case Western Reserve University. The outside group reviewed the program, provided objective perspectives, and made recommendations for future plans.

Later in 1985, the General Faculty voted to drop the physical education major altogether. In 1989, the long-standing faculty status and tenure-track career path classifications, dating to the early twentieth century, were eliminated for physical education instructors and coaches, to be replaced by appointments that were 51% professional and administrative staff. The "professionals" were defined as coaches; the "administrators" were all of the assistant coaches, trainers, and schedulers. A further recommendation was that the staff appointments be made with three-year renewable contracts. In 1989 the name of the unit was changed officially from the "Department of Physical Education and Athletics" to the "Department of Athletics and Physical Education."

Underlying this long sequence of events was a clear shift in philosophy. The foundational rationale for the combination of academics and exercise, which was a main feature of the college for more than a century and a half, was gradually eroding. As detailed in the next chapter, the purpose of athletics and some aspects of physical education became more about winning at all costs, though less enthusiastically at schools like Oberlin as compared to larger universities. This proved fatal for the major in physical education at Oberlin but opened the door for stronger competitive athletics with the focus shifted toward "winning." Individuals hired as coaches now could actively engage in recruiting. More practice time was granted for student participants in competitive sports. The NCAC, which was founded in 1983–1984 and became effective in 1984–1985, was more permissive in terms of off-campus recruiting. Oberlin was not as full-bore into this change in thinking as were some schools, because the college did not lower academic standards to accommodate its athletes or provide financial aid in the form of any type of athletic scholarships. Nonetheless, the college was not immune to the consequences of the sequence of events that occurred from the 1970s through the mid-1980s. This resulted in closing the 100-year-old, pioneering program to train top-notch physical educators. Some of Oberlin's peer institutions retain a major, minor, or program in physical education or related disciplines. Others, as covered in chapter 9, now feature health and wellness centers designed around physical exercise and a return to the mind–body relationship.

Sports as Entertainment

Athletics formed an ever-increasing part of life for many Americans. This included sports at all levels from recreational games to youth sports, high schools, colleges, and professional teams. With each upward step, the number of participants capable of performing at the elite level diminished. For the college and then professional teams, far more people became spectators, harkening back to the days in the second and third decades of the twentieth century and concerns about "spectatoritis." By the 1970s, attendance at sporting events was augmented not only by radio broadcasts or early television in the 1960s, but by games of a variety of sports on weekends, and by the 1980s on many weekdays sports were featured on television. Educational and Sports Program Network (ESPN) began operations in 1979 and covered sports on a virtual 24/7 basis. The major broadcast networks carried weekly games as well as some local coverage in cities with professional teams.

By the 1980s, the bigger colleges and universities moved to a larger stage. Broadcasts brought direct advertising revenue, and teams gained sponsorships from a variety of businesses for everything from advertising at their venues to naming rights for stadiums and arenas. Sales of team-related merchandise and program advertising provided other revenue sources. Sports venues, for universities and professional teams, either added special seating areas, usually enclosed and with various amenities and called "luxury" boxes or, as new facilities were constructed, these features were part of the design.

The following list of changes in intercollegiate athletics illustrates the ramping up of sports programs at larger schools. These trends characterize the way the overall philosophy governing many sports and the implementation of these shifting norms occurred from 1970 to 1990. For Division III institutions, like Oberlin, there was a moderate shift toward these actions. (1) The number of games scheduled each season for some sports increased. (2) Athletic contests, formerly played primarily on weekends, now occurred throughout the week. (3) Where some teams, most notably baseball, took spring trips in prior decades, by the 1990s more teams, for both men and women, traveled south over spring break to play other schools in preparation for the upcoming season. January trips are now included for some teams. (4) Many schools, including small colleges, engaged in out-of-season practices leading to limitations on the number of sports in which a student could participate. Issues pertaining to a "culture" surrounding athletics and athletes, with winning becoming the only satisfying outcome for college sports, is a major subject in chapter 8.

The desire to win existed for decades, but the intensity with which this goal was pursued increased in the years following World War II and grew even stronger by the 1970s and 1980s. At larger schools, members of the NCAA Division I, and in the medium-sized universities of Division II, there was a major increased emphasis on winning. This shift in philosophy started to pervade most sports at these schools, not just the prominent ones like football and basketball. A spillover effect became evident even at some Division III institutions, though many attempted to retain a core of the earlier philosophy embodying enjoyment and participation. The goal was to retain the underlying desire of all athletes and students to strive for excellence regardless of their natural ability. At a number of small colleges, winning games against principal rivals or achieving conference and national championships translates to more and larger gifts from alumni. Thus, the spirit of competition and winning was present here as well though with less intensity. By the mid-1980s, this trend toward winning as a primary focus began to impact women's intercollegiate sports as well.

Facilities

The period 1972–1990 included one major addition to the campus infrastructure pertaining to athletics. The Jesse Philips Physical Education Center, added in 1972, was funded from a generous donation by the man for whom the building is named (fig. 6.6; map, fig. 0.5). The facility includes two gymnasiums in which basketball, volleyball, and other sports are practiced, and intercollegiate contests are played. Courts for various types of racquet sports are included. The building incorporated a weight room, swimming pool, locker rooms, and offices for faculty and staff. There is a classroom and a conference room, the latter named for John Heisman. Some specialized areas, such as the climbing wall, aid the recreational functions of the center. In addition to serving the needs of intercollegiate athletics, most of the venues in the Philips Physical Education Center are used for intramurals, as well as exercise by students, faculty, and staff for recreational activities, including by residents of the City of Oberlin.

Among the older campus athletics facilities, Crane Pool was closed in 1973 soon after Carr Pool was opened as part of the Philips Physical Education Center. The Crane Pool space is now used mostly for storage. At Hales Gymnasium, some of the areas are or have been used for recreation by both women and men, intramural and club sports, various physical education classes, and as home for several departments and events. The Jazz Program was housed here for a period prior to the completion of the Kohl building. The Dance Program occupied portions of

FIGURE 6.6. The Jesse Philips Physical Education Center, located at the end of Woodland Avenue, houses sports venues including a basketball court; a second, smaller gymnasium; locker rooms; offices; and conference areas. (Oberlin College Archives)

the Hales structure, but now has its own home in the Warner Center (formerly Warner Gymnasium). The Theater Department was housed in a portion of this building for a time and held some performances there. The OCircus uses the main gymnasium for its practices and some performances.

Summary

Title IX, signed in 1972, providing for women's equality with men's athletics, became a requirement with a deadline of 1978 for full implementation. For colleges and universities, including Oberlin, this meant altering many aspects of their programs, with the new legislation covering facilities, budgets, the number of teams, training, travel, and more. The process was not fully completed until the 1980s. For Oberlin, the upheaval during this period involved dissolution of the Physical Education major in 1985. Letter grades were dropped for service classes and then the requirement was eliminated altogether. Hiring practices reflected a shift to engaging administrative staff and professional coaches who were familiar with the detailed methods for their sport(s) and with more liberal recruitment procedures. The staff and coaches were hired with appointments categorized as 51% administrative and professional staff and without tenure. The decline in the number of majors (and minors), the closing of the Department of Education at the college, and the inability to provide teacher certification all provided input for the committees whose charge it was to examine the major. Changing student interests also prompted shifts within the department. Most significant, however, was the departure from the underlying tenet that had stood the test of time in the twentieth century: that the mind–body duality required nurturing and support. Facilities were greatly enhanced with the addition of the Philips Physical Education Center. By the 1970s and 1980s, the culture surrounding intercollegiate athletics shifted more toward a "winning" mindset. Entertainment became a major focus with enhanced media coverage, sports merchandise for fans, and sports venues to accommodate major donors.

Sources Consulted for Chapter 6

Full citations are found at the end of the book.

Costa, D. M., and S. R. Guthrie (eds.). *Women and Sport: Interdisciplinary Perspectives.*

Galasso, O. J. *Philosophy of Sport and Physical Activity.*

Guttmann, A. *A Whole New Ballgame An Interpretation of American Sports.*

Kretchmar, R. S. *Practical Philosophy of Sport.*

Kretchmar, R. S., M. Dyerson, M. P. Llewellyn, and J. Gleaves. *History and Philosophy of Sport and Physical Activity.*

Lucas, C. J. *American Higher Education: A History.*

Mechikoff, R. *A History and Philosophy of Sport and Physical Education.*

Rudolph, F. *The American College & University: A History.*

Schwendener, N. *A History of Physical Education in the United States.*

Thelin, J. R. *A History of American Higher Education.*

Wushanley, Y. *Playing Nice and Losing The Struggle for Control of Women's Intercollegiate Athletics, 1960–2000.*

Zeigler, E. F. *History and Status of American Physical Education and Educational Sport.*

CHAPTER 7

Worldwide Sports and Winning Dominates

1991–2010

Period Events and Introduction

This chapter covers two decades with many significant national and international events. Among these were extensive space exploration built on efforts originating in the 1960s; military confrontations around the world; tremendous expansion of technology, most notably in terms of computers, telephones, and social media; and globalization of economics and many other aspects of Americans' daily lives. For intercollegiate athletics there was a continuation of trends that emerged in the previous decades. The basic underlying philosophy about winning did not change; it only intensified. Physical education remained as an academic major at most larger institutions, and at some smaller colleges, but Oberlin no longer offered that major.

Two brief quotes characterize the disparate philosophies about athletic competition and what occurred before, during, and after the two decades presented in this chapter:

> Henry Russell (Red) Saunders, legendary football coach at UCLA: *Winning isn't everything, it is the only thing.*

> Grantland Rice, sportswriter extraordinaire: *It's not that you won or lost but how you played the game.*

These two quotes exemplify the clashing approaches that emerged after World War II and became predominant by the last quarter of the twentieth century. The larger schools incorporated and maintained the philosophy expressed by Coach Saunders, while the approach favored by Rice, a journalist, was more in concert with what Oberlin and other smaller institutions favored. Much of the coverage in this chapter is concerned with the smaller schools, using Oberlin as a representative example.

Sports at both the larger university and professional levels was now a business, no longer maintaining any pretense of being about exercise and participatory enjoyment. Smaller schools tried to hold to the spirit of friendly competition; many succeeded, though some succumbed to the lure and challenge of going "big time." On the national level, professional sports grew ever more prominent, with teams added in all four major men's leagues—football, basketball, baseball, and ice hockey. Many other team sports developed ancillary outlets, such as indoor football and lacrosse. Professional golf and tennis for both men and women, which had strong roots prior to the 1970s, expanded, particularly on the international level. By the early 2000s, men's professional soccer was gaining a foothold in the US. For women, there were early starts for professional basketball and soccer. Despite some initial struggles, these became popular fixtures on the sports landscape, as have women's ice hockey and volleyball. Both the Summer and Winter Olympics are now large spectacles, attracting hundreds of millions of television viewers on six continents. Sports, in many forms, is now a dominant worldwide feature of life.

Much of this expansion is based on several factors, mostly tied to money and fostered by strong interest from fans supporting their favorite teams. Revenue generated from lucrative television contracts is the single most important source of increased funding. Tickets to games, special luxury boxes with amenities, inflated concession prices, and seat licenses all contribute to the funding. A third major revenue source is the sale of team-related merchandise. The steady population growth in the US means that there are more than twice as many potential sports fans in the US as there were seventy-five years ago. By the year 2000 the population exceeded 300 million people, which is more than double what it was in 1940 (140 million) and 40% greater than it was in 1970 (213 million). Modern stadiums and arenas abound; new ones continue to appear each year, many of them now specialized for just a single sport. More fans translates to more merchandise sales, larger media contracts, and an overall multifold increase in revenues. This change is evident not only at the professional level, but also at the university level. Contracts, in the millions of dollars for coaches in some sports at the larger universities, are primarily underwritten by alumni and commercial income, both of which are independent from state budgets and tuition funds.

Changes for Athletics

The effects of the shift in philosophy, from enjoyment to highly competitive contests, which occurred over several decades and reached a peak during the period 1991–2010, had far-reaching consequences for all sports competition. The need to win at any cost filtered downward to sports and games played by children and young adults, whether it be in junior soccer leagues, recreational baseball groups, or high school sports. Most people have witnessed or read the stories of disgruntled parents who argue with and berate coaches and officials at sporting events in which their children participate. Youth sports became big business as well, with estimates as high as $15 billion in expenditures each year based on equipment, travel, and other costs incurred by parents and their children. A quote from Lance Englelka, taken from his letter of resignation as high school football coach in Middletown, OH, in November 2017, aptly conveys the pernicious sentiment that now, all too often, governs our philosophy about sports, even among America's youth.

> The online death threats, threats of physical violence, personal and deceitful attacks from parents and community members, and verbal abuse leveled against myself, my family, and my coaching staff have devolved into an unsafe environment which I refuse to tolerate. These threats of physical harm and verbal abuse stem from the misguided community perspective on the irrational importance on winning high school football games, unrealistic expectations from parents related to their son's abilities and future prospects, and parental belief that bullying coaches is an acceptable method of communication. I understand the high-profile nature and acceptable criticism associated with being the head football coach at Middletown High School, however, winning and losing at the high school level should not be a life-threatening situation. (*Middletown Journal News,* October 30, 2017)

Across American colleges and universities, this philosophical shift produced changes in athletics. Most of these evolved gradually and involved recruiting, extended practice time, off-season practices, summer camps, and the elimination of most multisport athletes. Some of these were noted in the previous chapter. The profound changes, prompted by the "win at all costs" philosophy, continued to grow, now affecting even the smaller institutions like Oberlin, albeit at a much lesser level of intensity.

At the bigger Division I and II schools, recruiting students from secondary schools, which began in earnest in the 1950s, became a full-time occupation for scouts and assistants from many institutions in the 1970s. At smaller schools, like Oberlin, there was a shift in terms of attracting good athletes with superior academic credentials. Coaches and assistant coaches were assigned time devoted to recruiting. The practice of having assistant coaches in many varsity sports began after World War II and expanded in the late 1970s. In the case of the smaller schools, where Oberlin is a good example, recruiting involves contacting student applicants, showing potential students and their families the campus and athletics facilities when they come for an interview, and if they are admitted, encouraging them to come to the college. This extra time allocated for recruiting corresponds with several other changes in responsibilities for members of the Department of Athletics and Physical Education. Most coaches are now a head coach for only one sport, though some are assigned to both women's and men's teams in the same sports, including swimming and diving, cross country, and track and field. Assistant coaches, in sports that have them, are often only associated with one sport, and they too are involved in recruiting. Today, at Oberlin and most peer institutions, some coaches remain involved in the physical activities service classes offered for all students and some do classroom teaching for programs in physical education at colleges that chose to retain majors or minors in physical education and related fields.

Events involving scandals of one sort or another do not generally involve schools like Oberlin, but the larger university athletics landscape is littered with such occurrences. In terms of academics, the scandals run the gamut from phantom classes for athletes and the use of replacement students, to grades given but not earned, and papers written by outsiders on behalf of athletes. More recent years have witnessed significant problems with sexual harassment and domestic violence problems. Compensation, paid to athletes or their families in a variety of forms, has occurred in many instances. Fictitious summer jobs with high salaries, and gifts of merchandise are impermissible under current NCAA rules; yet they occur with regularity. The recent change to permit student athletes to receive payment for use of their name, image, or likeness (NIL) has altered these restrictions for some groups of college athletes.

To date, no problems of these types have been reported at Oberlin. Nor have they occurred at most small colleges, though information on this topic for peer institutions proved difficult to locate.

Oberlin College during This Twenty-Year Period

Throughout recent decades, as the goals for athletics at many levels shifted to the "winning is everything" approach, Oberlin and many similar colleges strived to promote and retain a philosophy that athletics should be more about competition as a form of maturation and preparation for life. Rivalries in some sports and between particular institutions often engendered strong competitive drives, but these did not rise to the levels just noted for bigger schools. Student athletes could arrive at places like Oberlin having participated in a culture at the youth sports or at the high school level that was all about winning. However, one of the reasons that they selected a small college was the ability to compete on a level playing field with scholar athletes from schools sharing the same philosophy, integrating a spirit of competition with an approach that balanced athletics with respect for their opponents. Such institutions also fostered a strong emphasis on combining the athletics with a foundational academic education.

The situation is nicely reflected in the athletics policy of 1975 given below. After the departure of Jack Scott from Oberlin and during the ongoing reorganization of the Department of Physical Education and Athletics, a new set of guidelines was promulgated.

1. Admissions based on academics should count first, but athletic ability should be a positive consideration.
2. Financial aid should be based entirely on need.
3. For recruiting, information can be dispensed to students once they have applied and then a visit to campus is encouraged. Some conference restrictions may apply.
4. The athletics budget should be part of that for the Department of Physical Education.

5. The General Faculty Committee should have an Athletics Advisory Committee to provide guidance on policy and schedules.
6. Intercollegiate Athletics involves no differences in treatment across all sports, the General Faculty voting on adding or dropping of any sport, and budgetary control by the department leadership.
7. Schedules should involve competition against schools with similar standards and policies.
8. Hiring coaches is handled by the Physical Education Department, with the proviso that those hired should be able to contribute to the academic program and intramurals. All appointments are to be approved by the Faculty Council.
9. There are no rules governing academic standing and eligibility to play for a team.

In 1996, President Nancy S. Dye received a report from a committee she appointed: Oberlin College Action Plan for Intercollegiate Athletics and Campus Physical Education. The report was, in part, a planning document for the twenty-first century. The main points included the following: (1) With respect to governance and oversight, the Director of Athletics would report directly to the college president. More support would be provided for the director, and the role of the Athletics Committee was to be examined. (2) To raise the competitiveness of Oberlin's athletics teams, steps were needed to ensure that better high school student athletes would choose to apply to and attend Oberlin. This, in turn, would promote those who were more likely to remain at Oberlin, and the college would garner more support from alumni. (3) With respect to the campus, additional use of the various facilities was to be promoted as a means of achieving and maintaining an atmosphere of physical well-being on campus. More funding for the intramural and club sports programs was deemed desirable. The report encouraged a greater integration of athletes into the campus community, while also striving to change faculty attitudes concerning scholar athletes.

Several changes at Oberlin reflected national shifts in the cultural landscape of college and university athletics. For some sports, most notably football but also occurring in other individual and team sports, out-of-season practices became more prevalent. The focus on a single sport for a young athlete nearly eliminates the multisport individuals of earlier decades. Many youths, through high school age, attend summer camps, where they become more specialized. Football and basketball are two good examples of the "need" for year-round training and conditioning offered to teenagers. There are still multisport athletes, but they are many fewer in number.

A cursory analysis of the membership (as of September 2021) of those who have been elected to the Heisman Club Hall of Fame at Oberlin serves as a test for change in the number of sports played by individual athletes. Data were collected with respect to four time periods and whether the individual elected to the Hall of Fame played one sport, or two or more sports. Males and females were combined, and for track and field and cross country, the individual was entered as competing in one sport. For all athletes who graduated in classes up to and including 1950 (all males), there are 55 members, of whom 35 (63.6%) were multisport participants. For the interval with classes from 1951 to 1970 (all males), there are 41 members, with 29 (70.7%) playing two or more sports. From the period 1971–1990, 43 individuals (both genders) were elected, with 21 (48.8%) competing in multiple sports. Lastly, for the 29 individuals (both genders) chosen from classes graduating between 1991 and 2011, only 9 (31%) played for multiple teams. Clearly, there is a strong trend to engage in just one sport.

The roster of teams for men's sports shifted during the past forty years. As of 1975, there were thirteen teams. In the late 1970s, wrestling, ice hockey, and fencing were dropped, and indoor track and field was added. A golf team at Oberlin existed until 1975 and was then revived from 2002 to 2013, when it was again eliminated, reducing the men's total to ten sports as of 2020. For women, the initial number of teams as of 1978–1979, when Title IX was implemented for intercollegiate athletics, was ten. Synchronized swimming was dropped in 1980; soccer and softball were later added to bring the current total to eleven. There are three reasons for dropping a team from the program: (1) insufficient funds; (2) lack of student interest; and (3) lack of available coaching. Hockey was discontinued as a varsity sport for lack of funding; it became a club sport for several decades. Wrestling, golf, and synchronized swimming were dropped because of a lack of student interest. Fencing was shifted from varsity to club status, mostly because of a lack of coaching.

Presently, the lineup of men's intercollegiate teams at Oberlin differs only slightly from a group of peer institutions within the North Coast Athletic Conference: Denison; Kenyon; Ohio Wesleyan; Wabash; and Wooster. Only Denison, Kenyon, and Wooster have golf as a varsity sport. Both Ohio Wesleyan and Wabash have wrestling teams. All of the colleges have teams for football, basketball, baseball, tennis, swimming and diving, indoor and outdoor track and field, lacrosse, cross country, and soccer. Wabash college is an all-male institution, and thus the comparisons for women are based on the other five schools. The women's teams at all of the colleges include basketball, field hockey, cross country, swimming and diving, track and field, volleyball, lacrosse, tennis, softball, and soccer. What little information was located concerning budgets for athletics at some of these schools suggests that the annual expenditures for all aspects of varsity sports—including field and facilities maintenance for venues also used for intramurals, club sports, and recreation—range from about $3.8 million to $4.8 million. These estimates do not include costs for construction or capital improvements.

Personnel for athletics and physical education at Oberlin College increased dramatically during the interval between 1985 and 2019, as shown in table 7.1. The data were gathered from college catalogues and directories. Assignments to staff or coaching/teaching/administrative positions are based on titles and duties, including coaching and class instruction. There was some ebb and flow evident in the personnel numbers prior to about 1990, and then both types of positions at least doubled in the ensuing thirty years. Many of the coaching additions took the form of assistants and some administrators. Staff increases reflect the addition of trainers and personnel needed to manage the athletics programs, including dissemination of sports information, and for facilities management. From an examination of the current coaching and staffing personnel listed on websites and consulting school directories, similar trends occurred for peer institutions.

Administration of the programs in men's and women's physical education and athletics underwent significant expansion in terms of titles and personnel filling the various positions between 1970 and 2010. The early 1970s were covered in the previous chapter regarding the merger of men's and women's physical education programs and the period when Jack Scott (fig. 5.7) was at Oberlin. Beginning in the mid-1970s, the combined department was chaired by Ruth Brunner (1974–1975; fig. 6.2); Patrick Penn (1975–1980; fig. 5.9); Richard Michaels (1980–1983); Don Hunsinger (1983–1986; fig. 7.1); and then, in acting capacities, by Lawrence Vance (1986–1988) and Joseph Gurtis Jr. (1988–1989). At this time, there was separate management for men's and women's intercollegiate athletics. Claudia Coville (1974–1977; fig. 6.5) and Mary Culhane

TABLE 7.1. The number of personnel in the program for physical education and athletics from the 1895-1896 year to 2015-2020

ACADEMIC YEAR	FACULTY, COACHES, AND ADMINISTRATORS*	STAFF AND SUPPORT PERSONNEL[†]
1895-1896	3	0
1900-1901	4	0
1905-1906	6	1
1910-1911	8	1
1915-1916	10	2
1920-1921	7	1
1925-1926	10	1
1930-1931	13	1
1935-1936	16	2
1940-1941	15	1
1945-1946	15	1
1950-1951	15	2
1955-1956	15	3
1960-1961	14	3
1965-1966	15	3
1970-1971	15	3
1975-1976	12	4
1980-1981	13	5
1985-1986	13	7
1990-1991	17	9
1995-1996	16	10
2000-2001	21	14
2005-2006	31	13
2010-2011	29	12
2015-2020	36	15

* Combined numbers for faculty, coaches, and administrators, with those holding dual roles counted only once.

[†] Includes trainers, equipment managers, and others.

(1977–1980; fig. 6.1) served as Coordinators of Women's Sports. The title changed to Director of Women's Athletics; Culhane held this office until 1988, after which Heather Setzler served a year before the men's and women's directorships were combined. The Directors of Men's Athletics were Tommie Smith (1974–1975; fig. 5.10), followed by Joseph Gurtis Jr. (1975–1988) and Don Hunsinger (1988–1989).

Beginning in 1989, all the administrative duties were combined under a Director of Athletics and Physical Education; this structure remains in place in 2020. A series of regular and interim appointments

FIGURE 7.1. Donald Hunsinger. (Oberlin College Archives)

FIGURE 7.2. Michael Muska. (Oberlin College Athletics)

began with James F. Foels (1989–1994), followed by Don Hunsinger (1994–1998), Michael Muska (1998–2002; fig. 7.2), George Andrews (2002–2003), Vin Lananna (2003–2005), and Joel Karlgaard (2005–2011). Muska was the first openly gay director of athletics in the nation. It was during the time when George Andrews served in an acting capacity that the position was endowed as the Delta Lodge Director of Athletics and Physical Education. James (J. D.) Donovan (fig. 7.3), though not an administrator, had a career with the college during which he recorded and edited all of the school's records and maintained the history of athletics at Oberlin.

Don Hunsinger held the directorship from 1994 to 1998. He had previously served as chair of the Department of Physical Education (1983–1986) and as Director of Men's Athletics (1988–1989). He joined Oberlin in 1972, departed during the Jack Scott era, and then rejoined the department in 1978, remaining at Oberlin until his retirement in 2008. He was a distinguished tennis coach; the current tennis courts off Woodland Avenue are named in his honor. The Hunsinger Award is made each year to a male athlete in the North Coast Athletic Conference (NCAC) who has distinguished himself throughout his collegiate career in the areas of academic achievement, athletic excellence, service, and leadership. A comparable award for females is named after

FIGURE 7.3. J. D. Donovan. (Oberlin College Archives)

Pam Evans, longtime women's tennis and basketball coach at Wittenberg College.

Michael Muska came to Oberlin in 1998 after stops at Auburn, Northwestern, and Brown Universities, where he coached track and field. He filled the position as Director of Athletics and Physical Education until 2002. He left Oberlin to start his own firm to advise preparatory schools in several states.

J. D. Donovan (OC 1961) had a twenty-six-year career teaching and coaching at Oberlin High School, retiring from that position in 1992. Beginning in 1983 and lasting until 2000, J.D. was the lacrosse coach at Oberlin College and an assistant coach for football. He remains active with Oberlin athletics, serving as the historian of the entire program and as a lead organizer for the annual Heisman Club Hall of Fame Induction Ceremony. He is an elected member of the Heisman Club Hall of Honor.

Football

Football has enjoyed a long history among colleges and universities, including several time periods when discussions, which occurred at many institutions, questioned the viability of the program including safety issues, costs, and cheating, among other factors. Oberlin was no exception to these conversations. The subject was addressed on a number of occasions, most recently in the 1990s. To enable the reader to best follow the flow of these events at one college, the story is gathered here, beginning with a brief introduction and proceeding through the decades up until today. The historical path of football as a premier intercollegiate sport begins with contests during the last decades of the nineteenth century. This was followed by widespread interest in the early decades of the twentieth century.

As the expansion occurred, some institutions disbanded their programs for football. Since the 1930s, more than eighty colleges and universities have eliminated football as an intercollegiate sport. Among these are the University of Vermont and Northeastern University, as well as smaller schools like Swarthmore College, MacMurray College, Urbana University, Haverford College, and Morris Brown College. Most recently, Earlham College, part of the NCAC, placed its football program on a suspended status for several years. The issues associated with football programs have some common threads.

Football at Oberlin began with contests played in 1891 against the University of Michigan, Case Tech, and two games with Western Reserve University. It was the second sport played at the intercollegiate level at Oberlin, following baseball. In its early years, Oberlin competed in football with a variety of institutions of all sizes. John Heisman coached the team in 1892 and again in 1894, with a perfect 7-0 record in 1892 that included two victories over Ohio State University and one over the University of Michigan. Oberlin was the last team from the state of Ohio to beat Ohio State University in football, having won the game in 1921 by a score of 7–6. In the first years of the new century, as competition heated up, concern about the spate of serious injuries to football players sparked much discussion and resulted in changes in equipment designed to preserve the game. There was a gradual shift so that by the 1920s bigger schools played each other and smaller colleges played like-sized institutions. Oberlin stopped competing against large universities in football in 1922, though they continued to compete against the bigger schools in minor sports like soccer and lacrosse as late as the 1970s.

Major concerns were that football would become commercialized and that gambling on various aspects of the games would interfere with the credibility of the competition. Small colleges like Oberlin and many others fought diligently to avoid the necessity of doing major recruiting or offering special scholarships to athletes. Beginning by the 1920s and continuing into the 1930s and beyond, the football team and its fortunes were the major focus of sports coverage in the *Oberlin Alumni Magazine*. By the early 1930s there was further discussion on the future of football, with proponents insisting that the college's reputation depended on having a football team; without it, there would be a decline in applications to Oberlin.

For Oberlin, football was the centerpiece of the fall sports calendar. The college remained steadfast in its determination to keep the sport competitive but friendly, so as to be enjoyed by players and spectators alike. In the early years, gate receipts provided sufficient funds to cover most if not all the costs of football and the other intercollegiate team sports. As football costs increased after World War II, this changed, and by the 1950s gate receipts failed to cover the financial needs of the football team, and there were certainly not enough funds to pay for the other men's sports. After about 1950, the college's general budget included a dedicated line item to support the athletics program.

Over the same years, the on-field success of the team declined. For the 1960s (25W-53L-2T) and 1970s (28W-63L), the teams had poor records. The fortunes declined further in the 1980s (24W-72L) and hit an all-time low in the 1990s (3W-95L). The first decade of the twentieth century witnessed some improvement (28W-72L), including three seasons (2003, 2006, 2007) when the team had 5 wins against 5 losses. Twice, there were extended losing streaks. From the last game of the 1992 season through the last game of 1996, the team lost 40 consecutive games. Then, for the period from the second game of 1997 until the sixth game of 2001, they lost 44 straight games. For several seasons, the team had very few players. There were just 16 on the team in 1975 and only 27 in 1977; this increased to 66 by 1979–1980. In the 1975 season, Coach Reindeau was able to say that Oberlin was the only school where he needed only to count the number of players on the bench to make certain that there were 11 men on the field.

Several reviews of the program were undertaken over a forty-year period. These included the Frank Report on the football program (1970), Dean Reich's summary report on the Rebuilding of Physical Education at Oberlin College (1972), the President's Committee on Athletics (1978), a review of Athletics at Oberlin (1983–1984), an outside review (1996), the Report of the Committee on Athletics (1998), and periodic discussions in and votes by the Education Plans and Policies Committee

(EPPC), along with debates in General Faculty meetings. A common theme in the reports, discussions, and recommendations from these groups was the possibility of dropping football as an intercollegiate sport at Oberlin College. There were strong proponents and sound arguments on both sides of the debate. It is noteworthy that the fortunes of some other intercollegiate varsity teams at Oberlin also suffered declines during this period and that portions of the reasoning presented in the following paragraphs can be applied to other sports as well. While men's athletics were the focus of the discussions, there were parallel effects on some women's teams in the last quarter of the twentieth century.

The case for dropping the football program involved at least six lines of thought: (1) A primary concern was the cost of the program. Football is always the most expensive collegiate sport, based on a number of factors, including equipment, maintenance of playing and practice facilities, the number of coaches and players needed, and travel. In the 1970s and 1980s there was increasing concern about the need to allocate equal funding for women's sports based on the requirements of Title IX. At several junctures over the decades, the college faced varying degrees of financial constraints; budget and program cuts were needed. Football was often the obvious and easiest choice when decreases to the athletics program funding were discussed. (2) A decline in student interest, evidenced for example by the numbers cited above, was coupled with issues surrounding the recruitment of student athletes for the program. (3) Attracting enough football players became a problem in the 1970s, with a total of only 31 men on the roster in 1974 and, as noted above, just 27 in 1977–1978. Even though this number had increased to 66 by 1979–1980, the squads from Oberlin, to the beginning of the third decade of the twenty-first century, almost always have fewer players than their opponents. (4) Finding a qualified head coach and a sufficient number of suitable assistants was sometimes an issue. (5) Another concern was for the health and safety of the players. With men of greater physical size on some of the opposing teams, the smaller Oberlin athletes could suffer serious injuries. It was often necessary for Oberlin, with limited players available, to use just one set of individuals playing both offense and defense compared to opponents who could field two platoons. (6) Finally, some who argued for dropping football expressed concerns about the likelihood of success for the future of the sport at Oberlin even if football remained as part of the athletics program.

On the other side of the question, those in favor of retaining football as an intercollegiate sport at Oberlin marshaled a series of arguments: (1) Football was a key drawing card to attract male applicants to the school. For much of the period under discussion, the potential applicant pool was shifting more toward female students, and some felt that steps needed to be taken to insure a continued interest in the college by males. (2) Athletics, including football, is a primary driver in terms of attracting male students from diverse backgrounds to enroll at Oberlin. (3) Having football is a way of attracting the attention of alumni and aiding the development office with fundraising. Associated with this was the perennial complaint from coaches and athletics administrators that alumni did not do an effective job of aiding the recruiting process by encouraging the best scholar athletes in their geographical areas to apply to the college. (4) The facilities for athletics also serve the entire college community and the people of Oberlin. (5) There was a consensus that improved, targeted recruitment of student athletes interested in playing football would boost interest in and performance by the team. One issue that arises when a team has a run of years of poor performance is that the school's athletics reputation suffers in terms of high school athletes wishing to apply for admission and their coaches providing less than stellar comments on the program at the college. (6) Supporters point to the Heisman Club with its fundraising efforts, commenced in the late 1970s, which resulted in one of the largest single-purpose funds ever at Oberlin. The perspective of those favoring retention of football was that concentrated efforts on and off the playing field would help resolve the funding problem, though it might take several years due to the "halo effect," whereby there is often a lag in terms of implementing changes and the actual response from students and their high school coaches.

In each instance, when debate ended with a vote, there was either a majority in favor of retaining football, or in at least one instance, a tie vote concerning a recommendation to be taken to the General Faculty from the President's Committee (1978).

A key event for keeping the football program was the founding of the Heisman Club. Started in 1978 to support athletics at Oberlin, the major impetus for the formation of this organization was a strong desire to aid the football program. At the outset, the club raised almost $250,000 for that purpose. The initial funds also enabled the college to hire new assistant coaches in one women's and one men's sport. Another factor that promoted saving football was dropping out of the Ohio Athletic Conference (OAC) to help found the North Coast Athletic Conference (NCAC). The new conference leveled the playing field for the weaker football schools that formed the new conference while the stronger football schools remained in the old conference.

Approaching the New Millennium

During the 1990s three reports were presented concerning athletics and physical education at Oberlin: (1) The first was commissioned by President Fred Starr; the response was authored by then Director of Athletics, James Foels, in September 1993. (2) A Report to the Committee on Athletics was submitted in 1998 by an outside group consisting of representatives from three liberal arts colleges—Carleton, Earlham, and Wittenberg. (3) A Strategic Planning Team consisting of individuals from Oberlin submitted a series of recommendations attached to the outside report. Many common threads appear in these documents. A summary of the combined recommendations provides insights regarding the prospects and plans for athletics and physical education at Oberlin College during the first decades of the twenty-first century. The major points include the following:

A. After fifteen years of playing sports in the North Coast Athletic Conference, Oberlin produced a single conference championship—in women's cross country. However, the college's record for attaining both team and individual All-American status was impressive. One proposed step toward addressing the problem of competitiveness involved admissions and financial aid. A practice that occurs at many Division III institutions involves allocation of some slots in each class for scholar athletes who meet all other criteria for admission. Oberlin offers admission and financial aid to students wishing to attend the Conservatory of Music, but not for scholar athletes. Appeals could be made to alumni both for assistance in the recruitment of qualified students with superior athletic abilities and for donating additional funds to the college to support financial aid.
B. Funding resource issues were addressed in all of the documents. More funds were needed to augment coaching staffs in a number of sports. Increasing facilities maintenance and operating costs occurred

without additional budget allocations. Monies were needed to maintain standards for uniforms, ancillary equipment, and transportation to away contests. Clearly, alumni would be a good source for such funds, but additional support from the general college budget was also needed. The creation of the Heisman Club in 1978 was noted in the previous section. This provided a new source for garnering enthusiasm and funding for Oberlin College athletics.

C. The first report noted that about 50% of the college population engaged in physical education department course offerings, through several different activities. The review felt that this level of participation could be enhanced by doubling the amount of credit awarded, from one-half credit to a full credit. Another report addressed what was labeled as the "Oberlin Culture." The issue centered on whether students at the college were not motivated to engage in physical activity, which resulted in some lack of individual self-esteem. Perhaps a survey of the students would provide valuable insight to guide changes that would enhance opportunities for enjoyment of physical exercise.

D. In one report, the club and intramural sports programs were generally lauded for their extent and levels of participation. Here also, recommendations pushed for additional funding and the hiring of a director to coordinate these activities. By contrast, another of the reports expressed concerns about the lack of participation in the club and intramurals programs. It was felt that a key root of the problem was the inability of the college to attract students with sufficient concern about their physical well-being.

E. A final theme concerned the need to expand the opportunities for health and wellness for students along with faculty and staff. This harkens back to the earlier philosophies that combined mental activity (mind) with physical activity (body). This issue was addressed by providing renewed emphasis on fitness programs. The strongest efforts to address the matter occurred in the second decade of the twenty-first century and are covered in chapter 9.

Two quotes, one each from the first two reports, nicely summarize the findings and hopes for the future:

A complete liberal education at Oberlin College should prepare students to succeed individually and as a member of a group combining physical and mental excellence.

Wellness programs increase productivity, decrease absenteeism, and reduce time lost to illness, accidents or injury resulting in a decrease in college personnel costs.

Facilities

Oberlin continued to make changes, through both new construction and renovation of existing facilities, during the twenty-year period covered by this chapter. Similar transformations occurred at all of the peer institutions. The current status of buildings and playing fields for sports on the Oberlin campus and at peer schools is reviewed in chapter 8. Several key structures were added during the period 1991–2010, replacing older locations and fields. The John W. Heisman Club Field House (fig. 7.4; map, fig. 0.5) opened in 1992. It is located behind and to the east of the Philips Center. This ended the last uses of Warner and Hales Gymnasiums for athletics competitions. The new facility, connected to the Philips Physical Education Center via a corridor and lounge, provided new venues for a number of sports (fig. 7.5). It has a six-lane 200-meter

FIGURE 7.4. The John W. Heisman Club Field House, located east of the Philips Center, features an indoor track and tennis courts. (Lee C. Drickamer)

FIGURE 7.5. Indoor track with a Super X surface (top) and indoor tennis courts (bottom) in the Heisman Club Field House. (Lee C. Drickamer)

indoor track and a set of four full-sized tennis courts. These provide for indoor practice and a venue for contests during inclement weather. The field house is used for a variety of other purposes, including banquets, meetings of professional groups, and community events.

FIGURE 7.6. An external view of the Williams Field House. The interior has a Tiger Turf surface. (Lee C. Drickamer)

Cross country meets were generally staged at the athletics fields for many decades, with a brief hiatus when the College Arboretum was used. The courses, which varied over time but differed for men's and women's teams, use portions of the North Fields (map, fig. 0.5), the solar array, adjacent woodlands, and existing playing fields, sometimes including "Oberlin Mountain" on the east side of Galpin Field (fig. 5.13) across from the Heisman Field House with its white roof.

When the college discontinued the varsity intercollegiate ice hockey program in 1978, a club team replaced it for some years, playing in Elyria after use of the ice rink at the college was discontinued. In 2006 the structure was converted to become the Williams Field House (fig. 7.6), an enclosed facility with artificial turf. It is a LEED Gold certified building and is the location for a variety of sports, recreational activities, and team practices.

With the completion of the Robert Lewis Kahn Track and Fred Shults Playing Field Complex in 2006, three sports, played by both men's and women's teams, moved to the new venue (fig. 7.7; map, fig. 0.5). The new facility, with lights, spectator seating, and a press box, hosts soccer, lacrosse, and track and field competitions. Fred Shults was a longtime member of the Physical Education Department and coach at

FIGURE 7.7. The Robert Lewis Kahn Track and Fred Shults Field. The grandstand is located on the east side, and the field is used for both soccer and lacrosse. (Oberlin College Athletics)

Oberlin (fig. 7.8). Robert Lewis Kahn is a significant benefactor of the college in the first decades of the twenty-first century.

Fredrick D. Shults (fig. 7.8) graduated from Oberlin in 1954, where he captained the baseball and soccer teams and was an All-American in soccer for 1953. The soccer team never lost a game during his three-year playing career. He later obtained a master's degree from Ohio State University (1959) and his doctoral degree from Indiana University (1967). He returned to Oberlin and taught Methods and Techniques of Physical Education, Sport Sociology, and The Competitive Ethic in the major program. He coached (1957–1959, 1961–1993) at his alma mater with a primary focus on soccer, though he also led the lacrosse team for some years (1961–1974, 1977–1980). He was a tireless advocate for the student athlete and adhered to strong feelings about his principles concerning the importance of the mind–body harmony involved in physical education and athletics. He was a successful coach, compiling an overall record with the soccer team of 220W-162L-52T. He also had a winning record with the lacrosse team of 88W-80L-6T. He and his older brother, Robert Shults, are both members of the Heisman Club Hall of Fame.

Today, the North Fields (fig. 7.9; map, fig. 0.5), covering more than seventy-five acres, serve multiple functions. Some varsity athletics teams use the area for practice. Both club teams and intramurals use the fields

FIGURE 7.9. A view of a portion of the North Fields with a soccer goal, a lacrosse goal, and goal posts all dotting the landscape, indicative of the variety of sports that are played and practiced on these grounds. (Lee C. Drickamer)

FIGURE 7.8. Fredrick D. Shults. (Oberlin College Athletics)

during fall and spring seasons. For a time, a stone wall on the North Fields was used for lacrosse, by throwing the ball at the wall and playing the carom. For soccer, the athlete kicked the ball against the wall and played the rebound.

Tennis courts for the college existed in at least eight locations and perhaps more since the sport first appeared on campus in the 1890s. These include Tappan Square, in front of Council Hall, at Athletic Park, at the corner of Morgan and Professor Streets (map, fig. 0.5), behind what is now Mercy Allen Hospital, a court on the west side of Savage Stadium, clay courts near the men's baseball diamond (fig. 4.12), and the present venue just east of Woodland Street at the western edge of Galpin Field (fig. 5.13). These courts were named for Don Hunsinger in 2008 (fig. 7.10).

Many of the college athletics facilities are shared with the local community. The various gymnasiums and other indoor areas—such as weight rooms—are used by college students, staff, and faculty for physical fitness and recreation. Club sports teams and intramurals have access to these same areas for their competitions. For four decades, people from the extended Oberlin area have been able to purchase a pass to access the various facilities. Venues like the football stadium, soccer field, track, tennis courts, and basketball court are scheduled by arrangements

FIGURE 7.10. The Hunsinger Tennis Courts, six pairs of outdoor courts with an all-weather surface. (Oberlin College Athletics)

between the college and Oberlin City Schools for interscholastic competitions and regional meets by state high school associations. The variety of venues at the college athletics complex serves as a bridge connecting the town and college and for the benefit of all who are part of the greater college community.

Summary

Set against a backdrop of world events that changed the way we live in terms of technology and globalization, some events in physical education and athletics also moved at a rapid pace. Winning at all costs became the predominant philosophy for bigger schools. This affects participation in sports at all levels, extending downward to youth leagues, and for both men and women. The almost-complete commercialization of college and university athletics resulted in a strong divergence between the small colleges like Oberlin and all other large- and medium-sized institutions following a path involving heavy emphases on recruitment, financial aid, and the emergence of a separate class of student athletes. Though Oberlin is successful in maintaining the balance between academics and athletics, there are ongoing shifts toward specialization in a single sport and holding off-season practices. The college athletic policy stresses the same goals as in previous decades—personal growth, leadership and teamwork, character development, physical fitness, and athletic excellence, to name just a few. Factors like specialization and recruitment have now emerged at smaller schools. Although Oberlin retains its primary philosophy regarding the combination of academics and physical activities, it now emphasizes serving the better athletes at the varsity team level over students at the bottom of the pyramid (fig. 0.3).

Sources Consulted for Chapter 7

Full citations are found at the end of the book.

Bowen, W. G., and S. A. Levin. *Reclaiming the Game: College Sports and Educational Values.*

Brandt, L. J. *The Evolution of Women's Intercollegiate Athletics at Oberlin College.*

Eitzen, D. S. *Sport in Contemporary Society.*

Guttmann, A. *A Whole New Ball Game: An Interpretation of American Sports.*

Hanford, G. H. *An Inquiry into the Need for and Feasibility of a National Study of Intercollegiate Athletics.*

Knight Foundation. *Report of the Commission on Intercollegiate Athletics.*

Mechikoff, R. A., and S. G. Estes. *A History and Philosophy of Sport and Physical Education.*

Shulman, J. L., and W. G. Bowen. *The Game of Life: College Sports and Educational Values.*

Shults, F. D. *The History and Philosophy of Athletics for Men at Oberlin College.*

Welch, P. D. *History of American Physical Education and Sport.*

CHAPTER 8

The Present and Future Directions

2011–2021 and Beyond

Period Events and Introduction

The last chapter examines the most recent period, from 2011 to the present. It explores the status of the department and programs, provides an update on Oberlin's recent additions to its venues for athletics and recreation, examines the growing interest in health and wellness, and concludes with some thoughts on current issues and what may lie ahead in future decades of the first half of the twenty-first century. Comparisons are made between Oberlin College and peer institutions for current facilities for athletic and recreation; regarding opportunities for study and majors in areas pertaining to physical education, health, and exercise science; and on developments in the area of health and wellness.

During the past ten years, the predominance of sports as a major cultural feature of peoples all around the globe continues to expand. With military and endemic conflicts occurring worldwide, many people surviving as refugees from such conflicts, and in areas where poverty is still the norm, sports has become a universal vehicle for goodwill, cooperation, and friendship. Played at all age levels across six continents, sports like soccer (football in most of the world), basketball, and tennis, among others, bring together people both within and between countries. The number of professional leagues for both men and women now encompasses more than a dozen sports in the US, Canada, and Europe; professional teams are playing worldwide. Media coverage of all types has proliferated, and fans follow their favorite teams on diverse electronic devices from televisions to computers to cell phones while using applications like Twitter and similar platforms to provide instantaneous communication.

Athletics on a Global Scale

For athletics, the underlying philosophy has remained as at the end of the previous century. Winning contests in almost all sports is the primary and, in many cases, the only goal. This attitude permeates all levels of competition, from pee wee football to professional sports. The only acceptable outcome and source of enjoyment is beating the other team or player. Some individual sports, like golf and tennis, exhibit more sportsmanship and friendliness than team sports. The momentum behind the win-at-all-cost has been passed on to second- and third-generation athletes and their supporters. There are several exceptions to this general statement. Many recreation leagues in, for example, basketball and softball, and events like weekend golf competitions do not have the same level of competitiveness just noted. Also, for many small liberal arts colleges and some smaller schools with religious affiliations, sports are still played for enjoyment, for gaining experience with traits such as cooperation and teamwork, and for character development.

The stakes are enormous in terms of the financial aspects of most sports. Large venues such as stadiums and arenas require funding in the hundreds of millions of dollars and even up to one billion or more in some instances, while salaries for coaches have ballooned budgets for athletics at many colleges and universities. Gambling is now legalized across much of the nation, adding another dimension to sports. Recall the days of Charles W. Savage and J. Herbert Nichols at Oberlin College, with their staunch opposition to the commercialization of athletics and the concerns about betting on college sports. This aversion diminished gradually over the last half of the previous century and then disappeared in the first two decades of the new millennium. Modern athletics at the college level bear little resemblance to those a hundred years ago. Just as society itself has changed, athletics have reflected trends and innovations in aspects of culture. The questions that arise now have more to do with what lies ahead. With money as a primary driver of all aspects of athletics, more scandals will emerge of the sorts that are being discovered and adjudicated each year. Does the continued expansion of sports on national and international stages, media coverage, and increased financial involvement from sponsors and advertisers portend problems? What if the growth passes some threshold for interest in major sports, and then declines, removing a significant portion of the financial underpinnings? What will happen now that some students are permitted to receive funds for their likeness and name?

Athletics at Oberlin

Joel Karlgaard (fig. 8.1) served during a transition into the twentieth century. He laid some of the groundwork for the years of changes that followed his departure in 2011. Initially, two coaches, Ray Appenheimer and Natalie Winkelfoos, shared the athletics directorship on an interim basis. The college then hired William Roth, who remained at Oberlin for just one year. Beginning in 2012, Natalie Winkelfoos (fig. 8.2) served one year as interim and, since 2013, as Delta Lodge Director of Athletics and Physical Education. She is the first woman to hold this role and is now the longest-serving person as athletics director since the position was established in 1989. She moved Oberlin's program forward in three ways. First, she played primary roles in raising funds for construction of the Knowlton Athletic Complex and the Shanks Health and Wellness Center, the remodeling of Carr Pool, and the updating of the Philips Physical Education Center. Second, Winkelfoos furthered the growth of interest in health and wellness. Third, she injected a winning spirit into the college athletics program.

Oberlin continues to strive to remain true to its founding philosophy, integrating academics and athletics. The guiding statement of principles, articulated as of 2018, provides the following goals and policies for sports at Oberlin:

1. The mission of the Department of Athletics and Physical Education is inseparable from the mission of Oberlin College.
2. The department will endeavor to instill in our athletes, student body, and other stakeholders the joy, power, and extraordinary personal growth that come to those who pursue athletic excellence, physical fitness, and overall wellness.

FIGURE 8.1. Joel Karlgaard joined the department in 2005 on an acting basis and became the Delta Lodge Director of Athletics and Physical Education in 2006. He served for five years, departing in early 2011 to become Associate Director of Athletics at Stanford University. Karlgaard was instrumental in improving the competitiveness of the college's athletics teams and in raising funds to support the program. He helped generate and implement ideas to foster a growing interest in health and wellness in everyday college life. (Oberlin College Athletics)

FIGURE 8.2. Natalie Winkelfoos is the Associate Vice President and Delta Lodge Director of Athletics and Physical Education. She received her B.A. degree from Baldwin Wallace, where she was a leading member of the basketball team, and an M.S. degree in education from Kent State University. Winkelfoos was named the Division III Under Armour Athletic Director of the Year for 2017–2018. (Oberlin College Athletics)

3. The department is committed to the personal development and well-being of the student body and college community.
4. The individuals who participate in our programs at all levels can learn the benefits of teamwork, discipline, goal-setting, physical fitness, character development, self-confidence, and the joy of achievement. We are committed to offering a competitive and recreational environment that fosters these personal attributes.
5. Therefore, it will be the purpose if the Department of Athletics and Physical Education to significantly improve its performance within this philosophical framework in order to strengthen the leadership position that Oberlin College has occupied among American educational institutions since its inception.

In addition to this general statement of goals, two documents govern activities in the department. The Title IX Policy spells out principles and procedures pertaining to efforts for establishing and maintaining equality for women in all matters involving athletics and physical education. It also defines the role of the Title IX Coordinator, who works with the Gender Equity in Athletics Review (GEAR) Committee. A grievance procedure is spelled out for anyone who feels that there has been a violation. The other policy, Guidelines for Inclusion and Respectful Treatment of Intercollegiate Transgender Athletes, covers overarching principles and important details about issues like privacy, participation in sports and intercollegiate athletics, availability of resources on specific topics pertaining to and assistance of transgender students, and compliance with all state and federal laws. The transgender policy incorporates the conditions under which individuals who have gone through a sex change procedure are eligible to participate on same and mixed-sex teams and the role of hormone treatments in these designations. Oberlin has a program for Preventing and Responding to Sexual Misconduct (PRSM), which involves trained peers who provide education to all students on topics that include gender-based discrimination and harassment, sexual and intimate partner violence, and stalking.

Some points from prior athletics policies at Oberlin and from peer institutions are incorporated into the rules and regulations promulgated by the North Coast Athletic Conference. These include matters pertaining to admissions, recruitment, and financial aid. Some peer schools now offer Leadership Scholarships, aimed at attracting students who have excelled in various aspects of student life during high school. This includes leadership roles in organizations such as student government, athletics, and community groups, among others. Some schools view this as a means to attract good athletes who have been team captains or primary stars at their high schools by providing them scholarships. However, Oberlin does not grant Leadership Scholarships. The Office of Admissions and Department of Athletics and Physical Education coordinate some activities to help identify and recruit students for the college who have strong abilities in various sports and who also hope to obtain a superior academic education. Oberlin coaches and assistants can, as part of the recruitment process, approach prospective students to encourage them to apply. Success in attracting well-qualified student athletes requires a thorough knowledge of and appreciation for the strong academic programs offered at Oberlin, as well as the successes enjoyed by graduates when they complete their B.A. degree and go forward to pursue careers or to further their education.

A worrisome issue exists between the athletics program, including both coaches and student athletes, and the general faculty and overall student body. Beginning with the change from faculty status to administrative and professional appointments for members of the Physical Education and Athletics Department in 1989, the lives of most coaches followed a separate pathway for interactions with members of academic departments and with much of the college administration. This isolation is problematic from the perspective of maintaining a viable community spirit with effective communication across the entire college.

In recent decades, the housing arrangements on campus involve particular dormitories that house predominantly athletes. Many of these housing units are located near the north end of the campus, where the athletics facilities are concentrated. Thus, the geographical proximity contributes to the perceived division between athletics and the general student body. Another factor for many sports, where figures are available, is that attendance at athletic events is much lower than at peer institutions. Students appear reluctant to participate as spectators for the intercollegiate contests. Ongoing discussions should address these issues and attempt to provide possible solutions.

Facilities and Peer Comparisons

The physical plant for athletics, physical education, club sports, and intramurals at Oberlin is excellent and on par with its peers. Virtually all buildings and playing fields that existed in 1970 have been replaced or upgraded. The Philips Physical Education Center was completed and opened in 1971 with just over 115,000 ft^2; its facilities were described in chapter 6. The main entryway includes an impressive display of historical photographs arranged down several hallways. The entire memberships of the Heisman Club Hall of Fame and Heisman Club Hall of Honor are featured on one wall, providing a fine welcome to everyone who enters the building. There is also a complete photo history for all teams in all sports dating back to the 1890s. Recently, the Carr Pool (fig. 8.3) was entirely rebuilt and now serves not only as a venue for regular swim meets, but also for conference and regional championships.

FIGURE 8.3. A view (2018) of the renovated Carr swimming and diving pool in the Jesse Philips Physical Education Center. (Lee C. Drickamer)

The baseball facility, Dill Field (fig. 8.4; map, fig. 0.5) has a newly added press box (named for Jack Dunn), recent irrigation work, and a new backstop and netting. Culhane softball field was dedicated in 2000, at the time the women's intercollegiate softball program began (fig. 8.5; map, fig. 0.5). Renovations in 2013 included irrigation changes and a new scoreboard. As of 2018, a new grandstand and press box were added, and the entire facility is named Dolcemaschio Stadium to recognize the donors for the upgrades. The area beyond these two facilities is called the North Fields (fig. 7.9). As covered in earlier chapters, the area is home to club sports, intramurals, and practice areas, and its perimeter is used as a portion of the cross country courses.

In February 2008, the George Jones Field House was deemed unusable because of a cracked structural beam; it was razed in 2009. At the conclusion of the 2013 football season, Savage Stadium and its related facilities were demolished. Construction of the Austin E. Knowlton Athletics Complex (fig. 8.6; map, fig. 0.5) commenced immediately and was completed in time for dedication and use in September 2014. The Knowlton Foundation provided $8 million of the $11.3 million funding

FIGURE 8.4. Dill Field, with the Jack Dunn press box, is the home of Oberlin College baseball. The press box is named in honor of a prominent Oberlin baseball player. The infield is a mixture of dirt and Turface. The outfield is blue grass (80%) and perennial rye grass (20%). (Oberlin College Athletics)

FIGURE 8.5. Dolcemaschio Stadium with Culhane Field is the home of Oberlin College softball, with new grandstands and a press box. The playing surfaces are the same combination of artificial and grass mixture as for Dill Field. The North Fields are visible at the top of the photo beyond the row of pines. (Oberlin College Athletics)

FIGURE 8.6. An aerial view of the Knowlton Athletics Complex, opened in 2015, looking southwest. Bailey Field and Knowlton Stadium have a social and meeting structure to the left of the grandstand. The south end zone structure features locker rooms for sports teams using the venues at the stadium and neighboring facilities. The Williams Field House is visible in the top center of the photograph, as is a corner of the Heisman Club Field House. (Oberlin College Athletics)

needed for construction. The Knowlton Foundation, started in 1981 by Mr. A. E. Knowlton, who owned a large construction company, provides funds to colleges in Ohio to promote and advance American higher education. This multifaceted set of structures features a new grandstand and press box, a smaller grandstand for the visiting team, a facility with spaces for social gatherings and meetings, and an extensive locker room building.

In addition to football and field hockey, the Dick Bailey Field at Knowlton Stadium (fig. 8.6) is used for soccer, lacrosse, and high school athletics. The state-of-the-art artificial grass is used for college events such as ultimate Frisbee and other club team contests. The social center portion of the Knowlton Complex frequently houses events of a variety of types staged by the Department of Athletics and Physical Education, by various units of the college, and for private functions.

In October 2018, Oberlin celebrated the opening of the new Patricia (OC 1963) and Merrill (OC 1961) Shanks Health and Wellness Center,

FIGURE 8.7. Entryway and outdoor patio of the Patricia (OC 1963) and Merrill (OC 1961) Shanks Health and Wellness Center. (Oberlin College Athletics)

constructed adjacent to the Philips Physical Education Center (figs. 8.7, 8.8; map, fig. 0.5). The primary funding for the new facility was provided by Mrs. and Mr. Shanks. It is located to the east of and is connected with the Philips Physical Education Center. A period of growing interest in physical well-being as a necessary part of education began several decades ago and intensified in the new millennium. The facility has a number of smaller rooms for classes, including yoga, Zumba, conditioning exercises, and boxing.

Facilities for athletics, physical education classes, and recreation are vital parts of every campus. They are critical for attracting and retaining students, providing spaces for club and intramural sports, and giving students, faculty, and staff places for exercise. They often serve as a bridge between a college and the local community. Given their importance, it is worthwhile to compare venues at schools that are peer institutions for Oberlin College: Allegheny College; Denison University; Earlham College; Kenyon College; Ohio Wesleyan University; College of Wooster; and Wabash College. Most of these schools have facilities and playing fields for sports which are concentrated in one area of the campus.

For the physical structures at Kenyon, Denison, Wooster, Wabash, and Oberlin, there is a single complex, sometimes with several inter-

FIGURE 8.8. Full view of the main exercise room in the Shanks Health and Wellness Center with multiple types of cardio exercise machines. (Lee C. Drickamer)

connected structures, that serves as the locus for all indoor athletics, as well as portions of the offerings for intramurals and club teams. At the other three schools, there are several facilities that combine to meet these same needs. The single most comprehensive and newest of these buildings is the Kenyon Athletic Center (2006). Other schools, including Oberlin, have made substantial renovations and upgrades in the past decade to buildings that range in age from twenty to more than fifty years old in terms of their original construction. Such is the case of the Philips Physical Education Center at Oberlin (opened in 1970), which combined with the Heisman Club Field House provides a full set of indoor venues for the college teams. An overall assessment of the available indoor infrastructure across campuses shows perhaps slight advantages for several of the schools, but there are no major differences in terms of the ability to attract athletes and those students who wish to engage in various form of recreation, exercise, and sports. There are, however, examples of stand-out programs, such as swimming at Kenyon, that have built reputations in terms of national championships for both teams and individuals. These serve as beacons for students interested in and skilled in a particular sport, guiding them to choose a specific institution.

For outdoor locations, there is perhaps more variation. The newest complex for football is the Knowlton Stadium at Oberlin (2015), though Earlham also has a relatively new stadium (2007). The other schools have all made renovations and upgrades in the last 10–15 years, including lights for nighttime activities. In addition to football, other sports, including field hockey, lacrosse, and soccer, are often played on the same surface at many schools, whereas others have separate playing areas for some of these competitions. At most locations, the outdoor track is part of the stadium complex. Oberlin's Kahn-Shults Field (2006), which serves track and field, soccer, and lacrosse, is unique among the conference schools. Others, like Kenyon, have made major renovations to their track facilities in the last ten years. Most schools established softball facilities when the conference added this sport for women in the late 1990s. Each institution has a baseball complex and a set of outdoor tennis courts. Several areas are mapped out for cross country courses, some located in proximity to the main campus and athletics venues, and several at a distance from campus. Fields for practice, intramurals, and club sports are present at all of the schools, though they vary in size. Oberlin's North Fields, along with Galpin Field, are likely the largest in terms of total acreage. As with the indoor capabilities, there do not appear to be any significant differences in terms of the outdoor venues and the ability to attract scholar athletes.

Health and Wellness

In 2008, Joel Karlgaard, Director of Athletics and Physical Education from 2005 to 2011, joined with the Division of Student Life to convene a two-week initiative to engage students, faculty, and staff in the pursuit of health and wellness. Under the sponsorship of the Office of the President, this event, termed "OB Fit," became an annual affair intended to foster a healthy culture and to promote lifetime participation in a variety of sports. Though the OB Fit is no longer a concentrated two-week period, the experience highlighted the need to consider physical activity as a necessary, important part of daily life. Both then President Marvin Krislov and current President Carmen Twillie Ambar are strong advocates for, and regular users of, exercise facilities offered at the college. The mind–body harmony, part of the original Learning and Labor motto, as embedded in the Oberlin College seal, is moving to a renewed level of importance.

A primary goal of the newly opened Shanks Health and Wellness Center is fostering healthy connections between mind and body. This, of course, has been a prevailing theme in this book and represents a process of coming full circle to the original philosophy for exercise and recreation at Oberlin, dating back to the mid-1800s. The need for this facility germinated over several decades. A driving force for its construction resulted from student demands for better access to facilities for their own physical well-being. In addition to exercise spaces, there is a room where the College Counseling Center holds drop-in hours for students, and areas for use as primary resource locations for the Office of Disability Support Services and the Center for Student Success. The major funding for this project, a visionary gift from Patricia and Merrill Shanks, was augmented by other donors. A wall in the entryway to the Shanks Center displays the names of those who helped make the Health and Wellness Center possible.

A new effort, initiated prior to opening the Shanks facility, but enhanced and expanded by the new spaces, is "YeoFit." This program features classes scheduled five mornings each week, taught by coaches, assistant coaches, college staff, and several community members. Sessions are held in various rooms and in the main exercise area of the Shanks Center. Activities include various forms and levels of yoga, aqua bootcamp and aquafit held in Carr Pool, first time fitness, cardio boxing, spinning and epic revolution using special bicycles, stretching and flexibility, and others. YeoFit became popular at its inception, and attendance has increased steadily with the new facility.

In addition, the college maintains a roster of physical activity classes "to contribute to the liberal education of students through experiences in movement and to encourage their physical and mental well being" (Oberlin YeoFit webpage, 2022). There are more than forty classes for everything from running and racquet sports to horseback riding and weight training. The list includes instruction and playing opportunities for almost all of the sports that are part of the men's and women's intercollegiate teams. Finally, there are classes in Exploring Personal Fitness, and Independent Fitness.

How do the facilities and programs for fitness and recreation at Oberlin College compare with similar endeavors at peer institutions?

With variations and differences in the ages of the buildings involved, all of the schools examined have more than sufficient facilities to accommodate the needs of the college community for physical fitness activities. The venues used at the seven schools used for this comparison ranged from buildings that served both the athletics program and exercise opportunities to separate, dedicated structures or designated portions of a building, for students and others to access spaces and equipment for physical activities. There was always some overlap with the facilities and fields for varsity teams and recreation, including intramurals and club sports, and for aquatics at all of these peer locations. The schools with dedicated facilities are Oberlin and Allegheny. Portions of indoor venues at Kenyon, Wooster, Denison, Ohio Wesleyan, and Earlham have special sections of their main athletics facility set aside for exercise and recreational use. Most schools have a fitness center with exercise machines and free weights, sometimes shared with athletics teams.

With respect to programs, each school has exercise classes and equipment, courts, and pool time for student, staff, and faculty use. The Kenyon Fit and Oberlin YeoFit offerings appear, from catalogues and websites, to be more complete at this time and are promoted more heavily to the campus community. In addition to these primarily indoor programs, all schools, except Wooster and Wabash, have both intramurals and club sports. The number of offerings in these two categories varies widely across institutions: Allegheny (12 intramurals/11 club sports); Denison (9/31); Earlham (8/7); Kenyon (14/10); Oberlin (10/19); Ohio Wesleyan (9/11); Wabash (5/0); and Wooster (0/14). Several values could not be determined. Also, schools use somewhat different definitions for what constitutes a club or intramural sport, and there is some year-to-year variation in the availability of particular sports. Using these observations, Oberlin would be classified among the top tier of schools in this group, in terms of its new facilities and the recreational offerings for exercise, intramurals, and club sports.

Future of Athletics and Physical Education at Oberlin

With strong support from the college administration and its president, Carmen Twillie Ambar, excellent leadership in the Department of Athletics and Physical Education in the person of Natalie Winkelfoos, and state-of-the-art buildings and playing fields, Oberlin is positioned to move forward into the third decade of the new century. The athletic programs, both men's and women's squads, are striving to improve their records and to produce team and individual champions in several sports.

The current roster of intercollegiate teams includes ten for men and eleven for women. Both genders have swimming and diving, track and field, basketball, soccer, cross country, lacrosse, indoor and outdoor track and field, and tennis. In addition, women have teams in volleyball, field hockey, and softball. Men also play football and baseball. Currently, there are more than 400 student athletes at the college (ca. 15% of the enrollment). This number has expanded over the past decade. The college remains a strongly committed part of the North Coast Athletic Conference (NCAC), of which it was a founding member in 1984. The NCAC became the first conference in the nation to provide fully equal treatment, in all matters, to both women and men. In this regard, it served as a model for many other campuses.

The current organizational structure of the Department of Athletics and Physical Education is headed by Natalie Winkelfoos, who serves as Associate Vice President and Delta Lodge Director of Athletics and Physical Education. She has eighteen people who report to her, including three associate directors, a director of sports medicine, an administrative assistant, and head coaches for the men's and women's varsity sports teams. Most coaches have one or more assistant coaches, some of whom are involved with teaching activities courses and YeoFit classes. Others serve in capacities such as building managers, media relations, and Title IX Coordinator.

Current Issues

Two partially interconnected issues are currently the focus of discussions at Oberlin. First is the tendency to view athletes and non-athletes as distinctly different populations of students on campus. Second is to continue to develop opportunities pertaining to health and wellness, including possible academic programs comparable to those at some peer institutions.

As noted earlier, a pattern of social division and separation has emerged in recent decades, between student athletes and their classmates at the college; this is of concern for several reasons. Oberlin has always been one united community, despite the existence of different interest groups. The social and physical divide seems to have expanded for the student athlete group. This pattern leads to an unnecessary and potentially harmful discrimination, relegating athletes to a lower-status category. Though the common stereotype of "jocks" is prevalent at bigger institutions, it is hoped that this would not be the case at places like Oberlin. However, it does exist and has been manifested in both oral comments and online discussions, with pejorative connotations assigned to athletes. Third, the open distinction of athletes and non-athletes could be detrimental to applications and admissions to the college. While this may seem counterintuitive, prospective students who visit the campus with their parents are sensitive to this division, either from their tour guides' comments or from interactions with current students. This can be off-putting for both athletes and non-athletes; it may discourage an individual from completing the application process or selecting Oberlin after being admitted to several schools. Efforts to change this climate of separation should be a focus of thoughtful and perhaps innovative efforts, both now and in the near future.

Of note is a comparable situation with students in the Conservatory of Music, which is sometimes referred to as the "other half" of the college. Here too, students engage in extensive, concentrated practice, provide performances, and exhibit a high degree of dedication. Music majors tend to live and eat in groups, mainly on the south campus near where the conservatory is located. There is a clear distinction between "connies" and liberal arts students. Thus, there is the same tendency to stereotype music majors as there is with athletes. Some consideration should be given to integrating these students into the general undergraduate population. Lessons may be learned from both groups in terms of how to maintain and foster the sense of community that is Oberlin College. For both athletes and musicians, there is a potential disconnect between the narrow, time-consuming focus on practice and performance accompanied by the required individual intensity and dedication which leads to a concomitant lack of interest in other ongoing activities and events in the greater campus community. What are the possibilities that lie ahead, to integrate these two student groups into the larger community? Oberlin is not unique in facing these issues. Exploring similar situations at other, peer institutions should provide helpful insights.

One promising development concerning the issue of stereotyping athletes was a course cluster, or learning community, arranged by Yago Colás, then a faculty member in the English Department. The cluster consisted of three interrelated classes encompassing Sport, Culture, and Society. Together, these topics addressed the issues raised by the separation of athletes from non-athletes. One class, 13 Ways of Looking at Sports, combined philosophy, literature, cultural studies, sociology, economics, and natural sciences, to examine sports and related cultural norms. A second class aided students wishing to assess sports critically as a social practice, holding possibilities for challenging social inequalities, especially those involving race and ethnicity, gender, social class, and gender identity. The third class, Sport and Community, probed academic concepts studied in the first two courses, through students participating in initiatives both across campus and in the Oberlin Public Schools. He also organized a series of discussions termed "Athletics 101," which explored ways in which stereotypes of athletes originate and what might be done to counter the cultural and community divide that this categorization appears to create. Colás left Oberlin College in the summer of 2019. Perhaps someone can follow up on this effort in the coming years.

Many student athletes from the college have gone on to graduate and medical schools, founded successful businesses, and performed significant service in the communities where they reside. Some have achieved national and international recognition, including membership in organizations like the National Academy of Sciences and renowned status in various performing arts. There is much to be learned from acknowledging the athletics portion of campus culture to promote an environment of inclusion.

A promising approach to coaching began in the spring of 2019 with the arrival of a new women's lacrosse coach, Kim Russell. Her philosophy is based on holistic wellness. A quote from Russell sums up her approach: "Now, Cheetos might not make you think of wellness, but when you look at the (Chester Cheetah) on the bag, this is what you want to look like. He's having fun and enjoying himself" (*Oberlin Review*, March 3, 2019). Being aware of your own body, physically and mentally, is a key facet of this philosophy. Emotional intelligence, a term that describes the core of this approach, aids team members in understanding each other and forging and cementing team cooperation and spirit. This philosophy certainly could have a broader appeal.

Recent developments at Oberlin portend a future that already includes new courses and directions for students and uses some foundational existing classes. An addition to the course offerings in Athletics and Physical Education, Exploring Personal Wellness, provides basic knowledge and practices for understanding and pursuing goals to remain healthy. Topics include nutrition, stress management, substance abuse, and sexual health. There are courses in the Dance Department, with enrollments by students from other majors, and new classes initiated in the last several years. One class offered through the Dance Department is taught by Jennifer Shults, a practicing chiropractor and daughter of Fred Shults. The course, Body Re-Education and Functional Anatomy, uses a variety of pedagogical practices, including hands-on laboratory situations to enable students to understand and practice principles of skeletal and muscular function. Another course, also offered as part of the program by the Dance Department, is Introduction to Somatic Studies—Exploration through Movement. This class focuses on wellness through acquiring a better understanding of our physical potential. By using a variety of movement modalities and learning, the course provides knowledge about individual uniqueness through combinations of muscular usage and thinking patterns. A third class, Physical Mindfulness, is a key topic for those interested in health and wellness. There are several classes in the Biology Department in anatomy and physiology which provide content matching the needs of students interested in health and wellness.

Oberlin has a long-standing option for students to design their own major, by packaging courses from various departments. One might expect, given the range of classes now available, that several students, individually or as a small group, would propose their own individual major. With the new Shanks Center adjoining the Philips Physical Education Center, Oberlin could, at some not-too-distant time, create a concentration or new program in areas pertaining to health, physical fitness, and recreation. The Environmental Science Program, now in existence for more than three decades, is an example of a curriculum that emerged through these steps. The major in Neuroscience began as a series of individually designed majors, progressed to a program, and, eventually became a major. One concern arises when a possible major involving health and wellness topics is considered: How would such a program be staffed? Duties and expertise among current personnel would cover only a portion of the topics that may be needed in the future.

In the context of changing perceptions and practices regarding physical exercise, it is important to explore what sorts of academic programs for physical education, health, wellness, and related topics are offered at other institutions of higher learning. In terms of current programming on these topics, Oberlin lags behind a number of its small college peers. Some schools offer majors such as Exercise Science, Health and Human Kinetics, Health and Wellness, or Health, Exercise and Sports Studies. These include Denison University and Ohio Wesleyan University. Examples of other small, midwestern schools with majors in these areas are Wittenberg, Baldwin Wallace, Hiram, Otterbein, and Mount Union. Wooster has a minor in physical education. Courses in coaching specific sports are taught at Wabash and Wooster, as well as some of those just noted that offer degrees in this broad area. At other institutions there are courses for students in physical education and health studies, but these are packaged as either a program in the subject or are simply available as part of the curriculum. Many larger, state schools offer similar majors and minors. These may serve as guidance for places like Oberlin as the twenty-first century progresses and student interests expand to help initiate curricular changes.

It is surely the case that modern American society exhibits both the need for and a growing interest in physical activity. As witnessed after both World Wars and in recent decades, the health of Americans will require substantial changes to stem both the major increases in health costs and the continued loss of productivity due to declining physical condition. As the population ages, the maintenance of good health is central to the well-being of the elderly. Oberlin students are becoming more aware of their need to meet both the academic and physical challenges in their lives. The lifelong desire to achieve an optimum balance in the mind–body continuum begins before the college experience. The Oberlin community recognizes this and strives to facilitate such goals. Much of the new push for well-being is driven by students concerned about the challenges in their lives, including the stress of concentrating on academics. This places undue burdens on their physical condition.

A quote from the Department of Athletics and Physical Education website summarizes nicely the thinking surrounding the newest facility for physical exercise on campus: "The Patricia '63 and Merrill '61 Shanks Health and Wellness Center is about more than revamping existing athletics facilities. The center was built with the intent of bringing the campus community together by fostering healthy connections between body and mind." It is noteworthy that the college's program began in the 1830s with a theme of "Learning and Labor" which was built around that same connection between physical activity and academic pursuits. In a sense, events have come full circle, returning to the roots of the educational process fostered more than 180 years ago by the founders of Oberlin. Developments in the coming decade will set a course that, driven in significant ways by the college's students, provides a balance in terms of physical education and athletic endeavors. A summary of words from Athletic Director Winkelfoos contained in the same press release cited above is an appropriate ending: "To carry out Oberlin's commitment not just to higher learning, but to social justice work as well, the interconnections of mental and physical wellness must be at the forefront of the conversation. By recognizing the pressure on students not only to perform academically, but to constantly think critically and thoughtfully about the world they live in, the center provides both a nexus and safe haven for students to prioritize taking care of themselves."

Summary

The second decade of the new century involved a continuation of the athletics philosophy based on the principle that winning is all that matters. At Oberlin, the current athletics policy makes some specific points about attempts to maintain a broader perspective. The mission is to benefit all of the people associated with the college, including students, be they athletes, participants in club sports or intramurals, or part of the general student body, and also faculty and staff. The several buildings that form the Knowlton Athletic Complex and the Shanks Health and Wellness Center, along with recent upgrades to other facilities, advance the goals of the college mission by providing new and renovated venues for athletics and for all members of the community to maintain the mind–body connection. Among its peers, Oberlin is well positioned for the coming decades in terms of its physical facilities, playing fields, and coaching staff, support services, and administration. Two important issues are at the forefront of current attempts to make Oberlin an even better place for students to attend school and remain physically fit. One involves the sensed separation of athletes from non-athletes with stereotypes that arise in these distinctions. Second, there is heightened interest in health and wellness, both for everyone at the college and in conjunction with educational opportunities. As at other schools in the peer group, it may be that Oberlin can now consider coming full circle in regard to the "Learning and Labor" motto on the college seal, which formed the basis for the origins of the institution.

Sources Consulted for Chapter 8

Full citations are found at the end of the book.

Coakley, J. *Sports in Society: Issues and Controversies.*

Edlin, G., and E. Golanty. *Health and Wellness.*

Hanford, G. H. *An Inquiry into the Need for and Feasibility of a National Study of Intercollegiate Athletics.*

Knight Foundation. *Report of the Commission on Intercollegiate Athletics.*

Mechikoff, R. A., and S. G. Estes. *A History and Philosophy of Sport and Physical Education.*

Welch, P. D. *History of American Physical Education and Sport.*

Wuest, D. A., and J. L. Fisette. *Foundations of Physical Education, Exercise Science, and Sport.*

APPENDIX A.1

Timeline for Pertinent National and International Events

Exercise in a variety of forms and including military drill began in antiquity. Presented here are some dates and hallmarks pertinent to this book on physical education and athletics. Also included are relevant dates for world events to provide a context for how the Oberlin experience fits into the bigger picture. No attempt was made to be inclusive. Key dates involving individuals and events associated with Oberlin are found in the second timeline specific to the college.

1600s   Cricket is first played in England

1749   Benjamin Franklin advocates for regular exercise

1774   Johann Simon credited with being the first modern physical education teacher and Johann Bernhard Basedow credited with developing the first modern sport lesson

1810   Friedrich Jahn, father of gymnastics, takes students outdoors for games and hikes

1814   Mandatory physical education in Denmark

1814   Pehr Henrik Ling begins teaching physical education at Lund in Sweden

1820   By this date there are many gymnasiums throughout Europe

1823 Round Hill School opens—Charles Beck is the first American physical education instructor—German gymnastics taught starting in 1825

1825 First men's physical education in the US

1832 Catharine Beecher founds the Hartford School—American-style calisthenics

1845 First comprehensive set of rules for baseball written

1848 First full set of rules for soccer (football) written

1848 First Turnverein (German gymnastics and exhibition) held in the US

1849 First physical education training solely for women founded in England

1851 First US YMCA, located in Boston

1853 Boston becomes first city to require physical education for school children

1855 First game of modern ice hockey is played at Kingston, Ontario

1858 First YWCA is founded in New York City

1859 First intercollegiate baseball game, with Amherst College defeating Williams College (73–32)

1861 Dio Lewis opens Normal Institute for Physical Education in Boston—first training school

1861 Amherst is the first college to establish a physical training program for men

1861 Vassar creates a physical training program for women

1862 Edward Hitchcock is appointed professor of Hygiene and Physical Education at Amherst College

1874 Lawn tennis is first played in the US

1874 First American football game is played between Harvard and McGill Universities

1875 Wellesley College constructs the first campus gymnasium for women in the US

1876 National League of Professional Baseball clubs is formed

1879 National Association of Amateur Athletics of America is formed (forerunner of AAU)

1882	Boston YWCA is location of first women's athletic games
1885	American Association for the Advancement of Physical Education (AAAPE) is founded
1885	YMCA College at Springfield, Massachusetts, opens
1887	Dudley A. Sargent begins his summer school at Harvard for training physical education teachers
1887	Softball is invented
1888	Amateur Athletics Union (AAU) is formed
1889	Boston Conference on physical training
1891	James Naismith invents basketball at Springfield, MA
1892	Ohio passes law mandating physical education
1894	First women's golf tournament is played in New Jersey
1895	First women's field day is held at Vassar College
1895	Volleyball is invented at Springfield, MA
1896	Modern Olympic Games begin in Athens, Greece
1896	First women's intercollegiate basketball championship, between Stanford and the University of California, Berkeley
1900	University of Pennsylvania becomes the first school with a physical education requirement
1900	Women first compete at the Olympic Games
1906	Founding of the Playground Association of America (later became the National Recreation Association)
1910	Origin of the National Collegiate Athletic Association (NCAA), initially formed in 1906 as the Intercollegiate Athletic Association of the United States
1910	Founding of Boy Scouts of America
1910	Founding of Camp Fire Girls of America
1912	Founding of the Girl Scouts of America
1917	Committee on Women's Athletics is formed by the American Physical Education Association

1920	Nineteenth Amendment to the US Constitution provides women the right to vote
1922	First AAU national women's track and field championships
1923	National Amateur Athletic Federation and Women's Division is formed
1924	Winter Olympics begin at Chamonix, France
1926	AAU sponsors the first women's national basketball championship
1927	Little League baseball is founded
1927	Organization of the American Academy of Physical Education (AAPE) is founded
1941	First woman's intercollegiate lacrosse game
1943	All-American Girls Softball League is formed
1945	National Association of Intercollegiate Athletics (NAIA) is formed
1946	First School of Health Physical Education and Recreation is established at Indiana University
1949	Formation of the National Basketball Association (NBA)
1953	Physical fitness tests in US reveal poor results for children relative to European countries
1954	Brown vs. Board of Education Supreme Court decision leads to the integration of schools
1956	President's Council on Youth Fitness is established
1957	Association of Intercollegiate Athletics for Women (AIAW) is founded in 1957 (later became AIAW, in 1972)
1968	Tommie Smith and John Carlos finished first and second in the 200 yd. dash at the Mexico City Olympics, followed by their protest during the medal ceremony
1970s	National Intramurals Sports Council is founded
1971	Women's basketball switches to five players, full court, and with a shot clock
1972	Title IX of the Educational Amendments of 1972
1982	NCAA holds the first women's intercollegiate championship

1990   Americans with Disabilities Act mandates accommodations for physical education for all
1991   First Women's World Cup Soccer tournament is won by the US
1994   Physical Best fitness testing program is established
1997   Founding of the Women's National Basketball Association (WNBA)
2001   No Child Left Behind Act provides for testing of basic physical skills for grades 3–8
2011   Healthy People Initiative

APPENDIX A.2

Timeline for Physical Education and Athletics at Oberlin College

Entries were selected for inclusion in this timeline based on their importance and relevance to the material covered in the book with special reference to Oberlin College.

1833–1834	Founding and opening of Oberlin Collegiate Institute
1836	Faculty established class work groups for manual labor
1840s–1870s	Tappan Square (College Green/College Park) used for many sports activities and games
1850	Name changes to Oberlin College
1861	First Men's Gymnasium built with funds collected by students
1870s	Recreation Ground being used for outdoor exercises and athletic contests
1873	Second Men's Gymnasium built with funds collected by students
1874–1880	Music Hall used for women's physical training—First Ladies Gymnasium
1874	Cabinet Hall used for some physical training activity
1878	Football plays first external match against a team from Wellington
1878	Oberlin College takes over control of the Men's Gymnasium and athletics

1880	Field behind (west of) Cabinet Hall prepared as baseball grounds
1881	Student Athletic Association (for men) approved
1881–1882	Moses Fleetwood Walker plays baseball for Oberlin (played professionally in 1884)
1885	Tennis courts laid out on Recreation Ground north of town
1885	Delphine Hanna hired as Director of the Ladies Gymnasium
1886	Annex to Second Ladies Hall becomes part of the Second Ladies Gymnasium
1886	Men's baseball becomes an intercollegiate sport
1886	College acquires land north of campus and Athletic Park is built
1888	Fred E. Leonard is first appointed as Director of Men's Gymnasium
1890	College joins Ohio College Athletic Association on limited basis—baseball and tennis only
1890	Delphine Hanna is asked to sit with the college faculty at their meetings
1890	First track meet held at Athletic Park
1890s	Women's basketball is first played as an intramural sport
1892, 1894	John W. Heisman coaches and plays football for Oberlin
1892	First course offered for women to train as physical education instructors (one-year course)
1892	Teacher training course is also offered to men
1892	Men's football becomes an intercollegiate sport
1893	Ms. Julia Dickinson donates substantial funding to the college and Dickinson Field is later named in her honor
1894	Fred E. Leonard is made Professor of Physiology and Director of the Men's Gymnasium
1895	Rockefeller Skating Rink opens—connected with the Second Ladies Gymnasium
1896	Teacher training class program is expanded to two years with certificate

1896	Ohio Inter-Collegiate Athletic Association is approved—only for track and field
1899	Teacher course is combined with four-year college major for A.B. degree for women
1901	Warner Gymnasium for men opens
1901	Men's outdoor track and field becomes an intercollegiate sport
1902	Men's physical education training program listed in college catalogue
1902	First student graduates from the four-year teacher training course
1902	Formation of the Ohio Athletic Conference (OAC)
1903	Men's basketball becomes an intercollegiate sport
1904	Formation of the Gymnasium and Field Association (GFA) for Women
1904	Delphine Hanna is appointed as Director of the Teacher's Course in Physical Education for women
1904	Women's tennis is first noted as an intramural sport
1905	First Yale–Princeton basketball game is played on court behind the Second Ladies Gym
1905	Charles W. Savage is first approved as Assoc. Prof. of Physical Training and Dir. of Athletics
1905	Men's tennis becomes an intercollegiate sport
1906	Rockefeller Skating Rink is converted to be part of the Second Ladies Gymnasium
1906	First male graduates of physical education teacher training program
1908	Julia A. Dickinson Field begins to be used for women's outdoor physical activities
1908–1924	Dickinson House (first) is used as women's field house
1910	College faculty votes to retain football: part of a major national discourse
1912	Major addition to Warner Gymnasium is completed

1913	New football stadium opens
1913	New outdoor track opens—first used in spring 1914
1914	Skating rink is established by flooding Dickinson Field
1915	Men's cross-country becomes an intercollegiate sport
1915	First intercollegiate soccer match is played against Baldwin Wallace
1915–1939	Yale–Princeton games played in Warner Gymnasium
1916	Women's softball is first noted
1917	Tennis courts are located at Morgan and S. Prospect Streets
1918	Women's soccer is first introduced
1918–1919	Student Army Training Corps (SATC) activities replace aspects of physical education
1921	Oberlin beats Ohio State 7–6 in football—last time an Ohio school beat OSU
1922–1923	Women's volleyball is first listed as a regular activity
1923	Whitelaw Reid Morrison is appointed as Director of the Men's Gymnasium
1924	Galpin Field used for the first time for women's sports activities
1924–1931	Dickinson House (second) is used as women's field house and social gathering place
1925	Savage Stadium is remodeled and opens with a quarter-mile cinder track
1930	Lysle Butler joins the faculty as football coach, later became Director of Athletics
1930	Men's soccer becomes an intercollegiate sport
1931	Crane Pool for Women opens—closes in 1973
1933	Golf becomes an intercollegiate sport
1933	Men's swimming and diving becomes an intercollegiate sport
1934	Men's fencing becomes an intercollegiate sport
1935	John Herbert Nichols is appointed as Director of Athletics

1939	Hales Memorial Gymnasium for Women opens
1948	George M. Jones Field House opens—closes in 2009
1949	Men's lacrosse becomes an intercollegiate sport
1950–1955	Men's soccer wins forty-one consecutive games
1951	Men's wrestling becomes an intercollegiate sport
1957	Nichols Gateway to the athletic complex is dedicated
1958	Hales Memorial Gymnasium Annex is completed
1963	Williams Ice Rink opens
1964	Men's ice hockey becomes an intercollegiate sport
1965	Men's ice hockey wins Midwest Conference Championship
1969–1970	Arrangements are completed for the merger of the Men's and Women's Departments
1970	Men's basketball team wins the Ohio Athletic Conference tournament
1971	Jesse Philips Physical Education Center is completed
1972	Jack Scott is hired as Chair of the Department of Physical Education
1973	Dick Michaels runs two women in a men's cross-country meet
1974	Cass Jackson is hired as men's football coach—second African American to hold such a position at an NCAA school
1976	Oberlin Ultimate Frisbee club team is founded
1977	Women's basketball, volleyball, field hockey, outdoor track and field, cross-country, tennis, and lacrosse all become intercollegiate sports
1978	John W. Heisman Club is founded
1979	Men's indoor track and field becomes an intercollegiate sport
1980	Women's indoor track and field becomes an intercollegiate sport
1984	Formation of the North Coast Athletic Conference (NCAC)
1985	Major in Physical Education is dropped
1985	Women's soccer becomes an intercollegiate sport

1986	First class of inductees to the Heisman Club Hall of Fame
1989	Appointments in the Department of Physical Education are changed from faculty to administrative and professional status and no longer come with tenure
1989	Name is changed to Department of Athletics and Physical Education
1992	John W. Heisman Club Field House opens
2000	Culhane Field for women's softball opens
2000	Women's softball becomes an intercollegiate sport
2006	Fred D. Shults Soccer Field and Robert Lewis Kahn Track open
2008	Tennis courts are named in honor of Don Hunsinger
2009	Williams Ice Rink is converted to Williams Field House
2014	Alfred E. Knowlton Athletic Complex is completed
2014	First class of inductees to the Heisman Club Hall of Honor
2018	Dolcemaschio Stadium is dedicated—home of Culhane Field and women's softball
2018	Patricia and Merrill Shanks Health and Wellness Center opens
2018	Completely renovated Carr Pool opens

APPENDIX B

Administrators for Physical Education and Athletics

The listings here are taken from: http://oberlinarchives.libraryhost.com/index.php?p=collections/controlcard&id=151. The positions are listed in the chronological order in which they were created. Note that, at times, the same individual filled two positions. There are sometimes gaps, indicating that either no one held that position or possibly that someone was named to the position for an interim period or on an acting basis and the information was not fully recorded.

Department of Physical Education for Women

DIRECTOR, WOMEN'S GYMNASIUM (1887–1955)

1887–1897 Delphine Hanna
1903–1920 Delphine Hanna
1911–1913 Helen Finney Cochran (acting)
1920–1923 Helen Finney Cochran
1923–1945 Gertrude Moulton
1946–1954 Lera B. Curtis
1954–1955 Betty F. McCue

DIRECTOR, DEPARTMENT OF PHYSICAL TRAINING FOR WOMEN
(1887-1903)

1887–1903 Delphine Hanna

DIRECTOR, TEACHER'S COURSE IN PHYSICAL EDUCATION FOR WOMEN
(1904-1936)

1904–1920 Delphine Hanna
1911–1912 Helen Finney Cochran (acting)
1920–1923 Helen Finney Cochran
1923–1936 Gertrude Moulton

CHAIR, DEPARTMENT OF PHYSICAL EDUCATION FOR WOMEN
(1955-1970)

1955–1964 Betty F. McCue
1964–1965 Helen Domonkos (acting)
1965–1970 Ruth Brunner

Department of Physical Education for Men

DIRECTOR, MEN'S GYMNASIUM
(1888-1951)

1888–1889 Fred E. Leonard
1892–1922 Fred E. Leonard
1923–1951 Whitelaw Reid Morrison

DIRECTOR OF ATHLETICS
(1905-1974)

1905–1918 Charles W. Savage
1918–1920 T. Nelson Metcalf
1920–1935 Charles W. Savage
1935–1955 John Herbert Nichols

1955–1970 Lysle Butler
1971–1972 Julian L. Smith
1972–1974 Jack Scott

DIRECTOR, TEACHER'S COURSE IN PHYSICAL EDUCATION FOR MEN
(1906-1935)

1906–1922 Fred E. Leonard
1923–1925 Whitelaw Reid Morrison
1925–1935 Charles W. Savage

DIRECTOR, INTRAMURAL ATHLETICS
(1928-1936)

1928–1936 John Herbert Nichols

CHAIR, DEPARTMENT OF PHYSICAL EDUCATION FOR MEN
(1955-1970)

1955–1969 Lysle K. Butler
1969–1970 Billy Tidwell

Combined Department of Physical Education

CHAIR, DEPARTMENT OF PHYSICAL EDUCATION
(1970-1989)

1970–1971 Billy Tidwell
1971–1972 Julian Smith (acting)
1972–1974 Jack Scott
1974–1975 Ruth Brunner
1975–1980 Patrick Pen
1980–1983 Richard Michaels
1983–1986 Don Hunsinger
1986–1988 Lawrence Vance (acting)
1988–1989 Joseph W. Gurtis Jr. (acting)

**DIRECTOR OF MEN'S ATHLETICS
(1974-1989)**

1974–1975 Tommie Smith
1975–1988 Joseph W. Gurtis Jr.
1988–1989 Don Hunsinger

**COORDINATOR, WOMEN'S SPORTS
(1974-1980)**

1974–1977 Claudia Colville
1977–1980 Mary Culhane

**DIRECTOR OF WOMEN'S ATHLETICS
(1980-1989)**

1980–1989 Mary Culhane
1988–1989 Heather Spicer

**DIRECTOR OF ATHLETICS AND PHYSICAL EDUCATION
(1989-PRESENT)**

1989–1994 James F. Foels
1994–1998 Don Hunsinger
1998–2002 Michael Muska
2002–2003 George Andrews (interim) (became Delta Lodge Director of Athletics and Physical Education)
2003–2005 Vin Lananna
2005–2006 Joseph P. Karlgaard (acting)
2006–2011 Joseph P. Karlgaard
2011   Natalie Winkelfoos and Ray Appenheimer (co-acting)
2011–2012 William Roth
2012–present Natalie Winkelfoos

REFERENCES AND SOURCES

Books

The books and other documents listed here include all of those cited as sources at the end of each of the chapters and some titles that were used for basic background and reference information.

Barnard, J. 1969. *From Evangelism to Progressivism at Oberlin College, 1866–1917.* Columbus: The Ohio State University Press.

Barrows, I. C. 1890 (2017 reprint). *Physical Training: A Full Report of the Papers and Discussions of the Conference Held in Boston in November 1890.* Boston: George H. Ellis.

Baumann, R. J. 2010. *Constructing Black Education at Oberlin College: A Documentary History.* Athens: Ohio University Press.

Bosco, J. S., and M. A. Turner. 1981. *Encyclopedia of Physical Education, Fitness, and Sports.* Salt Lake City: Brighton.

Bowen, W. G., and S. A. Levin. 2003. *Reclaiming the Game: College Sports and Educational Values.* Princeton: Princeton University Press.

Brandt, L. J. 1992. *The Evolution of Women's Intercollegiate Athletics at Oberlin College.* Honors Thesis for the Department of History at Oberlin College.

Brandt, N. 2001. *When Oberlin Was King of the Gridiron.* Kent, OH: Kent State University Press.

Bucher, C. A. 1972. *Foundations of Physical Education.* St. Louis: C. V. Mosby.

Chessman, G. W. 1957. *Denison: The Story of an Ohio College.* Granville, OH: Denison University.

Chessman, G. W., and W. M. Southgate. 2003. *Heritage and Promise: Denison, 1831–1981.* Granville, OH: Denison University.

Coakley, J. 2009. *Sports in Society: Issues and Controversies.* Boston: McGraw-Hill.

Cohen, A. M., and C. B. Kisker. 2010. *The Shaping of American Higher Education: Experience and Growth of the Contemporary System.* New York: Josey-Bass.

Committee on Athletics. 1998. *Report of the Committee on Athletics.*

Consentino, F., M. Dinning, K. Jones, and G. Malszecki. 1988. *A History of Physical Education.* North York, Ontario, Canada: Cactus Press.

Costa, D. M., and S. R. Guthrie (eds.). 1994. *Women and Sport: Interdisciplinary Perspectives.* Champaign, IL: Human Kinetics.

Dewey, J. 1884. "The New Psychology." *Andover Review* 2:278–289.

———. 1916. *Democracy and Education: An Introduction to the Philosophy of Education.* New York: Macmillan.

Dorgan, E. J. 1934. *Luther Halsey Gulick 1865–1918.* New York: Columbia University.

Edlin, G., and E. Golanty. 2010. *Health and Wellness.* Burlington, MA: Jones & Barrett Learning.

Eitzen, D. S. 2014. *Sport in Contemporary Society.* 9th ed. Oxford, UK: Oxford University Press.

Elcombe, T. 2005. "Reformist America: 'The Oberlin Experiment'—The Limits of Jack Scott's 'Athletic Revolution' in Post-1960s America." *International Journal of the History of Sport* 22:1060–1085.

Fairchild, J. H. 1883. *Oberlin: The Colony and the College, 1833–1883.* Oberlin, OH: E. J. Goodrich.

Fletcher, R. S. 1943. *A History of Oberlin College from Its Foundation through the Civil War.* Chicago: R. R. Donnelly & Sons.

Foiels, J. 1993. *A Report on Athletics and Physical Education at Oberlin College.*

Footlick, J. K. 2015. *An Adventure in Education: The College of Wooster from Howard Lowry to the Twenty-First Century.* Kent, OH: Kent State University Press.

Fuess, C. M. 1935. *Amherst: The Story of a New England College.* Boston: Little, Brown, & Co.

Galasso, P. J. (ed.). 1988. *Philosophy of Sport and Physical Activity: Issues and Concepts.* Toronto: Canadian Scholars' Press.

Gerber, E. W. 1971. *Innovators and Institutions in Physical Education.* Philadelphia: Lea & Febiger.

Goerler, R. E. 2011. *The Ohio State University: An Illustrated History.* Columbus: The Ohio State University Press.

Gulick, L. H. 1920. *A Philosophy of Play.* New York: Charles Scribner's Sons.

Guttmann, A. 1988. *A Whole New Ball Game: An Interpretation of American Sports.* Chapel Hill: University of North Carolina Press.

Hackensmith, C. W. 1966. *History of Physical Education.* New York: Harper & Row.

Hanford, G. H. 1974. *An Inquiry into the Need for and Feasibility of a National Study of Intercollegiate Athletics.* New York: Carnegie Foundation.

Harvey, R. S. (ed.). 1982. *These Fleeting Years: Wabash College, 1832–1982.* Crawfordsville, IN: Wabash College.

Hayes, W. 2006. *The Progressive Education Movement: Is It Still a Factor in Today's Schools?* New York: Rowman and Littlefield.

Heisman, J. M., and M. Schlabach. 2012. *Heisman: The Man Behind the Trophy.* New York: Howard Books.

Hetherington, C. W. 1921. "Special Objectives of Physical Education with Relationships in Public Health." *American Journal of Public Health* 11:520–528.

Horger, M. 1996. "Basketball and Athletic Control at Oberlin College, 1896–1915." *Journal of Sport History* 23:256–283.

Hubbart, H. C. 1943. *Ohio Wesleyan's First Hundred Years*. Delaware: Ohio Wesleyan University.

Keeler, H. L. 1912. *The Life of Adelia A. Field Johnston*. Miami, FL: Hard Press Publishing.

Kinsey, D. C. 1935. *The History of Physical Education in Oberlin College 1833–1890*. M.A. Thesis, Oberlin College.

Knight Foundation. 1993. *Report of the Commission on Intercollegiate Athletics*. Miami, FL: Knight Foundation.

Kornblith, G. J., and C. Lasser. 2018. *Elusive Utopia: The Struggle for Racial Equality in Oberlin, Ohio*. Baton Rouge: Louisiana State University Press.

Kretchmar, R. S. 1994. *Practical Philosophy of Sport*. Champaign, IL: Human Kinetics.

Kretchmar, R. S., M. Dyerson, M. P. Llewellyn, and J. Gleaves. 2017. *History and Philosophy of Sport and Physical Activity*. Champaign, IL: Human Kinetics.

Ladd, T., and J. A. Mathisen. 1999. *Muscular Christianity: Evangelical Protestants and the Development of American Sport*. Grand Rapids, MI: Baker Books.

Lee, M. 1983. *A History of Physical Education and Sports in the U.S.A.* New York: John Wiley & Sons.

Leonard, F. E. 1915. *Pioneers of Modern Physical Training*. New York: Association Press.

Leonard, F. E., and G. B. Affleck. 1947. *A Guide to the History of Physical Education*. 2nd edition. Philadelphia: Lea & Febiger.

Lewis, D. 1862. *The New Gymnastics for Men, Women, and Children*. Boston: Ticknor and Fields.

Lucas, C. J. 2006. *American Higher Education: A History*. New York: Palgrave MacMillan.

Lyn, M. 1937. *An Historical Analysis of the Professional Career of Delphine Hanna*. M.A. Thesis. University Park: Pennsylvania State University.

Mechikoff, R. 2010. *A History and Philosophy of Sport and Physical Education*. Boston: McGraw-Hill.

Mechikoff, R. A., and S. G. Estes. 1998. *A History and Philosophy of Sport and Physical Education*. Boston: McGraw-Hill.

Morris, J. B. 2014. *Oberlin: Hotbed of Abolitionism*. Chapel Hill: University of North Carolina Press.

Moulton, G. 1930. The Scientific Development of Physical Education. *Oberlin Alumni Magazine* 26:197.

Nash, J. B. 1948. *Physical Education: Interpretations and Objectives*. New York: A. S. Barnes.

———. 1960. *Philosophy of Recreation and Leisure*. Dubuque, IA: William C. Brown.

Oberlin College. 1948. *Catalogue of Graduates*. Oberlin, OH: Oberlin College.

———. 1960. *Graduates and Former Students, Teaching and Administrative Staff of Oberlin College 1833–1960*. Oberlin, OH: Oberlin College.

Pollard, J. E. 1959. *Ohio State Athletics 1879–1959*. Columbus: The Ohio State University Press.

Putney, C. 2001. *Muscular Christianity: Manhood and Sports in Protestant America, 1880–1920*. Cambridge, MA: Harvard University Press.

Reich, D. 1972. *Rebuilding Physical Education*. Report to the Faculty at Oberlin College.

Rice, E. A., J. L. Hutchinson, and M. Lee. 1969. *A Brief History of Physical Education*. New York: John Wiley & Sons.

Rudolph, F. 1990. *The American College and University: A History*. Athens: University of Georgia Press.

Schwendener, N. 1942. *A History of Physical Education in the United States.* New York: A. S. Barnes.

Scott, H. A. 1951. *Competitive Sports in Schools and Colleges.* New York: Harper and Brothers.

Scott, J. 1971. *The Athletic Revolution.* New York: Free Press.

Shepardson, F. W. 1931. *Denison University, 1831–1931: A Centennial History.* Granville, OH: Denison University.

Shulman, J. L., and W. G. Bowen. 2001. *The Game of Life: College Sports and Educational Values.* Princeton: Princeton University Press.

Shults, F. D. 1959. *The Life of Fred Eugene Leonard, M.D: His Contributions and Influence on the Profession of Physical Education.* M.A. Thesis, The Ohio State University.

———. 1967. *The History and Philosophy of Athletics for Men at Oberlin College.* Ph.D. in Education Dissertation, Indiana University.

Smith, R. A. 1988. *Sports & Freedom: The Rise of Big-Time College Athletics.* New York: Oxford University Press.

Smythe, G. F. 1824. *Kenyon College: Its First Century.* New Haven: Yale University Press.

Thelin, J. R. 2004. *A History of American Higher Education.* Baltimore: Johns Hopkins University Press.

Trekell, M. 1926. *Gertrude Evelyn Moulton, M.D.: Her Life and Professional Career in Health and Physical Education.* Ph.D. Dissertation, The Ohio State University.

Van Dalen, D. B., and B. L. Bennett. 1971. *A World History of Physical Education.* Englewood Cliffs, NJ: Prentice Hall.

Waite, C. L. 2002. *Permission to Remain Among Us: Education for Blacks in Oberlin, Ohio, 1880–1914.* Westport, CT: Praeger.

Wayman, A. R. 1938. *A Modern Philosophy of Physical Education.* Philadelphia: W. B. Saunders.

Welch, P. D. 2004. *History of American Physical Education and Sport.* Springfield, IL: Charles Thomas.

Weston, A. 1962. *The Making of American Physical Education.* New York: Appleton-Century-Crofts.

Williams, J. F. 1922. *The Organization and Administration of Physical Education.* New York: Macmillan.

———. 1932. *The Principles of Physical Education.* Philadelphia: W. B. Saunders.

Williams, J. F., and W. R. Morrison. 1939. *A Text-book of Physical Education.* Philadelphia: W. B. Saunders.

Wuest, D. A., and J. L. Fisette. 2012. *Foundations of Physical Education, Exercise Science, and Sport.* New York: McGraw Hill.

Wood, T. D. 1910. *Health and Education. The Ninth Yearbook of the National Society for the Study of Education.* Philadelphia: W. B. Saunders.

Wood, T. D., and R. F. Cassidy. 1927. *The New Physical Education.* New York: Macmillan.

Wushanley, Y. 2004. *Playing Nice and Losing the Struggle for Control of Women's Intercollegiate Athletics, 1960–2000.* Syracuse, NY: Syracuse University Press.

Zeigler, E. F. 1974. *A History of Physical Education & Sport in the United States and Canada.* Champaign, IL: Stipes.

———. 2005. *History and Status of American Physical Education and Educational Sport.* Victoria, British Columbia: Trafford.

General Sources for Oberlin College

Oberlin Alumni Magazine (1904–2019)
Oberlin Review (1904–2018)
Oberlin College Catalogues (1885–2019)
Hi-O-Hi Yearbooks (1894–1970)

Websites

Allegheny College
Amherst College
Baldwin Wallace University
College of Wooster
Denison University
Earlham College
Harvard University
Kenyon College
Mount Union University
North Coast Athletic Conference
Oberlin College Athletics
Ohio Athletic Conference
Ohio State University
Ohio Wesleyan University
Otterbein University
Springfield College
Wabash College
Williams College

Oberlin College Archives—Files Used for Physical Education and Athletics History

RG0—COLLEGE GENERAL RECORDS

Series 1—Miscellaneous Publications and Printed Materials
Series 2—Miscellaneous Publications Relating to Instruction and Recruitment
    Subseries 1—General Catalogues
Series 15—Commencement

244 • References and Sources

RG5–OFFICE OF THE SECRETARY RECORDS

Subgroup I—Administrative Records (General)
    Series 3—Buildings and Grounds
        Subseries 2—General Files
    Series 5—Faculty and Personnel Records
        Subseries 1—Faculty Records
    Series 6—Subject Files
Subgroup II—Administrative Records of Departments and Offices
    Series 1—Academic Departments and Programs
        Subseries 1—College of Arts and Sciences
Subgroup V—Athletics and Athletic Associations
    Series 1—Athletic Associations
        Subseries 1—Oberlin College Athletic Association
        Subseries 2—Ohio Athletic Conference

RG9/006–PHYSICAL EDUCATION DEPARTMENT

Subgroup I—Administrative Files
    Series 1—Annual Reports
    Series 2—Minutes
    Series 4—Oberlin Athletic Policy
    Series 5—Financial Records
    Series 10—Facilities and Equipment
    Series 12—General File
    Series 13—Files of the Heisman Club
        Subseries 2—Files of Mickey Cochrane (Heisman Club Historian)
Subgroup II—Instruction and Evaluation
    Series 1—Curriculum
Subgroup III—Intercollegiate Sports
    Series 1—All Sports
    Series 2—Baseball
    Series 3—Basketball
    Series 4—Cross Country
    Series 5—Fencing
    Series 6—Football
    Series 7—Golf

Series 8—Ice Hockey
Series 9—Lacrosse
Series 10—Soccer
Series 11—Swimming and Diving
Series 12—Tennis
Series 13—Track
Series 14—Wrestling
Series 15—Field Hockey
Subgroup IV—Intramurals
Series 3—Miscellaneous
Subgroup V—Athletic and Professional Associations
Series 1—Oberlin College Athletic Association
Series 3—NCAA
Series 4—Other Athletic and Professional Associations
Subgroup VI—Department of Physical Education for Women
Series 1—Minutes
Series 4—Gertrude Moulton
Series 5—Delphine Hanna Foundation
Series 6—Curriculum
Series 9—Women's Athletic Association
Series 10—Facilities
Series 13—Printed Material
Series 15—Historical File
Series 16—Annual Reports
Subgroup VII—Publications and Publicity
Series 2—Articles, Talks, and Studies
Series 3—Clippings and Scrapbooks
Subgroup VIII—Non-print Media
Series 1—Photographs

RG9/019–THEATER AND DANCE PROGRAMS

RG19/03/05–STUDENT LIFE: WOMEN'S ORGANIZATIONS RECORDS

RG19/03/08–STUDENT LIFE

Series 1—Miscellaneous and Social Organizations
Series 2—Sailing Club

RG30 PERSONAL PAPERS

/047—Fredrick E. Leonard
/094—Lysle K. Butler
/131—John Herbert Nichols
/145—William S. Chambers
/174—Sara Houston
/195—Fredrick D. Shults
/230—Helen Domonkos
/290—Barbara Calmer
/324—Delphine Hanna
/330—Leland Brandt
/404—Mary Jane Culhane

RG31/044 OBERLIN COUNTRY DAY CAMP PHOTOGRAPHIC COLLECTION

RG 36 POSTCARDS

Interviews/Conversations with

George Andrews
Roland Baumann
Yago Colás
Norman Craig
James D. Donaldson
Anne Elder
Ken Grossi
Prudy Hall
Carol Hart
Norman Henderson
Don Hunsinger
Mike Mancini
Thelma Morris
Nancy Hawley Morrison
Anne Cuyler Salsich
Ann Stevens
Ed Vermue
Kevin Willbond
Natalie Winkelfoos

INDEX

Note: Italicized page numbers indicate illustrations and their captions. Tables are indicated by *t* following the page number.

Academy of Physical Education, 52
African Americans: on early football teams, *57*; first Black professional athletes, 91; first colleges to award degrees to, 43; firsts in professional sports, 59; Jack Scott's focus on, 163; at Oberlin, 1, 42, 44; and reforms to Oberlin's PE programs, 141
AIAW. *See* Association for Intercollegiate Athletics for Women (AIAW)
Allegheny College, 78, 211, 215
alumni and fundraising, 192, 194
Amateur Athletic Union (AAU), 106
Ambar, Carmen Twillie, 213, 215
American Academy of Kinesiology, 93
American Academy of Physical Education, 93, 97, 100
American Association for Health, Physical Education, and Recreation, 94, 97, 157
American Association for Physical Education, 35
American Association for the Advancement of Physical Education, 52, 90
American Folk Dance Society, 52
American Physical Education Association, 66, 95

American School Hygiene Association, 52
American Society for Research in Physical Education, 92
American Society of Physical Education, 92
Amherst College, 28, 55, 89, 157
Anderson, William G., 90
Andrews, George, 187
Annapolis–West Point field hockey game, 83, *119*
anthropometrics, 32–33, 36, 53, 113
Appenheimer, Ray, 204
archery, 81, 111, 117, 132
Association for Intercollegiate Athletics for Women (AIAW), 133, 157
athletic competitions, emergence of, 26–28
Athletic Park, 49–50, *50*, 86, 199
athletics: definitions of, 9; in pyramid of activities, 10; reflection of culture in, 203
Athletics Advisory Committee, 114
Athletics at Oberlin, 190
athletic scholarships, 76–77, 116, 117, 131, 167, 173
Austin E. Knowlton Athletics Complex, 87, 119, 166, 204, 208–9, *210*, 221

247

248 • Index

Bailey Field. *See* Dick Bailey Field
Ballantine, William G., 31–32
Bancroft, Jessie Hubbell, 90
baseball: and athletic associations, 58; class competition in, 55; coaches for, *142*; dominance of, 131; and early intercollegiate sports, 44; facilities for, 122, 213; first intercollegiate matches, 28, 55–56, *56*, 74; as national pastime, 105; origins of, 7; prominence of professional leagues, 179; Resolutes team, *27*; Shults and, 198
basketball: academic credit for, 163; advent of, 52; as big business, 67; coaches for, *137*, *142*, *161*; dominance of, 131; early participation by women, 57, 79, 81; facilities for, 175; intercollegiate teams for, 216; Oberlin's teams, 74, *78*, 164; origins of, 7; out-of-season practice for, 183–84; prominence of professional leagues, 179; as urban game, 105; in women's athletics, 132; women's championships in, 157; Yale–Princeton game, 81–83, *82*, 111–12
Beck, Charles, 18, 90
Beecher, Catherine, 19, 90
bicycle clubs, 55, *55*
bowling, 58, 81
Boy Scouts of America, 65
Brunner, Ruth, 160, 161, *161*, 185
Buchern, C. A., 9
Burchenal, Elizabeth, 90
Butler, Lysle: career of, 134–35; disagreements with Jack Scott, 144–45; educational athletics of, 134, 135–36; as football coach, 107; as men's department chair, 133; photograph of, *135*

calisthenics, 17, 24, 28. *See also* gymnastics
Calmer, Barbara, 160, *161*, 161–62
Camp Fire Girls, 52, 65
Camp Hanna, 37–38, 100, 122–24
Camp Pemigewassett, 97–98
Carr, Robert K., 139
car racing, 105
Carr Pool, 166, 204, 207, *208*, 214
Centennial Athletic Conference, 164
Center for Student Success, 214
championship games: establishment of, 79; and fundraising, 175; hockey team's win in, 149; increased numbers of, 106; for swimming, 207, 212; in women's sports, 133, 157, 172, 193
Chance Creek recreational area, 89
Chenoweth, Laurence, 99
Civil Rights Act of 1964, 156
Clark W. Hetherington Award, 93, 94
Cleveland Alumni Club of Oberlin, 87
Colás, Yago, 217–18
College Counseling Center, 214
College Faculty Council, 146
College of Wooster: admission to, 131; as coeducational, 78, 158; comparison of Oberlin to, 11; courses on coaching at, 220; emergence of, 30; facilities at, 211–12, 215; men's teams at, 184; and NCAC, 164; religious heritage of, 154; requirements of PE major at, 134
College Physical Education Society, 97
commercialization of athletics: continued expansion of, 203–4; football and, 189–90; opposition to, 78, 96, 97; revenue sources in, 179, 180; small colleges and, 201
Commission on Intercollegiate Athletics for Women (CIAW), 133
Committee for the Regulation of Athletic Sports, 49, 114
Conservatory of Music, 21, 156, 193, 217
Cosell, Howard, 146
Coville, Claudia, 160, 162, *162*, 163, 164, 185
Craig, Norman, 98
Crane family, 117
Crane Pool: addition of, 117–18, *118*, 148; closure of, 175; location of, *148*; women's athletics and, 100, 138, 163, 166
cricket, 26
cross country, 144, 157, 193, 208; academic credit for, 163; courses for, 151; facilities for, 197, 213; intercollegiate teams for, 216; teams added for, 74; women's varsity teams, 164
Culhane, Mary Jane, 160, *160*, 164, 185–86
Culhane Field, 160, 208, *209*
Curtis, Henry, 92
Curtis, Lera B., 109, *110*

dance, 81, 132; Calmer's teaching of, 162; Domonkos and, 109–10; facilities for,

175–76; women's performances, 81, 156; in women's program, 79, 132

Dance Department, 219

Danenberg, Emil, 170

degree programs: courses for PE majors, 112–13, 163, 168–69; curricular changes to, 133, 144; expansion of PE teacher training programs, 134; first with PE major, 41; graduation data for PE major, 169t; majors in, 12; new PE and wellness programs, 219–20; Oberlin's discontinuance of PE major, 154, 169–72, 176; Oberlin's first men's PE program, 41; proficiency exemptions in, 138; requirements of Oberlin's PE major, 134; shifts in Oberlin's PE major, 76; student-designed majors, 219

Delphine Hanna Foundation, 38, 109–10

Delsarte, François, 30

Delta Lodge Director of Athletics and Physical Education, 187, 204, *205*, 216

Denison University (previously, Denison College): admissions at, 131; athletics and PE facilities at, 89, 117, 215; combining of men's and women's programs at, 158; comparison with Oberlin, 11; facilities at, 211–12; manual labor at, 21; men's teams at, 184; new PE and wellness degree programs at, 220; religious heritage of, 1, 154; requirements of PE major at, 134; shifts to calisthenics at, 24; student-initiated PE organizations at, 49; teacher training classes at, 72; women at, 78

Department of Athletics and Physical Education: coaches' responsibilities in, 181; department's name change to, 173; director positions in, 186–87; organizational structure of, 216; on Shanks Center, 220

Department of Physical Education and Athletics: as combined men's and women's department, 136; policy of 1975, 182–83

Department of Physical Education for Women, 81, 92, 99, 112, 135, 141

Descartes, René, 16

Dewey, John, 28, 32, 52, 67, 106

Dick Bailey Field, 119, 166, 210

Dickinson, Julia, 37, 86

Dickinson Field, 71, 86, 87, 92

Dickinson House, 81, 86–87

Dill, Judge James Brook, 122

Dill Field: addition of, 102; history of, 87–88; naming of, 122; upgrades to, 71, 208, *209*; view of, *122*

diversity and multiculturalism, 154–55

Division I and II schools, 181

Division III colleges, 131–32, 167, 174, 175, 193. *See also* small colleges

Dolcemaschio Stadium, 208, *209*

Domonkos, Helen, 109–10, *111*

Donovan, James D. "J. D.," 187, 188, *188*

Dunn, Jack, *209*

Dye, Nancy S., 183

Earlham College, 78, 158, 189, 211, 213, 215

Ederle, Gertrude, 79

Educational and Sports Program Network (ESPN), 174

Educational Plans and Polices Committee (EPPC), 114, 170–71, 190–91

emotional intelligence, 218

Englelka, Lance, 180

EPPC. *See* Educational Plans and Polices Committee (EPPC)

Evans, Pam, 187

exercise physiology, 92

exercise science, 9, 39

facilities and buildings for athletics and PE: during 1896 to 1925 period, 83–89, 102; during 1926 to 1950 period, 117–24; during 1951 to 1974 period, 147–51; during 1972 to 1990 period, 175–76; during 1991 to 2010 period, 195–200; during 2011 to 2021 period, 207–11; compared to peer institutions, 207, 211–13; cost of, 203; evolution of, 7; fields used by specific sports, 166; first facilities, 44–50, *45–48*, 86, 87; and increases in recreational facilities, 65; large stadiums, 69; local community's use of, 199–200; maps of, 13, *14–15*; and Oberlin's mission, 221; for professional sports, 179–80; sports facilities for increased revenue, 174

Fairchild, James H., *Oberlin: The Colony and the College, 1833–1883*, 22–23, *23*

Federal Office of Compliance guidelines, 158

fencing, 77, 79, *80*, 113, 163, 184

field hockey: academic credit for, 163; Annapolis–West Point game, 83, 119; athletic facilities for, 119, 213; in intercollegiate competitions, 157; in intramural sports, 81; in service classes, 111; in women's sports, 59, *59*, 79, 132; women's teams, 164, 216

Finney, Charles Grandison, 20, 22

First Ladies Gymnasium, 44

Fisette, J. L., 9

Five College Consortium, 11

Foels, James F., 59, 187, 193

folk dancing, 90

Follis, Charles, 91

football: athletic facilities for, 150, 212; budget for, 165; class competitions for, 55; coaches for, *137, 142, 143*; dominance of, 66–67, 131; as early sport at Oberlin, 26; and funding of intercollegiate athletics, 77, 191; growth in culture of, 105; historical path of, 188–93; Oberlin's elimination of, 171; Oberlin's first teams and games, 55, 56, *57*, 74; and Oberlin's Four Horsemen, *96*; origins of, 7; out-of-season practice for, 183–84; and prominence of professional leagues, 179; undefeated 1892 team, 60

Frank Report, 170, 190

Fred Shults Playing Field Complex, 197, *198*

Fuller, Robert W.: and reform at Oberlin, 139, 141, 151, 170; tenure of, 147; as youngest Oberlin president, *140*

Galpin, W. A., 87

Galpin Field: addition of, 71, 100, 102; and field hockey, 119, 166; improvements to, 148; and "Oberlin Mountain," 197; size of, 213; sports using, 87; views of, *122, 148*

gambling on sports, 58, 203

games and sports: definitions of, 9; growing popularity of, 33; in pyramid of activities, 10; transition from gymnastics to, 54, 68; winning at any cost in youth, 180. *See also* intercollegiate athletics; men's sports; sports; women's athletics

gendered divisions at Oberlin: and coeducational classes, 76; in faculty and coaching responsibilities, 112, 135, 140–41, 145; in management of men's and women's athletics, 185–86; in office, gymnasium, and fields space, 138; in PE curricula, 71–72; in physical education requirements, 73; in sports, 66. *See also* Title IX

Gender Equity in Athletics Review (GEAR) Committee, 206

gender inequality: and attracting male applicants, 192; in budgeting of athletics, 165; and coaching contracts, 167; and male dominance of PE profession, 125; and "Muscular Christianity" movement, 43; in PE career tracks, 130; Title IX and, 117; and wartime opportunities for women, 155–56, 157

gender parity in athletics, 165, 216

George M. Jones Field House, 117, 120–22, *121–22*, 127, 166, 208

German gymnastics: about, 17–18; Beck and, 90; decline of, 69; in men's PE, 31; in nineteenth century, 30, 33–34; teacher training schools for, 40

Girls Scouts, 65

golf, 157; appearance as college sport, 57; coaches for, *137*; elimination of, 184; expansion as college sport, 106; in intercollegiate athletics, 113; in intramural sports, 81; professionalism in, 179; in service classes, 111; sportsmanship in, 203; women's competitions in, 79, *80*, 157

golf course, 150

Gray, Glen, 131

Grice, William "Bill" J., 136, *137*, 138, 172

Guidelines for Inclusion and Respectful Treatment of Intercollegiate Transgender Athletes, 206

Guide to the History of Physical Education, A (Leonard), 38

Gulick, Luther H., 42; books written by, 92; career of, 51; and development of physical education field, 51, 62, 91; emphasis on scientific aspects of PE, 53; and New Physical Education, 69; as Oberlin alumnus, 51, *51*; *A Philosophy of Play*, 53; as student of Hanna, 36, 62. *See also* Luther Halsey Gulick Award

Gurtis, Joseph, Jr., 163, 185, 186

gymnasiums: establishment of, 17–18, 19; Ladies' Gymnasiums, 44; Oberlin's first, 24–25; Second Men's Gymnasium, 46–47, *48*, 49, 83; stock certificate for, *25*; women's gymnasiums, 24, 35–36. *See also* Hales

Gymnasium Annex; Hemenway Gymnasium (Harvard University); Second Ladies Gymnasium; Warner Gymnasium

gymnastics: decline of, 69, 102; description of, 17–18; Fairchild's skepticism about, 22–23; Leonard as proponent of, 38–39; as PE at Oberlin, 28; and physical training, 8; public schools and, 33–34; replacement of manual labor by, 24, 31, 71; for women, 79, 111; women's exhibitions of, 156

Hales, G. Willard, 119

Hales Gymnasium Annex, 148, *149*

Hales Memorial Gymnasium: addition of, 117, 148; aerial view of, *148*; description of, 119, *119*, *120*; end of athletics competitions in, 195; Institute for Study of Sport and Society in, 145; for intramural and club sports, 175–76; for women's athletics, 100, 127, 138, 163, 166

Hall, G. Stanley, 67–68

Hanna, Delphine: anthropometrics in programs of, 32–33; background and honors for, 35; and Camp Hanna, 122, 124; and development of physical education field, 51, 62, 91, 92; as director of women's PE facilities, 36, 45; as first female PE professor, 4–5; influence on Gulick and Wood, 51–52; Oberlin Beach Club, 89; and Oberlin's physical education curriculum, 35, 97; PE programs developed by, 36–37, 40, 71, 74; photograph of, *36*; salary increases and faculty recognition for, 58; and swimming facilities, 117; training of Fred Leonard, 36, 38; use of Swedish gymnastics, 31

Harkness Bowl, 118

Hartford Seminary (CT), 90

Hartwell, Edward M., 90

Hayes, Woody, 91

health and wellness programs: benefits of, 195; expansion of, 194; facilities for, 210–11; at Oberlin, 213–15, 218, 219; physical activity in, 20; renewed interest in, 220–21; return to mind-body philosophy in, 173; among small colleges, 215; strengthening of, 216; Winkelfoos and, 204

health and wellness studies, 7

health education, 64, 90, 170

Heisman, John, 5, *57*, 60, *61*, 175, 189

Heisman center, 175

Heisman Club Field House, *195*, 195–96, *210*, 212

Heisman Club Hall of Fame: data on multi-sport athletes in, 184; displays in Philips Center, 207; founding and mission of, 192; and fundraising, 192, 194; members of, 97, 109, 135, 188, 198

Heisman Trophy, *61*

Hemenway Gymnasium (Harvard University), 40, 49

Hetherington, Clark W., 69–70; *The School Program in Physical Education*, 93

higher education: and broadcasts of athletic events, 174; career training in, 154; curricular changes in, 104; demographic changes in, 153–54; disciplinary specializations in, 129–30; distinctions between small and big schools in, 66; expansion of athletics programs at, 68; focus on winning in, 174–75; four-part mission for physical education in, 72–76, 102; gradual control over college athletics, 107; increased numbers of academic institutions in, 129; PE graduate degrees established in, 65; philosophies of PE in, 179; physical exercise in, 18; professionalism in athletics, 66–67; reforms in, 139; secularization in, 154; shift to sports and games, 55; social freedoms in, 155; sports as big business in, 180; types of physical education programs in, 11–12. *See also* commercialization of athletics; degree programs; physical education; small colleges

Hitchcock, Edward, 19, 32, 90

Horn, Joe, *143*

Houston, Sara, *143*, 144, 169

Hunsinger, Don, 144, 185, 186, 187, *187*, 199

Hunsinger Award, 187

Hunsinger Tennis Courts, 87, 199, *200*

ice hockey: athletic facilities for, 149, 166; coaches for, *143*; competitions in, 77; discontinuance of varsity team, 184, 197; prominence of professional leagues, 179

ice skating, 79

Institute for Study of Sport and Society, 141, 145

Intercollegiate Athletic Association (later, NCAA), 65

intercollegiate athletics: and coaches' contracts, 177; eastern schools' lead in, 55; emphasis on winning in, 154, 178; as entertainment and big business, 105, 174–75, 177; evaluations of, 7, 190–91; expansion of, 105–6, 126, 127; funding of, 77–78, 109, 191, 193–94; guidelines for Title IX compliance, 158; and "hair rule," 139–40; in higher education PE programs, 12; in larger versus smaller schools, 64, 66, 102, 106, 130–31, 178–79; and mind-body harmony, 10; in mission for physical education, 74, 102; Oberlin's commitment to, 74–76, 77; Oberlin's teams and competitions, 55–59, *56–57, 59*, 216; off-season practices for, 201; people of color in, 43; recruitment for, 131, 173, 181, 193, 201, 206–7; scandals in, 181–82; scheduling of competitions in, 58; schools' elimination of football, 189, 191–92; women's competition in, 157, 164. *See also specific sports*

intramural and club sports: athletic facilities for, 119, 175, 199, 208; continued support for, 183, 194; early forms of, 62; emergence of, 69; forerunners to, 55; in higher education, 12, 106; in mission for physical education, 74, 102, 106; in PE pyramid, 10, *10*; at small colleges, 215; ultimate Frisbee, 210; women's participation in, 81, 156

Jackson, Cass, 142, *142*
Jahn, Friedrich, 18
Jesse Philips Physical Education Center, 144, 163; addition of, 150, 163, 177; description of, 207; designed for men's PE and athletics, 166; funding and use of, 175, *176*; renovations to, 204, 212; women's locker rooms in, 167
Jones, George M., *121*
Jones Field House. *See* George M. Jones Field House

Kahn, Robert Lewis, 198
Kahn-Shults Field, 213
Karlgaard, Joel, 187, 204, *205*, 213
Kenyon College: admissions to, 131; athletic facilities at, 49, 117; athletics and PE facilities at, 89, 211–12, 213, 215; comparisons with Oberlin, 11; manual labor at, 21; men's teams at, 184; and NCAC, 164; Protestant religious revival and, 1; requirements of PE major at, 134; swimming at, 212; transition to coeducation at, 157; and women's sports, 78
Knowlton, A. E., 210
Knowlton Athletics Complex. *See* Austin E. Knowlton Athletics Complex
Knowlton Foundation, 208–9
Knowlton Stadium, 210, *210*, 212
Kretchmar, Robert, 98
Krislov, Marvin, 213

lacrosse: academic credit for, 163; athletic facilities for, 199, 213; coaches for, *143*; competitions in, 77; in intercollegiate athletics, 57, 113; intercollegiate teams for, 216; women's varsity teams, 164
Ladies Grove, 89
Lananna, Vin, 187
Lasell Gymnasium (Williams College), 49
Lawn Tennis Association, 56
Leadership Scholarships, 206
"Learning and Labor": as college motto, 4, 214, 221; and Shanks Center, 220–21; as theme in early years, 9, 71, 220
Leonard, Fred E., 5; contributions to Oberlin's PE programs, 35, 38–39, 62, 71; courses taught by, 41, 74; and development of physical education field, 5, 36, 51, 91, 125; education of, 38; *A Guide to the History of Physical Education*, 92; photograph of, *39*; *Pioneers of Modern Physical Training*, 92
Lewis, Dio, 26, 40, 90
Ling, Pehr Henrik, 18
Little, George, 90–91
Luther Halsey Gulick Award: establishment of, 53; recipients of, 54, 91, 93, 94, 95, 97, 125, 126; recognition of Gulick through, 92

Mahan, Asa, 19, 20, *21*, 22
manual labor as exercise: and construction of gymnasiums, 21, 49; continuing proponents of, 26, 33; and exemption from physical training classes, 54–55; gymnastics' replacement of, 17, 24; and "Muscular Christianity," 42; at Oberlin, 4, 28, 71; Oberlin's shift from, 22–24; objectives of, 19, 20; philosophy behind, 3; at small colleges, 21

McCue, Betty F., 132–33; *Physical Education for Women, 132*
Mechikoff, R. A., 64
Megyessy, Dave, *Out of Their League,* 145
Men's Department of Physical Education, 112, 115, 140, 145
Men's Gymnasium and Athletic Committee, 114
Men's Gymnasium Association, 47
men's sports, 69, 79, 113, 184–85, 216. *See also* intercollegiate athletics; *and specific sports*
Michaels, Dick, 144, 158–59
Michaels, Richard, 185
military drills, 26, 33
mind-body duality, 2, 16, 54, 130, 156, 163, 177
mind-body harmony: and development of physical training programs, 2–3; disappearance from Oberlin's PE philosophy, 177; lifelong desire for, 220; New Physical Education rooted in, 73; Oberlin's commitment to, 221; proponents of, 22–23, 31–32, 198; and reductionism, 16; in Renaissance, 3; renewed interest in, 213–14; and reviews of athletics programs, 8, 194; and scientific approach to PE, 51–52; and Title IX changes, 163; and women's athletics, 111
Morrill Act of 1862, 30
Morrison, Whitelaw Reid, 8, 96, *99*, 111, 125; *Basketball,* 99; *Community Health, Normal and Elementary Physical Diagnosis* (with Chenoweth), 99; *Community Hygiene* (with Chenoweth), 99; *Physical Diagnosis* (with Williams), 98; *A Text-book of Physical Education,* 98–99
Moulton, Gertrude E., 36, 96, 99–100, *100*, 110–11, 125
"Muscular Christianity" movement, 17, 42, 43
Muska, Michael, 187, *187,* 188

Naismith, James, 52
Nash, Jay Bryan: Hanna's mentorship of, 36; *Interpretations of Physical Education,* 93, 125; model PE program set up by, 93–94; and New Physical Education, 69; *Philosophy of Recreation and Leisure,* 93; *Physical Education,* 93; and standards for teacher training, 94
National Academy of Kinesiology, 125, 126

National Amateur Athletic Federation, 66
National Association for Intercollegiate Athletics (NAIA), 106
National Association of Directors of Physical Education for Women in Colleges and Universities, 100
National Collegiate Athletic Association (NCAA): championships started by, 106; Committee on Football Rules, 97; and control of AIAW functions, 157; divisional classifications adopted by, 131; formation of, 5; prior name of, 65; rules for athletes, 181–82. *See also* Division I and II schools; Division III colleges
NCAA. *See* National Collegiate Athletic Association (NCAA)
NCAC. *See* North Coast Athletic Conference (NCAC)
New Physical Education: as change in methods, 54, 69; elements in, 64–65; emergence of, 30, 102; focus on big muscle activities in, 70; influence of pragmatism on, 68; Oberlin's leadership in, 5, 69; philosophical tenets of, 62, 68–69; transition to, 61
Nichols, John Herbert, 78; and Camp Pemigewassett, 97–98; contributions to Oberlin's PE programs, 96, 97; as director of athletics, 111; and Oberlin's athletic policies, 115–16; opposition to commercialization of athletics, 203; philosophy of PE, 134; photograph of, *98*
Normal Institute for Physical Education, 40
North Coast Athletic Conference (NCAC): changes in competitions in, 77; Culhane and, 160; and Hunsinger Award, 187; Oberlin and founding of, 11, 193, 216; and recruiting, 173; rules and regulations of, 206; women's teams in, 164
North Fields, 150, 198–99, *199,* 208, 213

OAC. *See* Ohio Athletic Conference (OAC)
Oberlin Academy, 12, 135, 164, 204
Oberlin Alumni Magazine, 190
Oberlin Beach Club, 89
Oberlin Beach Colony, 92, 117, *123,* 124
Oberlin College (previously Oberlin Collegiate Institute): aerial view of, *84;* affiliations with other schools, 58; athletics policies

254 • Index

at, 58, 114–17, 170, 171, 204–5, 206, 221; calisthenics and gymnastics at, 17, 23–24, 31; combined men's and women's PE department at, 136, 138, 151, 173; competition against larger schools, 76–77; curricular incorporation of PE by, 31; first baseball and football teams at, 55–56; first four-year PE training program at, 37; funding for PE programs at, 191, 193–94; future of athletics and PE at, 215; graduates with PE majors, 71; increases in PE personnel at, 185, 186*t*; isolation of PE and athletics at, 141, 207, 216–17, 221; list of PE influencers from, 101–2, 110–11, 125–26; maintaining community at, 216–18, 220; mind-body philosophy of, 3–4; moniker of "Yeoman" for sports teams at, 97; New Physical Education at, 70–71; PE faculty attrition at, 172; religious heritage of, 1; unrest in combined PE department, 138, 139–41, 144–45, 151, 170. *See also* degree programs; Department of Athletics and Physical Education; facilities and buildings for athletics and PE; Fuller, Robert W.; games and sports; gymnastics; intercollegiate athletics; "Learning and Labor"; manual labor as exercise; Men's Department of Physical Education; men's sports; philosophies of physical education; reviews of Oberlin's athletics and PE programs; Scott, Jack; students; Title IX; women's athletics; women's physical education

Oberlin College Action Plan for Intercollegiate Athletics and Campus Physical Education, 183

Oberlin College Archives, 12

Oberlin Collegiate Institute, 1–2, 19–20, 28

"Oberlin Experiment," 151

Oberlin Hall, 2

Oberlin Mock Conventions, 120

"Oberlin Mountain," 117, 197

Oberlin Review: coverage of women's basketball game, 81

"OB Fit," 213

OCircus, 119, 176

Office of Disability Support Services, 214

Ohio Association for Intercollegiate Sports for Women (OAISW), 157

Ohio Athletic Conference (OAC), 77, 158, 159, 164, 192–93

Ohio College Athletic Association, 58

Ohio Inter-Collegiate Athletic Association, 58

Ohio State University, The, 21, 49

Ohio Wesleyan College: admissions at, 131; athletic facilities at, 49, 117, 211; athletics and PE facilities at, 89, 215; gymnastics at, 49; manual labor at, 21; men's teams at, 184–85; new PE and wellness degree programs at, 220; religious heritage of, 1, 78, 154; requirements of PE major at, 134; women's program at, 158

Ohio Wesleyan University, 11

Olympic games: establishment of, 3, 65–66; expansion of, 106; raised fist protests at, *143*; women in, 79

Patricia and Merrill Shanks Health and Wellness Center: funding for, 204, 211; goals of, 214, 220–21; opening of, 210–11; photographs of, *211*, *211–12*

Penn, Patrick, 142, *142*, 163, 185

pentathlons, 52

people of color: and admission to Oberlin, 42; in Oberlin's athletics programs, 43, 44; and reforms to Oberlin's PE program, 141

Perrin, Ethel, 90

Philips, Jesse, 175

Philips Physical Education Center. *See* Jesse Philips Physical Education Center

philosophies of physical education: gender differences in, 130, 167; holistic wellness, 218; mind-body paradigm as focus in, 3, 6, 204; Plato's dichotomy, 18; Sargent's American system, 40; shift to winning, 58, 106, 127, 173; "win at all costs," 6, 131, 174–75, 178, 180–81, 200–201, 203

physical culture, growth of, 30–31, 124

physical education: administration of Oberlin's PE programs, 72, 110–11; as career, 91; clothing for, 45, *46*; courses in, 71–72, 194; credentials for PE faculty and coaches, 113, 171, 177; as distinct from health education, 54; early faculty views, 26; elimination of Oberlin's requirement for, 172; evaluations of, 190–91; faculty status in, 97, 172–73; four-part mission of, 112; the Greeks and, 2; key individuals in development of, 89–91; Nash's summary of objectives of, 94; Oberlin's leadership in development of, 4–5, 7, 124–25; professionalization of, 66, 92, 102; pyramid of stages and activities in, 9–10, *10*; reforms to Oberlin's programs, 138–40, 141, 145; scientific approach to, 51–52, 74; terminologies and definitions of, 8–10; themes underlying historical changes in, 5–8; twentieth-century curricular changes in, 71–72; types of programs for, 40. *See also* degree programs; facilities and buildings for athletics and PE; games and sports; gendered divisions at Oberlin; intercollegiate athletics; intramural and club sports; manual labor as exercise; men's sports; philosophies of physical education; service classes; Title IX; women's athletics; women's physical education

Physical Education Library, *120*

Physical Education Society of New York City, 53

Physical Education Training Program for Women, 40–41, 62, *73*, 74

physical examinations at Oberlin, 169–70

physical fitness: anthropometrics and, 32–33; efforts to improve, 133, 134; renewed interest in, 220; of US children, 32, 65, 133

physical training: beginnings of, 25–26; centrality of gymnastics in, 30, 60; first programs for, 40; in mission for physical education, 73, 102; shift to sports and games, 55; as term, 8

Pioneers of Modern Physical Training (Leonard), 38

Plato, 2, 18

Play Days (Sports Days), 156

Playground Association of America (later, National Recreation Association), 5, 52, 65, 92

playgrounds, 74

pragmatism, 16–17, 28, 52, 67–68, 106

President's Commission on Physical Fitness, 134

President's Committee for the Study of Athletics Policy, 170, 171

President's Committee on Athletics, 190

professional sports, 59, 69, 105, 179, 202–3

Progressivism, 31, 42, 66, 67

Protestant evangelism, 42

public school systems, PE in, 40, 90, 134

Rebuilding of Physical Education at Oberlin College, 190

recreational activities, increased participation in, 65

Regal, Howie, *96*

Reich, Donald, 141, 146

Reindeau, Coach, 190

Report of the Committee on Athletics, 190, 193

reviews of Oberlin's athletics and PE programs: issues noted in, 141; list of, 170, 190–91; recommendations from, 170–72, 193–95

Rice, Grantland, 178, 179

Rickey, Branch, 90

Robert Lewis Kahn Track, 197, *198*

Rockefeller, John D., 46

Rockefeller family, 148

Rockefeller Skating Rink: conversion of, 118; funding for, 46; Hanna and, 37, 92; incorporation into Second Ladies Gymnasium, 79; views of, *45, 47, 82, 84*

rodeos, 105

Roth, William, 204

Round Hill School (Northampton), 90

rowing, 79

Russell, Kim, 218

Sargent, Dudley A.: and anthropometrics, 32; and development of PE, 89–90; early training school of, 40; gymnastics systems and, 30–31; as Hanna's mentor, 33–34, 35, 43; PE program of, 39; and Playground Association of America, 92

Sauer, George, 145

Saunders, Henry Russell "Red," 178, 179

Savage, Charles W.: contributions to PE and Oberlin College by, 74, 95–97; directorships of, 76, 96, 111; and New Physical Education, 71; opposition to commercialization of athletics, 78, 96–97, 203; organizational contributions by, 97; philosophy of, 76; photographs of, *96*; principles and goals of PE outlined by, 114–15, 134; and professionalism of college sports, 96; stadium honoring, 87

Savage Field, 88
Savage Stadium, 87, 88, *88*, 97, 102, *121–22*, 208
scandals, 181–82, 203
scholarship in physical education, 91–94, 98–99, 100, 124, 125, *143*
Schwendener, Norma, 95
Scott, Harry A.: *Competitive Sports in Schools and Colleges*, 68–69
Scott, Jack: abrasive practices of, 146–47; and admission to athletic events, 172; *The Athletic Revolution*, *140*, 141; and budgeting for women's teams, 165; changes implemented by, 139, 142–43, 144, 151; clashes with others, 144–45; controversy around, 129; and gender parity, 159, 166; hiring of, 139, 141; philosophy on sports, 145–46; reform activism of, 141, 170; relationship with College Faculty Council, 146; reputation developed by, 145; resignations due to hiring of, 138, 144; and Sara Houston, 144; termination agreement for, 147; and Title IX, 162–63
Second Ladies Gymnasium: construction of, 35; Physical Education Library in, *120*; removal of, 118; renovation of, 79; use by military, 107; views of, *45*, *46*, *47*, *84*
Second Ladies Hall, 35, 44
Second Men's Gymnasium, 46–47, *48*, 49, 83
Semple, Carl, *96*
service classes: coaches involved in, 181; coaching and, 135, 167, 181; gender roles in teaching, 135, 160; grading of, 138, 171, 176; in historical PE pyramid, 10, *10*, 11–12; in men's career tracks, 130; in Oberlin's PE program, 112; in PE curriculum, 102; requirement for, 176–77; skills needed to teach, 113; sports in, 111
Setzler, Heather, 186
sexual misconduct, 206
Shanks, Merrill, 211, 214
Shanks, Patricia, 211, 214
Shanks Health and Wellness Center. *See* Patricia and Merrill Shanks Health and Wellness Center
Shipherd, John Jay, 1, 19, 22
Shults, Fredrick D.: about, 197–98; at Camp Pemigewassett, 98; and "hair rule," 139–40; photograph of, *199*; view of Scott, 141, 146–47
Shults, Jennifer, 219
skiing, 106
small colleges: and commercialization of sports, 201; competition levels at, 76–77; emergence of, 1, 30; increases in PE personnel at, 185; intramurals and club sports at, 215; new PE and wellness degree programs at, 215, 220; pedagogy changes 1972–90, 155; PE philosophies at, 182, 203; sports teams at, 184–85; Title IX and, 157–58
Smith, Julian, 136, *137*, 138
Smith, Tommie, 142, *143*, 186
soccer: athletic facilities for, 151, 199, 213; fields for, 150; immigrants and, 105; intercollegiate teams for, 216; professional teams in, 179; in service classes, 111; Shults and, 198; in women's sports, 79, 83, 184; women's varsity teams, 164
Society of Directors of Physical Education, 125
Society of Health and Physical Educators (SHAPE), 53, 92
softball: athletics facilities for, *209*; in intramural sports, 81; women's championships in, 157; in women's sports, 83, 111, 132, 184, 216; women's varsity teams, 164
"spectatoritis," 67, 94, 174
spectators, 106, 127, 173–75, 180
sports: college regulations for, 49, 50; cultural predominance of, 202; definitions of, 9; emergence of competitions in, 26–28; and exemption from physical training classes, 54–55; growing popularity of, 33, 104–5; inventors of, 7; in PE pyramid, 10; schools' control over, 67; transition from gymnastics to, 37, 54, 68
Sports Days, 132, 133
sports injuries, 189, 191
Springfield College training program, 25, 40, 49, 72, 102
Stanford University, 93
Starr, Fred, 193
stereotyping issues, 217–18
Stewart, Philo P., 1
Strategic Planning Team, 193
Student Gymnasium Association, 24

Index • 257

students: and athletes' separation from general student body, 207, 217, 221; and changes in PE focus, 107; civil rights petition filed by, 167; and housing for athletes, 207; inclusion in departmental decisions, 142, 145, 172; and inconsistent grading, 171; interest in social causes, 171; low attendance at competitions, 207; as managers and coaches, 108; PE program contributions initiated by, 26, 47, 49, 155; protest against Scott's changes, 145; and self-designed majors, 219

Swarthmore College, 189

Swedish gymnastics, 18, 30, 31, 33, 34, 69

swimming and aquatics: academic credit for, 163; athletics facilities for, 117, 175; coaches for, 144, 160; intercollegiate teams for, 216; in men's sports, 113; von Wenck and, 110; in women's sports, 111, 132, 184; women's varsity teams, 164. *See also* Carr Pool; Crane Pool

Talcott Hall, 45, *45, 47,* 84

Tappan, Arthur, 2, *3*

Tappan Square: athletics facilities on, 24–25, 26, *27,* 49, 50, 86, 199; interpretive dance in, *34;* naming of, 3; restrictions on games in, 26; team competition on, 28; views of, *84*

teacher training: coursework and practice teaching, 72, 74, 102; expansion of programs of, 134; new focus on, 66; Oberlin's discontinuance of, 171, 173, 177; Springfield College's program of, 72; standards in, 99–100

television broadcasting, 179

tennis: academic credit for, 163; and athletic associations, 58; championships for, 79; coaches for, 187; in early club sports, 55; intercollegiate teams for, 74, 106, 216; Oberlin's first intercollegiate competitions, 56, 57; professional players in, 179; sportsmanship in, 203; in women's sports, 111, 157, 164

tennis courts: Hunsinger Tennis Courts, 87, 187, *200;* locations of, 199; views of, *47–48, 122, 122–23, 148, 196, 200*

Terrell, Mary Church, 59–60

therapeutics, Gulick's studies of, 53

Thorndike, Edward, 67

Throner, Guy C., 109, *110,* 134

Tidwell, Billy, 136, *137,* 138

timelines in PE history, 12, 223–38

Title IX: budgetary changes needed for, 165; effect on Oberlin's athletic policies, 117, 157; and funding of football, 191; Oberlin's implementation of, 159–60, 162–63, 166–67, 176–77; Oberlin's oversight of compliance with, 206; passage of, 154, 158; purpose of, 176

track and field: and athletic associations, 58; athletics facilities for, 196, *196,* 213; coaches for, *137,* 142, *143;* and cross country, 184; in expansion of collegiate sports, 106; first meet, 55; intercollegiate teams for, *75,* 216; Oberlin's first intercollegiate competitions in, 56–57; teams added for, 74; in women's sports, 111, 132; women's varsity teams, 164

transgender athletes, 206

uniforms, *57, 78, 82*

University of Nebraska, 37

US Navy V-12 units, 107, *108*

US Office of Civil Rights (OCR), 167, 168

US Olympic Committee, 97

Vance, Lawrence, 185

Veeck, Bill, 91

volleyball: academic credit for, 163; all-star game in, 83; athletics facilities for, 175; origins of, 7; in women's sports, 83, 179, 216; women's varsity teams, 164

Von Wenck, Katherine, 109, 110, *111,* 118

WAA. *See* Women's Athletic Association (WAA)

Wabash College: admissions to, 131; as all-male, 78; athletics facilities at, 211–12; courses on coaching at, 220; emergence of, 30; intramurals at, 215; manual labor at, 21; men's teams at, 184–85; shift to gymnastics at, 24

Walker, Moses Fleetwood, 5, 59, *60*

Warner, Dr. and Mrs. Lucien C., 21–22, *22,* 83

Warner, Karen Osborne, 21

Warner Gymnasium (now Warner Center): addition of, 5, 102; description of, 83–86; as early facility, 5, 49; Leonard's role on,

38, 92; and New Physical Education, 71; physical examinations in, 169; replacement of, 138, 166, 195; views of, *84–86*
Wellesley College, 43
Wignall, Janet, 160, 162, *162*
Williams, Beatty B., 149
Williams, Carl, *96*
Williams, Jesse Feiring: *The Administration of Health and Physical Education,* 95; definition of PE, 8; Hanna as mentor for, 36; on importance of mind-body harmony, 94–95; *Manual of Elementary Physical Diagnosis,* 95; and New Physical Education, 69; philosophy of, 94–95; photograph of, *95*; *Physical Diagnosis* (with Morrison), 98; *Principles of Physical Education,* 95; as scholar, 94, 125
Williams College, 89, 157
Williams Field House, 149–50, *150*, 166, 197, *197*, 210
Williams Ice Rink, 148–49, *150*, 166
Wills, Helen, 79
Winkelfoos, Natalie, 204, *205*, 215, 216, 221
women: admission to midwest colleges, 78; civil rights petitions filed by, 167, 168; increases in college attendance by, 153–54; key PE influencers among, 126; in nonsanctioned sports exhibitions, 158–59; and reforms to Oberlin's PE program, 141; teaching of PE classes, 111–12
Women's Athletic Association (WAA): exhibitions of gymnastics and dance, 156; founding of, 79; Hanna and, 37; headquarters for, 87; and Hi-O-Hi yearbook, 81; regulatory responsibilities of, 111, 133; renaming of, 163–64
women's athletics, 44; aquatics facilities and, 118; assumptions about women in, 81; and coaching requirements for women faculty, 163; expanded opportunities in, 78–79, *80*, 102, 127, 132, 165; gender parity in, 168; history of women's participation in athletics, 158–59; increased recognition for, 58–59; increased support for, 171–72; key women in Title IX transitions in, 160–62, 164; locker room space for, 166, 167; male coaches in, 159–60; mind-body philosophy in, 79, 111, 156; Moulton on competition in, 100–101; in nineteenth century, 156; organizations established for,

66; Play Days, 156; professional teams in, 179; recruiting for, 165; Scott's promotion of equality in, 144; teams at Oberlin and small colleges, 184–85. *See also specific sports*
Women's Female Institute at Cincinnati (OH), 90
Women's Gymnasium and Field Association (GFA) (later, WAA), 79
women's physical education: Hanna's pioneering role in, 37; Oberlin students in, *73*; philosophy behind, 111; proponents of, 90; Sargent's view on, 43; Swedish gymnastics in, 34, *34*
Women's Recreation Association (WRA) (formerly, WAA), 163–64
Women's Sports Committee, 159
Wood, Thomas D.: career of, 53; and development of physical education field, 51, 54, 91; Hanna as mentor for, 36, 62; *Health and Education,* 53; and New Physical Education, *53*, 64, 69; *The New Physical Education,* 54, 93; philosophy of, 54; and Stanford University, 93
world events and societal changes, 153; from 1896 to 1925, 65, 102; from 1926 to 1950, 104; from 1951 to 1974, 129; in 1960s, 139; from 1991 to 2010, 178; from 2011 to 2021, 202; and sports as entertainment, 173–75
World War I: athletic competitions during, 65; and men's lack of fitness, 65, 67
World War II: athletic competitions during, 108–9; effect on PE programs, 126; impact on college athletics, 107; physical fitness and military rejection rate, 133
wrestling, 106, 184
Wuest, D. A., 9

Yale–Princeton women's basketball game, 81–83, *82*, 111–12, 133
YeoFit, 214, 215
YMCA: first, 19; Gulick and, 42, 92; need for instructors at, 74; Oberlin's use of pool at Elyria, 117, 118; role in men's development, 52; training programs for staff of, 40
Young Men's Christian Association Training School, 25, 40, 49, 51–52
youth sports, 180, 182, 200

Zaharias, Babe Didrikson, 79